T0319888

Corporate Governance and Ethics

NEW HORIZONS IN LEADERSHIP STUDIES

Series Editor: Joanne B. Ciulla
Professor and Coston Family Chair in Leadership and Ethics,
Jepson School of Leadership Studies, University of Richmond, USA

This important series is designed to make a significant contribution to the development of leadership studies. This field has expanded dramatically in recent years and the series provides an invaluable forum for the publication of high quality works of scholarship and shows the diversity of leadership issues and practices around the world.

The main emphasis of the series is on the development and application of new and original ideas in leadership studies. It pays particular attention to leadership in business, economics and public policy and incorporates the wide range of disciplines which are now part of the field. Global in its approach, it includes some of the best theoretical and empirical work with contributions to fundamental principles, rigorous evaluations and existing concepts and competing theories, historical surveys and future visions.

Titles in the series include:

Corporate Governance and Ethics

An Aristotelian Perspective

Alejo José G. Sison

University of Navarra, Spain

NEW HORIZONS IN LEADERSHIP STUDIES

Edward Elgar
Cheltenham, UK • Northampton, MA, USA

Published by
Edward Elgar Publishing Limited
The Lypiatts
15 Lansdown Road
Cheltenham
Glos GL50 2JA
UK

Edward Elgar Publishing, Inc.
William Pratt House
9 Dewey Court
Northampton
Massachusetts 01060
USA

A catalogue record for this book
is available from the British Library

Library of Congress Control Number: 2008927948

ISBN 978 1 84542 746 7

Printed and bound in Great Britain by MPG Books Ltd, Bodmin, Cornwall

For J.P. II, *i.m.*,
and J.E.R, P.O.D.

Contents

Foreword

There is little evidence that reforms in corporate governance have made any difference. The salaries of chief executives continue to soar in the U.S. and elsewhere as well, even though compensation committees must be independent and even though there is more disclosure of what people earn. Companies are still restating financial results at a prodigious rate and balance sheet and income statement surprises continue, even though accounting standards have presumably been tightened, audit fees have gone up, and CEOs must personally attest to the accuracy of the reports their companies release. And in the workplace, distrust of management and disengagement and diminished job satisfaction persist, resulting in ever higher levels of turnover and, as a result, lower levels of productivity and service – just fly on most airlines to see these facts at close range – even though most observers recognize a coming labour shortage and the importance of intellectual capital for business success in the modern economy.

For the most part, we have attacked the symptoms rather than the root cause of the problems. Reforms have been concerned with form instead of substance, with ensuring compliance instead of changing mindsets, with promulgating 'minimum standards' rather than with stimulating excellent and thoughtful leadership. The mindset that seems to dominate current discourse all over the world is one that emphasizes ends, achievements and objectives, and plays down the means and processes employed in their attainment. In business and in society more generally, we do not look too hard at the price paid for 'success'. Robert Reich's new book on *Supercapitalism* argues that, even as we achieved lower prices through globalization and deregulation, we have diminished citizenship and impoverished community and social life. Dennis Bakke, co-founder of the large independent power producer, AES, has argued that there are things we should do in creating our workplaces not to make them more efficient or effective, but simply because to do otherwise is inconsistent with the values we should hold for locales that can either diminish or uplift the human spirit.

Alejo Sison believes that we ought to elevate the consideration of our 'philosophy' of management and governance to centre stage. As part of that elevation, we need to educate people in leadership roles to be as expert in thinking about purpose, values and the philosophical underpinnings of their choices as they are in the more technical aspects of management such as understanding financial statements and probability. And as part of the role of philosophy, we should subject organizations and their leaders to scrutiny – not just through the lens of compliance and law, but also through the great moral ideas that form the basis of philosophical discourse and analysis.

This is an argument and an analysis that must be true. To move beyond the obsession with results that has resulted in environmental degradation, enormous increases in income inequality and, in many countries, outright corruption in the service of getting deals done, management needs to reconnect with its fundamental moral purposes. Rakesh Khurana's recent book, *From Higher Aims to Hired Hands*, provides an historical account of how management education has lost its way. This book by Sison provides a way forward to rethink what companies are about, how they are to be governed, and what it means to be a leader in an organizational world where people's financial, physical and mental well-being are inextricably tied to what happens to them in organizations. *Why* we do what we do is as important as *what* we do. Understanding why entails revisiting questions that have occupied philosophy over the ages. There is no more important task in today's world.

Jeffrey Pfeffer
Thomas D. Dee II Professor of Organizational Behavior
Graduate School of Business
Stanford University

Introduction and acknowledgements

I suppose that most people write to convey information and knowledge they already possess. I write primarily to begin to learn about something that interests me; as part of an effort to try to make sense of matters which everyone else may be talking about, but – to my mind – rather aimlessly and without reaching any robust conclusions. This was how I started my research on corporate governance. (To what extent I still am very much of a novice or learner in the field, even after finishing this book, I leave to the kindly reader to respond.) Once more, to guide me in my inquiry, I chose Aristotle, particularly his treatise on *The Politics*. In the same way that my previous work, *The Moral Capital of Leaders. Why Virtue Matters* could be considered a reading of Aristotle's *Nicomachean Ethics* addressed to a business audience, this present volume may be taken as a digest of *The Politics* for members of corporate boards and directors of organizations.

The first two chapters identify my point of departure, that is, the dominant, commonplace understanding both of the firm – a 'money-making machine' – and of corporate governance – compliance by 'box-ticking'. I challenge this peacefully accepted and widespread notion of the firm by presenting a case that serves as a counterexample: *Tasubinsa* certainly seeks profits, but only in a manner subservient to its main goal, the complete social integration of the mentally handicapped who constitute more than 90 per cent of its workforce. To be sure, this single case would not be enough to topple the prevalent and long-established model, yet, at the very least, it could still raise serious doubts while opening up space for the development of a new theory of the firm. Any business organization should exist, above all, in order to contribute to the common good of society. Rather than as a machine, a company should be thought of as a community of workers who seek their own integral human development by producing the goods and services that society needs. Profits should be regarded as a supervenient prize for a job well done, not something to be gained at all costs, regardless of the means. As for the box-ticking corporate governance model that Sarbanes–Oxley has set, perhaps the strongest argument against it lies in the fact that Enron itself could have been essentially a Sarbanes–Oxley-compliant company. Conformity with the welter of purely formal structures, rules and procedures obviously was not sufficient to prevent the company's meltdown, covered in a haze of financial and managerial scandals. The problem lay, not in the form, but in the substance, in the lack of moral integrity of those ultimately entrusted with the company's direction.

Necessary for constructing my argument is the recognition that 'governance' comes from 'government' and, as such, is normally associated with the running of a state. It was in this context that Aristotle developed his treatise on *The Politics*. Chapters three and four represent the effort to extend the meaning of 'government' analogously from its original turf in Greek city-states to the realm of modern corporations, including multinational enterprises. The comparison is carried out on a triple basis: the people who comprise them, their forms of organization and the specific ends they pursue. Special attention is directed to the notion of citizenship as it applies not only to the business organization or firm as a whole (corporate citizenship) but also to the different shareholders and stakeholder groups as citizens of the corporate polity.

In continuation, chapters five to seven flesh out the analogy between different state and corporate regimes, using Aristotle's classification grounded on a twofold criterion: the number of rulers and whether those rulers seek the common good or their own individual good. Each kind of regime is later on exemplified by an actual corporation: Fiat (corporate tyranny), Cheung Kong Holdings and Whampoa Limited (corporate monarchy), Abelardo Investment and Manufacturing Corporation/AIMC (corporate oligarchy), Banco Popular Español (corporate aristocracy), United Airlines (corporate democracy) and IDOM Engineering Consultancy (corporate polity). Corporate narratives come from the world over – Italy, China, Philippines, Spain and the United States – and they stand for a variety of sectors, from the automotive industry through finance, flour-milling and real estate to airlines. Furthermore, companies come in all sizes, from relatively small, family-owned ones to huge publicly listed multinational corporations, leaders in their field.

Chapter eight brings together some concluding remarks on the true nature of corporate governance, now envisioned to be a form of Aristotelian *praxis* (roughly, 'practice'). Steps are outlined to initiate an authentic and effective corporate governance reform premised on the education of board directors, particularly on the ethical and political aspects of their function. It is indeed remarkable that, in the end, the secret of good corporate governance can be found in the governors' education in the virtues, for, without the virtues, neither the goods nor the objectives that a corporation should seek could be properly identified, nor the the rules, procedures and structures it should follow correctly formulated, interpreted and implemented.

Perhaps unconsciously, the majority of prescriptions for corporate governance reform draw inspiration from a political theory obsessed with finding justifications for the uneven distribution of power, and hence, one that is constantly looking for ways to avoid abuse. Ultimately, what this political theory endeavours to do is to prevent one party from eliminating the others, simply because of divergent views of the good. The solution proposed consists in the rules of procedural justice. Purportedly, we cannot help but arrive and agree on them, departing from an original position of ignorance regarding our own particularities and preferences. Abstract reason and a desire for equality are the only useful guides. Another version of this theory insists on a fundamentally market-based approach to sort out our differences, without having to renounce them. After all, in a properly functioning market, needs are satisfied and conflicts resolved, not through the use of power but through free exchange. Moreover, personal beliefs are kept safe because they are apparently of no interest to other market players. Nonetheless, sufficient experimentation has been carried out with these alternatives to realize that they lead to a dead end.

Classical political theory, on the other hand, inquires above all about the best regime in the understanding that that would represent the best life for man, who is by nature a social creature. Such a regime not only allows for the satisfaction of material, external goods, but, more importantly, it permits citizens to develop themselves spiritually and internally, that is, to acquire and to perfect the requisite human virtues or excellences. This is what good government consists in; not in the mere provision of material goods or in the mechanical observance of purely formal and procedural rules. Good corporate governance should not be very far from this. It comes as no surprise, therefore, that classical political theory emphasizes the education of the prince as its main concern. In the corporate context, we would do well to take the cue and concentrate before anything else on the ethical and political education of corporate rulers, board members and directors.

I was indeed fortunate to be appointed Visiting Scholar at the Policy and Leadership Studies Department of the National Institute of Education of Singapore in the final stretch of my research and writing in the summer of 2007. I would like to take advantage of this opportunity to thank the members of the department for their support, stimulating conversation and, most of all, friendship. I wish to acknowledge a special debt of gratitude to Professor Ong Kim Lee, the Department Chair, and to Professor Jude Chua Soo Meng, who introduced me to this distinguished team of scholars. During my all too brief stay with them, I certainly felt inspired and empowered with their dedication to education. I could only hope that this book qualifies as a fitting contribution to their noble efforts.

Alejo José G. Sison
Ravenahl
Singapore
Summer of 2007

1. Changing conventional wisdom: the firm is not a money-making machine

I BUSINESS 'COMMON SENSE'

There are a few simple things that anyone who comes in contact with a firm – and past a certain age, that makes almost everybody – should know: in a firm there are people or groups of people called 'owners'. They are the ones who put in the money, thanks to which the firm is able to operate and, in exchange, the rest of society recognizes their right to call the shots. In other words, despite the boss's self-sufficient airs and penchant for ordering everyone else around, he's a mere stand-in for his own boss, the real boss, that is, the owners.

Next is that owners put their money in the firm expecting some rewards. They do not do so out of selflessness, love of neighbour or some other lofty ideal. They just expect to earn more money after a given time, hopefully, not too long. That is the logic of investment. Owners are entitled to the surplus money the firm generates for having parted with their money in the first place and allowing other people (managers and workers) to use that capital productively. Of course there are several ways of investing money and, generally, the risk each one entails is directly proportional to the possible gains. Nonetheless, a keen investor is precisely the one who is able to choose from among the different options that which yields maximum returns. In principle, therefore, business owners or capitalists wager their money on the best investment opportunity, the one that, in their minds, would probably give them the greatest profits.

Thirdly, an individual begins to form part of a firm once he has signed a contract. For some it would be an employment contract, for others, a supplier's contract, and for still others, a buyer's contract, and so on. From a legal perspective, therefore, the firm is nothing more than a bundle of such contracts, and these more or less formal agreements 'to do X in exchange for Y' are the links that bind any given party to it. It is presupposed, moreover, that anyone who enters into a contract with a firm does so by his own free will and volition, and not under duress. Whatever his particular motives may be is nobody's business, as long as he abides by the terms and conditions of the contract. It is sufficient that the two parties to a contract freely give their consent for such an agreement to be binding and enforceable. Kibitzers are admonished to hold their peace and refrain from interfering.

And finally, just as owners invest in a firm to maximize returns, correspondingly, firms are supposed to maximize value for investors as a whole. Oftentimes this means doing whatever it takes to raise a firm's share price, above all. Certainly there may be other things that a firm can do in the process, such as producing goods and services that the market demands at a price with which consumers would be agreeable. But that is simply a means to the end of increasing share or investment value. This is the one true standard with which a firm's success is to be measured.

These truisms form the kernel of what are perhaps the three most influential theories in our understanding of the modern firm, namely, 'the nature of the firm' according to Ronald Coase, 'agency theory' from Michael Jensen and William Meckling, and the 'shareholder or financial theory' of the firm as formulated by Milton Friedman. Their inclusion in what has come to be business 'common sense' is very revealing of how these doctrines have triumphed in shaping our thinking.

In the article 'The nature of the firm', first published in 1937, Ronald Coase attempted to respond to what was in fact a very simple question: why carry out production through the firm instead of the market (Coase, 1937)? Given an efficient market where the value of goods and services is determined through free exchange, why not allow the price mechanism itself to coordinate production? Why have recourse to an entrepreneur to manage production through a hierarchical organization such as the firm?

Coase's response was equally plain, although not completely satisfactory, as we shall see later on. A firm exists in order to reduce 'transaction costs'; its true 'nature' lies in its ability to drive 'transaction costs' down and thereby improve production efficiency compared to the market. Transaction costs are the 'extra costs' associated with conducting a deal, be it in terms of money, time or any other inconvenience. These could refer, for example, to the 'extra costs' incurred by the entrepreneur when scouting around for workers in the open market and having to negotiate short-term contracts with them. Such costs could be saved if workers were somehow locked in already in the firm by virtue of employment contracts. In response to changing market demands, workers could then simply be ordered around by superiors to carry out different tasks instead of renegotiating with them each time. In a commentary more than half a century later, Coase remained unmoved in that the purpose of 'The nature of the firm' was to establish cost as the deciding factor in producing goods and services through the firm instead of the market (Coase, 1991b: 61–74).

While Coase may have given an interesting first response to the question why firms exist, he nevertheless admittedly failed to explain how exactly firms reduce transaction costs (Coase, 1991a, 1991b). For this we will have to turn to the work of Michael Jensen and William Meckling.

In their ground-breaking article, 'The theory of the firm: managerial behavior, agency costs, and ownership structure', Jensen and Meckling (1976) pick up from where Coase had left off and affirm that firms reduce transaction costs largely through the establishment of so-called 'agency relationships'. Agency relationships generally take the form of contracts, although not necessarily explicit or formal ones. These stipulate that one party (the *agent*) is to perform a specific service on behalf of another (the *principal*), receiving from the latter some decision-making power for this purpose (Jensen and Meckling, 1976). In the context of the firm, we could think of the owners and other investors as the principals, and of the managers and other employees as the agents. In other words, it is through the hierarchy implicit in the agency relationship or contract that transaction costs within the firm trump those of producing in the open market.

The problem, however, is that principals cannot be continually monitoring agents. Hence, two sorts of difficulties arise: one is called 'adverse selection' and the other 'moral hazard' (Eisenhardt, 1989: 58). Adverse selection describes the case in which an agent misrepresents his ability to do the work agreed upon or adopts decisions inconsistent with the contractual goals or the principal's preferences. For example, because prospective employers cannot accurately gauge beforehand the quality of work candidates to a certain post could perform, these could always claim to do a better job than what they are in fact able to do. It could even be that they are out of a job and seeking employment precisely because of their incompetence. In such a situation, bad workers would have been 'adversely selected' to be the only ones available in the labour market, to the dismay of principals or employers.

Moral hazard occurs, on the other hand, when agents shirk their tasks or do not put forth their best efforts. For instance, if a factory worker received the same daily wage as another, regardless of the quantity and the quality of the output, we could say that he has no incentive whatsoever to improve productivity. On the contrary, he faces the 'moral hazard' of exerting the minimum indispensable effort to earn the agreed upon salary. Once again, it is the principals or employers who stand to lose.

As we have seen in the discussion of adverse selection and moral hazard, there is no guarantee that agents will always act in the best interests of principals. Rather, agents are under a constant temptation to maximize their own interests, even at the expense of the principals themselves. This divergence between the actual interests of principals and those of agents inevitably generates additional costs. These agency costs are the residual costs incurred either by the principal, when implementing measures to control the agent's behaviour, or by the agent, when striving to demonstrate commitment to the principal's goals. Whichever way, these agency costs result in a failure to maximize the principal's wealth or resources.

The challenge now lies in devising a mechanism that ensures, to the extent possible, an effective alignment of interests between agents and principals, thereby reducing the aforementioned agency costs (Shankman, 1999: 321). This is achieved through the careful formulation of contracts, so much so that principals are able to protect their interests and maximize their utility in the event of conflicts. To do so contracts should be crafted taking into account several assumptions regarding agents (self-interest, limited rationality, risk aversion), organizations (goal conflict among members) and information (assymetry) (Shankman, 1999: 332).

In a famous essay, 'The social responsibility of business is to increase its profits', the Nobel laureate economist Milton Friedman defends the role of shareholders as the owners or principals of the firm (Friedman, 1970). Therefore, the primary obligation of managers as agents of shareholder–owners is 'to conduct the business in accordance with their desires, which generally will be to make as much money as possible while conforming to the basic rules of the society, both those embodied in law and those embodied in ethical custom' (Friedman, 1970). In a free-enterprise system, there is no room for such a thing as 'the social responsibilities of business', for responsibilities could only accrue to individuals, never to groups such as corporations. Certainly, as an individual, a manager or executive may recognize or voluntarily assume some 'social responsibility' towards his community or church, for instance. 'But in these respects he is acting as a principal, not an agent; he is spending his own money or time or energy; not the money of his employers or the time or energy he has contracted to devote to their purposes' (Friedman, 1970). At best, the 'social responsibility of business' should be set aside as an empty rhetorical flourish.

Let us now examine how these business truisms square with a firm called Tasubinsa.

II TASUBINSA: AN UNCOMMON BUSINESS

Tasubinsa (Talleres Auxiliares de Subcontratación Industrial Navarra, Sociedad Anónima) was constituted as a not-for-profit 'special employment centre' on 29 December 1989 through an agreement between the

Navarre Regional Autonomous Government and ANFAS (Asociación navarra a favor de las personas con discapacidad psíquica), a local association that works in favour of people with mental disabilities. Special employment centres were created by the Spanish Law on the Social Integration of the Handicapped (Ley 13/1982 of 7 April, articles 41 to 46) to provide these members of society with productive and gainful work in keeping with their personal characteristics. This law obliges both state and privately owned companies with more than 50 employees to set aside at least 2 per cent of the total number of jobs for the handicapped. Alternative measures consist in the purchase of goods or services from special employment centres or from a self-employed worker with a disability, or in donations to a foundation dedicated to the integration of the disabled (Real Decreto 27/2000 of 14 January). Failure to comply with these provisions results in substantial fines and exclusion from government contracts. Tasubinsa engages in the manufacturing and assembly of parts for automobiles, home appliances, vending machines, electronic apparatuses, and paper and plastic products. Tasubinsa also offers logistics, landscaping and janitorial services to different companies within Navarre. Towards the end of 2005, it had around 90 firms in its portfolio of clients, some of which were even located abroad.

More than 90 per cent of Tasubinsa employees have mental, physical or sensorial handicaps as certified by the Labour Ministry. The rest of the workers are the professionals indispensable for the proper functioning of the organization. The great majority of the mentally handicapped have a dysfunction equivalent of around 33 to 65 per cent less than normal. Associated with Tasubinsa are several 'occupational centres' for those whose mental disability currently impedes them from working in a special employment centre. Some occupational centres prepare individuals for future work in a special employment centre, helping them acquire the requisite skills, while others cater to those already past their productive years and who most likely suffer from premature aging, which among the mentally disabled sets in at around 45 years of age. Other formulas used by Tasubinsa for the integration of the handicapped include 'work enclaves' (enclaves laborales), 'mobile brigades' (brigadas móviles) and 'jobs with individual support' (empleo con apoyo individual). Work enclaves were set up by the Labour Ministry (Real Decreto 290/2004 of 20 February) as some sort of half-way house between a job in a special employment centre and ordinary employment. Work enclaves allow groups of workers from a special employment centre to render services to a partner-firm within the latter's premises for a period of between three months and three years, after which the partner-firm is expected to hire at least some of those workers permanently. Mobile brigades typically provide cleaning or gardening services to clients within Navarre. And, lastly, jobs with individual support from Tasubinsa staff represent the maximum integration of handicapped employees in an ordinary working environment.

In corporate documents, Tasubinsa has set for itself a three-fold objective (Tasubinsa, 2005: 2–3). First is the creation and management of special employment centres and occupational centres; second is the provision of services for the personal and social growth or occupational therapy of mentally handicapped people with great difficulties in obtaining employment; and third, the generation of stable, good quality employment for the mentally disabled. In consequence, Tasubinsa runs three different programmes simultaneously: an occupational programme for the mentally disabled whose productive capacity is scarce to nil; a work training programme to develop the productive capacities of those who could be prepared for a job; and a special employment centre programme, properly speaking.

In December 2005, Tasubinsa had 733 workers in special employment centres, distributed among 13 shops and four work enclaves throughout Navarre, and 552 other mentally disabled people in occupational centres, making it the fourth-largest firm in the Navarre region in number of employees.

Tasubinsa, like all other special employment centres, receives government subsidies for the creation and maintenance of jobs (Orden of 16 October 1998). It receives €2000 for each new employment created and further financial assistance to cover salaries, social security contributions and expenses related to the elimination of architectonic barriers and the adaptation of work stations to the handicapped. However generous this may seem, it is not all that different from the help that any other Spanish firm could expect from government for hiring handicapped workers.

According to Óscar González, a consultant to Tasubinsa and himself a former managing director of a special employment centre, five key traits set this organization apart in its corporate culture from other businesses (González, 2006: 77–9). First is the unequivocal determination to adapt production processes to workers instead of the other way around. This is shown in the extraordinary degree of flexibility of infrastructure and installations, as well as of job designs and job descriptions. Second is the rapidity in accommodating innovations in manufacturing in tune with the ever-changing environment. Just like any other company competing in the market, Tasubinsa incorporates automation and robotics, 'just-in-time', Kanban and other production techniques meant to improve quality. It even possesses the ISO 9001:2000 and the ISO 14001:1996 certifications for customer satisfaction and environmental management systems, respectively. Third is the importance laid on worker recognition. Acknowledgement is made explicit for a job well done as the result of a constant and sincere concern on the part of managers for individual workers and the teams they form. Praise is a crucial component of the handicapped worker's psychological income. Aside from strengthening vital emotional bonds between handicapped workers and their immediate superiors, approving words also enhance motivation.

Fourth, in Tasubinsa there is a keen awareness and clear understanding of what it means to be 'different'. The relationship between a professional for the time being spared of disabilities, and a mentally handicapped worker, is never one among equals. Rather than deny this difference, it rests upon the professional untiringly to lend a hand to the disabled employee through demonstrations of affection, closeness and a sense of professional and personal responsibility. And, lastly, Tasubinsa is also characterized by its courage in resisting the widespread and easy temptations of putting profits before people in its list of priorities, giving in to unfounded prejudices regarding the capacity of workers and, consequently, engaging in counterproductive 'paternalistic' measures.

These features of Tasubinsa's distinctive business culture bear very heavily on the areas of operations and in what is commonly known, for want of a better term, as 'human resources'.

González underscores the following hallmarks in Tasubinsa's operations (González, 2006: 79–81). Complex production processes are conscientiously broken down into simple units such that corresponding movements could easily be carried out by disabled workers. 'Poka yoke' techniques – 'mistake or error-proofing' in Japanese – are employed in the design of procedures, equipment and tools so that operations literally cannot be performed incorrectly. Because of poka yoke, for instance, a 3.5-inch floppy cannot be inserted into the external disk drive of a computer unless oriented correctly. The bevelled corner of the diskette pushes a stop in the disk drive out of the way, allowing the diskette to be inserted. This feature, along with the fact that the diskette is not a perfect square, makes incorrect orientation virtually impossible. Analogous 'lock and key' specific procedures are used in Tasubinsa production processes.

As mentioned earlier, Tasubinsa also subscribes to the 'Kanban' – 'card-signal' in Japanese – production system. The basic idea is that the supplier or warehouse should only deliver components when needed by the production line, so that there is no build-up of inventory or storage in the production area. Workstations along the production line only produce or deliver components upon receipt of an order card with the specifications (part name, description, quantity and so forth) and the corresponding empty container. Unlike the forecast-oriented method, where parts are pushed to the production line, in Kanban the delivery of components is pulled along by the production line itself. Kanban therefore bears the advantage of being a simple and understandable process that provides quick and precise production information at a low cost. This allows Tasubinsa to generate a quick response to market changes, avoiding both overproduction and underproduction, while minimizing waste. More importantly, Kanban allows for the delegation of responsibility to line workers, their disabilities notwithstanding.

Moreover, Tasubinsa employs 'cellular manufacturing' techniques, such that groups or 'cells' of people work together on particular parts of the production process. This means they do not only handle practical production, for instance, but also manage stock and try to figure out for themselves how to improve their own performance levels. The strict separation between thinking and doing as advocated by Taylorism, together with its dehumanizing effect, is thus avoided. Besides, cellular manufacturing techniques complement the other Total Quality Mangement (TQM) and Just in Time (JIT) initiatives.

Given the workers' limitations, ordinary accident-prevention measures are insufficient for Tasubinsa's needs. Special attention is paid to ergonomics which takes into account workers' health, fitness and well-being in the postures they adopt and the activities they realize. In Tasubinsa, both work and rest zones are clearly marked with vertical and horizontal signs; barriers to mobility are removed. And a pleasant, conducive environment is created with the help of picture frames, indoor plants and functional (although sober) furniture.

In paying attention to the disabled workers' emotional and social needs, workstations are arranged in a manner that encourages communication. Easy and fluid dialogue, in turn, favours an atmosphere of good humour, camaraderie and friendship, essential for a good working ambience. Such teamwork, apart from being good in itself, also drives up productivity.

Valuable insights into Tasubinsa's employment practices and personnel policies could be gained from two sources: a formal one, consisting in its second Collective Bargaining Agreement (Expediente 91/2004 of 16 March 2005), and an informal one, related to the experience of the 'personal and social development teams' (Equipo de Desarrollo Personal y Social) which operate in tandem with the supervisors or middle managers (González, 2006: 81–3).

The first thing that calls one's attention in Tasubinsa's Collective Bargaining Agreement is the degree and extent of worker representation and participation. Included among the signatories are representatives from the major national unions, Comisiones Obreras (CC.OO.) and Unión General de Trabajadores (U.G.T.). A whole section of the Agreement spells out workers' and union rights (articles 44–8): the right of members of the

Worker's Council to use company time for Council business, the right of workers to call and attend meetings, and the obligation of the company to provide the Worker's Council with the resources to carry out its tasks (an adequately furnished office, bulletin boards, pigeon-holes or mailboxes, and so forth).

The Agreement establishes five professional groups, one of which corresponds to the mentally handicapped workers (article 8). Their general job description consists in 'tasks executed according to instructions that are precise, concrete and clear, with a high level of dependence, repetitive; [jobs] which require physical effort or attention but do not need any special training aside from the one necessary for a correct adaptation to the post' (article 8). The document adds that their job comprises 'operations in accordance with a precise work-method, [done] under a high degree of supervision, and which normally demands elementary knowledge and a period of adaptation' (article 8).

Another innovation the Agreement introduces is the so-called 'low performance contract' (contrato a bajo rendimiento) (art. 11 and Real Decreto 1368/1985 of 17 July). This is meant for workers who, for whatever circumstance certified by a multiprofessional team, perform at 25 per cent less than their normal capacity, while clocking a regular workday. Although this contract allows for corresponding wage deductions, it nonetheless safeguards all other employee rights and benefits. In addition, the Agreement contains generous provisions for the continuing training of employees (article 26). Tasubinsa commits itself to offer a yearly training plan to all the different worker groups, either within company premises, during company time and at company expense, or outside. In the latter case, if it was upon Tasubinsa's initiative, the firm will shoulder from 50 per cent to the total amount of expenses.

And lastly, just like any other Collective Bargaining Agreement, there are stipulations concerning work-hours and the work calendar, leaves, vacations, salary scales and professional ranks, worker mobility, family assistance, health, insurance and retirement benefits.

Personal and social development teams are composed of psychologists, social workers and supervisors or middle managers. They meet regularly for the purpose of tracking the progress or development of each disabled worker in the professional and personal realms; they also set individual objectives or targets for a given period. It is vital that the management team work in unison. Middle managers take responsibility not only for meeting production quotas, deadlines and quality standards, but also for the evolution of each and every member of their team. For this reason they keep a formal record or logbook of 'incidents' covering health and sickness, emotional stress, behavioural alterations, performance at work, relationship with other team members, changes in family relations and so forth. They have to keep an eye open, for example, when a worker starts his decline and would be better off if sent to an occupational centre instead of the special employment centre.

An essential function of personal and social development teams relates to employee evaluation. In the previous Collective Bargaining Agreement (Expediente 69/1999 of 4 February 2000) performance evaluation was carried out in accordance with five different parameters – cooperation and attitude, perseverance and capacity, quality of work, flexibility and discipline – each of which corresponded to a bonus. Note that the criteria do not include any reference to the number of parts produced by an individual worker. Accordingly, personal and social development teams also intervened in meting out sanctions such as suspensions, salary deductions and terminations of employment for 'grave' and 'very grave violations' committed by workers (arts. 39–42).

In the present set-up, the attitudinal parameters have disappeared. According to Rosa Jaso, Tasubinsa's Managing Director and former Human Resource Head interviewed in December 2005, this does not mean that such factors have ceased to count. Rather, supervisors have grown so accustomed to their team members that a positive attitude among them had turned into a 'given' or something that could be taken for granted. It was no longer effective as an incentive. Instead, promotion within the same professional group or among different professional groups now takes place in accordance with more 'objective' criteria such as work merits and experience.

The time has now come for us to test the tenets of what we have called business 'common sense' against the Tasubinsa case. Who owns Tasubinsa? What is the owner after? How does the owner envision Tasubinsa as a firm? And what does Tasubinsa as a firm seek? The bigger question is, of course, given all its peculiarities, does Tasubinsa really qualify as a firm at all? And if in the end it does, how should our common-sense understanding of the firm change to meet the Tasubinsa challenge?

When Tasubinsa was founded in 1989, 100 per cent of the capital was provided by ANFAS, the Navarre association of families and friends of the mentally handicapped. Ten years later, in 1999, there was a change in capital structure such that ANFAS reduced its holdings to 78 per cent and Fundosa, the investment arm of Fundación ONCE, the national organization of the blind in Spain, took over the remaining 22 per cent. Legally speaking, one might say, therefore, that Tasubinsa's capital comes from ANFAS and Fundosa. However, both ANFAS and Fundosa themselves are broken down into a myriad of constituents, brought together by a special interest in the full social integration – particularly through work – and the overall welfare of the mentally disabled and the blind, respectively.

The Board of Directors of Tasubinsa is composed of 13 members: three worker representatives, three from ANFAS, three from the Navarre Regional Autonomous Government (the Director General of Social Welfare, the Director General of Labour, and the Director of the Employment Service), one from Fundosa, with the remaining three seats reserved for prominent civic leaders such as the President of the Regional Chamber of Commerce, and so forth. Reporting to the Board is the Executive Committee, headed by the Managing Director, together with Directors from the different departments, such as Marketing, Finance, Industrial Operations, Human Resources, Quality, Work Safety and Environment, and Personal and Social Development. Under the Industrial Operations department are the persons in charge of the different workshops, made up of special employment and occupational centres, which in turn could be further broken down into various teams or 'cells' with their corresponding supervisors. And, just like the characteristics of any other firm in Spain, Tasubinsa also has a Workers' Council actively involved, among others, in the design and implementation of its Collective Bargaining Agreement.

Thus, in the case of Tasubinsa, it is fairly plain to say who provides capital and who carries out the productive work. What is not so easy to determine is who *owns* the firm, or even if there is any such person or group of persons, in the strict sense of 'ownership'. For Tasubinsa's owners seem to be whoever possesses a stake in the integration and well-being of the mentally disabled in Navarre, and contributes to this end with money or work. Certainly, from this perspective of ownership, the place of prominence belongs to Tasubinsa workers and, in particular, to those who have mental disabilities themselves. Ownership, therefore, connotes something more than mere provision of capital or sporadic attendance in board meetings, although it does not exclude any of these. Above all, it indicates identification with an organization's objectives and commitment to further them with one's work or money.

What are Tasubinsa's owners, in this qualified sense, after? What is it they seek in the end? Tasubinsa's five-year strategic plan, beginning in 2006, states the following mission, vision, values and lines of action (Tasuvida, 2005: 6–7). Its corporate mission, purpose or reason for being, is 'to achieve the full professional and social integration of all people with intellectual disabilities in Navarre, and to provide a service that promotes their personal and social growth and development' (Tasuvida, 2005: 6). Over a period of five years, the corporate vision consists in Tasubinsa having transformed itself into 'the standard or benchmark among all the different special employment and occupational centers in the country, capable of offering the best service and providing employment to the mentally handicapped to respond to their needs, capacities and expectations through the different stages of their life, while achieving utmost customer satisfaction' (Tasuvida, 2005: 6).

Among its corporate values Tasubinsa lists the *independence* or *autonomy* of its governing bodies, notwithstanding the respect and cooperation owed to all the legitimate actors of Navarre society. Next comes the recognition of *the mentally disabled person as the axis or reference point* of all of Tasubinsa's endeavours, which are carried out with a view to improving his quality of life, day by day. As an organization, Tasubinsa is committed to *integrity in its decision making* and in managing capital in the service of its people. Also, it pledges to respond adequately to the needs of clients and to *guarantee the quality of its products*, while *fully respecting the freedom and self-determination of its mentally handicapped workers*. Lastly, all Tasubinsa workers strive towards the common goal of *leadership in its sector* through a high level of motivation in their activities and deference towards people in their diversity.

In accordance with the European Foundation for Quality Management (EFQM) guidelines, Tasubinsa has established the following strategic objectives (Tasuvida, 2005: 7): first, consolidation and stability as a business; second, growth and substantial improvement of competitiveness; third, profitability; fourth, the development of a new system for evaluating results and stakeholder satisfaction; fifth, advancement in both external and internal communication; and sixth, further enhancement of quality management. In this way Tasubinsa would reach its goal of becoming a transformative organization centred on the human person.

It is quite surprising that, for an organization that considers itself a business firm, profits are absent in its mission and vision statements, and are mentioned only in third place among its strategic objectives. From this we could infer that profits do not occupy the top slot among the priorities of Tasubinsa's owners; that belongs to the full social and professional integration of the mentally handicapped in Navarre, to the constant improvement of their quality of life. But neither does this mean that Tasubinsa or its owners are indifferent, much less inimical to profits. Is Tasubinsa a profitable business?

Any response to such a question has to be limited to a given time frame in order to be significant or valid. At the time of this writing (in early 2006) Tasubinsa is a profitable, financially healthy and ongoing concern. That has not always been the case, however. In 2001, Tasubinsa posted a profit of €18 802; yet 2002 and 2003 were dismal years, with the firm reporting total losses of €19 322 and €166 063, respectively (B.O. del Parlamento de Navarra, n. 112/ 28 December 2004). Its operating losses had ballooned from €725 293 in 2001 to €1 345 260 in 2003. During that same period,

Tasubinsa's assets had been reduced to a fifth, from €253 349 in 2001 to €51 147 in 2003. Such a downward trend certainly posed a threat to Tasubinsa's solvency as an organization and everything else that it stood for, most especially, its uncommon business model centred on the mentally handicapped person.

This turn of events provoked inquiries in the regional parliament regarding possible financial irregularities in mid-2004 (B.O. del Parlamento de Navarra, n. 112/ 28 December 2004). Opposition politicians claimed that, although Tasubinsa was in principle a non-state company, the lion's share of its income (between 35 and 45 per cent) came from Navarre government subsidies (Roncal, 2004; Diario de Navarra, 2004). There was even an insinuation that the numbers in red could be due to some of Tasubinsa executives' helping themselves to the company's coffers. In any case, the opposition parties thought the Navarre government had the duty to exercise greater control and supervision over Tasubinsa's finances.

At the root of this problem was the bankruptcy of Interisa, one of Tasubinsa's major clients, for which it manufactured telephone parts (B.O. del Parlamento de Navarra, n. 112/ 28 December 2004). In 2002, Interisa owed Tasubinsa €895 151 (about 75 per cent of the latter's operating losses that year) and another €829 981 in 2003. While negotiations were being undertaken with Interisa's representatives, Tasubinsa solicited a subsidy from the Navarre regional government to cover losses. In the end, the local parliament agreed to grant €660 000 in 2003, roughly half of the firm's operating losses in the previous year.

In his response before parliament, José Ignacio Palacios, then regional welfare minister, began by emphasizing that Tasubinsa was a 'sociedad anónima', that is, a company independent from state control, despite its 'public utility' (B.O. del Parlamento de Navarra, n. 112/ 28 December 2004). Therefore, the only ones responsible for Tasubinsa's operations and finances were its board directors and management team, not the members of the Navarre government. Palacios then clarified that the welfare department only extended subsidies to the occupational centres, in particular, to their personal and social development activities meant to prepare individuals for work in the special employment centres. Funds were never provided by the Navarre government to the special employment centres directly, since these are conceived to be just like any other firm competing in the market, notwithstanding their peculiarities. Moreover, the welfare department had only granted subsidies of €2 119 492 in 2001 and €2 116 502 in 2002, equivalent to around 12 per cent of Tasubinsa's income for each year, and far below the 35 to 45 per cent claimed by the opposition parties (Roncal, 2004).

Nonetheless, the promoters of the parliamentary inquiry had a point, because the remainder of the funds still came from the Navarre treasury, albeit from a different department, that of Industry (Diario de Navarra, 2004). In reply the Navarre government simply referred to the audited accounts which showed no basis for suspicions of shady dealings.

These parliamentary proceedings serve to emphasize a couple of truths about Tasubinsa's owners and their purpose in establishing the firm. They are also useful in settling whatever doubts remained regarding Tasubinsa's identity as a business organization. Tasubinsa is not a government welfare agency meant to look after the mentally disabled, neither is it a not-for-profit NGO working for a similar end. If it were so, it should be entitled to protection and subject to intervention by whoever has the public good under his care. Instead, it is an independent business set up to provide goods and services produced by mentally handicapped people, and as such is recognized by the state. Tasubinsa workers, management and board directors enjoy the same freedom and responsibilities as their colleagues from other business firms; they are subject to the same market pressures to survive, compete and grow. That Tasubinsa experienced downturns caused by the bankruptcy of clients is proof, just as in any other business firm, of its vulnerability.

In a December 2005 interview, Tasubinsa's managing director, Rosa Jaso, explained the firm's profitability in terms of its 'return coefficient'. A full 74 per cent of Tasubinsa's income proceeds from its own revenues and only 26 per cent comes from state aid in whatever form. Let us not forget that most, if not all, of that state aid is available to any individual or company that hires handicapped workers: in this Tasubinsa enjoys no privilege. It so happens that, from the total amount of state aid that it receives, Tasubinsa returns a hefty 56 per cent through taxes and social security contributions for its professionals. This is its 'return coefficient' for the state aid received: more than half of it is paid back.

There are other measures of a firm's profitability aside from the crudely objective indicator of income minus expenses for any given year. In the case of a special employment centre with a not-for-profit statute, such as Tasubinsa, there may be other more relevant benchmarks in determining how efficiently it makes use of resources. Between 2002 and 2004, sales revenues rose by 35 per cent (Ernst & Young, 2002, 2003, 2004). The percentage of subsidies to sales revenues correspondingly decreased from 63.24 per cent in 2002 to 52.21 per cent in 2004, reflecting lesser dependence on state aid. There was also a proportionate decrease in the percentage of subsidies to salaries during these years. In fact, in 2004, the increase in sales revenues was even accompanied by a diminution in salaries to a level inferior to that of 2002. In other words, with fewer labour costs, Tasubinsa was registering greater sales. Nonetheless, these gauges of productivity, apart from purely financial profitability, should always be compared to the ultimate standard the firm has set for itself, which is the complete integration of the mentally handicapped through work.

And if only to belabour the point that Tasubinsa welcomes profits, although it is not obsessed by them, Jaso disclosed a profit-sharing provision that benefits the members of ANFAS – the Navarre association for the mentally handicapped and part owners of Tasubinsa – once profits in a given year surpass a certain multiple of the firm's capital. Until then, whatever profits earned are duly reinvested in the company. So much for the issue of profits and their place among the objectives of Tasubinsa owners.

The next question that concerns us refers to the way Tasubinsa sees itself as a business firm. Is it essentially a 'nexus of contracts' as the dominant line of thinking suggests? Probably not, judging by the way Tasubinsa workers (both the disabled and those currently free from disabilities) comport themselves and by what they say. Of course the employment contracts are entirely above board, just like all the other transactions and agreements the firm enters into with its customers, suppliers, partners and so forth. Being a special employment centre, these are subject to scrupulous scrutiny by government agencies to avoid abuse. Beyond these formal legal accords, however, given the gruelling challenges of working with mentally handicapped people, one would expect a very high turnover rate among Tasubinsa professionals. Yet the complete opposite is true and the turnover rate for the past five years has been zero. Taking into account that pay and benefits, although comparable to those of similar firms, are not exceptionally high, something else must be keeping these professionals in Tasubinsa, despite the additional difficulties and personal demands. Theirs is what one may call almost a 'vocational commitment' that clearly surpasses the limits of strict reciprocity and enforceability established by contracts. Tasubinsa professionals give more of themselves than the letter of their contracts state and require. Perhaps it is also because they receive a lot more, although this plus factor cannot be accounted for in euros.

The experience with Tasubinsa's mentally disabled employees in terms of loyalty is very similar, Jaso recounts. Thus they seem to respond as best they can to the dedication and commitment manifested by management and their colleagues. Many of the disabled workers who, after training, qualify for a 'job with individual support' elsewhere or for the status of a 'self-employed disabled worker' prefer to remain instead on Tasubinsa's rolls. And those who do actually leave always return to Tasubinsa workshops during their free time and holidays: that is where their friends are found. Tasubinsa provides them with the nurturing environment they need for their development and growth, not only as disabled workers but also as integral human persons. For them Tasubinsa is a lot more than just a place of work, with its retinue of contracts, rights and obligations; it is their community, almost like their family. This is especially true because the great majority of Tasubinsa's handicapped workers never get to form families of their own.

Thus Tasubinsa may be understood as an umbrella community with three distinct complementary groups working side by side, in close contact with each other (Tasubinsa, 2005: 3). First is the group formed by mentally handicapped people in the occupational centre, who undergo occupational therapy as well as personal and social development programmes which prepare them for future work. Then come those in the special employment centre, who have work contracts with the firm and are subject to performance criteria such as productivity, quality, flexibility and so forth. And finally, we have the group of professionals without disabilities whose work is absolutely necessary for the running of Tasubinsa.

And how about Tasubinsa's goal as a business organization, as opposed to the individual motives of its owners? Does it conform to the conventional business wisdom of maximizing shareholder value?

Once more, Tasubinsa's business philosophy here seems wide of the beaten track. Firstly, it is not the interest of shareholders that reigns supreme, but that of mentally disabled workers. The place of prominence among the members of the Tasubinsa community belongs to them and everyone who partakes in this collective effort knows that he is at their service: their well-being and flourishing is his reward; it is the value he seeks to maximize. Secondly, and because of this, there is no divergence between the individual purposes of those who would qualify as Tasubinsa's owners and the end of the organization as whole. The good which individual members of the organization seek and that which the organization as such is after, is one and the same. It is a 'common good'. Everyone identifies with this purpose and commits himself to furthering it with his work in the firm. Not that everyone does the same thing, but, whatever it is he does, he does it for the same end. Thirdly, this common good is not something exclusively material, and that is why, perhaps, it can be properly shared among many. Clearly the common good of the firm must have a material basis (disabled workers should be adequately paid for their efforts, for instance), but much else goes beyond that, such as a sense satisfaction over one's achievements with the help of others and the joy of their loyalty and friendship. The material aspect is merely the tip of the iceberg compared to the other elements of a mentally handicapped person's full flourishing.

Jaso has her own version of what the end or purpose of Tasubinsa as a business firm is. As a special employment centre, it is not to be just a 'place of transit' which prepares mentally disabled individuals to work somewhere else, but a real alternative in itself for their complete social integration. She would like Tasubinsa to be a community of working persons embedded in society and positively contributing to its good, to the wider common good.

III TOWARDS A NEW THEORY OF THE FIRM

The Tasubinsa experience cannot but raise some doubts regarding what we, uncritically, may have taken as true of business organizations. The responses we have garnered from it to the fundamental questions about the firm are radically different. Shareholders should not be considered as the sole owners of the firm; perhaps firms do not even have owners, strictly speaking, but just different groups of people contributing to the ends of the firm through their work and money. Some have suggested that they be called 'stakeholders' (Freeman, 1984), but this term is also burdened by a load of implicits with which we cannot fully agree, as will be explained later on. 'Participants' or 'members' may be the best names among those available to designate the people who take part in the collective effort or who form part of this distinctive human institution called a firm.

The participants or members of a firm do not pursue economic interests or profits exclusively, nor are their ends limited to their own advantage or benefit. They could just as well strive for wider goals in which they do not figure as direct or primary beneficiaries: for instance, the social integration and well-being of the mentally disabled in Navarre in the case of Tasubinsa. Firms need not be understood predominantly in the legal mode as a 'nexus of contracts'. It is plain that they need an adequate legal figure or personality to operate in civil society, but this does not capture their essence or deepest meaning. Rather, business organizations seem to be more aptly defined as a 'community of workers'; they are a 'nexus of relationships' among human beings on the occasion of (and not necessarily confined to) work. Implicit is the recognition that the human activity called 'work' gives rise to a host of results aside from the goods or services produced. Many of these results are intangible and difficult to account for. Workers themselves are notably enriched through the habits, skills, dispositions, relationships, satisfactions and so forth they acquire, none of which is exclusively material in nature.

And lastly, with the Tasubinsa case in mind, the purpose of the firm can no longer be circumscribed to something as narrow as the maximization of shareholder value. Instead, it should be the achievement of the organization's particular end, the growth and development of the mentally handicapped, for example, insofar as it contributes to the common good of society, which is the full flourishing of all its members individually and as a whole; that is, in relation to one another. This is the sole and ultimate justification of a firm: its ability to promote integral human flourishing through organized work, in terms not only of the goods and services produced but also of the excellences of mind and character or virtues acquired by its participants. As we hope to demonstrate further on, these acquired human excellences or virtues that accrue to the workers themselves are even more important than the objective or material goods – including profits – that they produce.

These conflicting accounts of the business organization somehow force us to go beyond the questions themselves and to reconsider the underlying premises identified earlier, namely, Coase's 'Nature of the firm' (1937), Jensen and Meckling's 'Agency theory' (1976) and Friedman's 'Shareholder theory' (1970). Each one of these doctrines has received a barrage of criticisms in recent years, presaging a thorough revision of the neoclassical 'Theory of the firm' they have supported up to now. By means of the adjective 'neoclassical' we refer to that dominant school of thought in economics which holds the following assumptions regarding the economic agent or *homo economicus*: individuals have rational preferences among outcomes that can be identified with a value; individuals maximize utility in the same way that firms maximize profits; and individuals act independently of each other (and firms are nothing more than the aggregate of individuals) on the basis of full and relevant information (Weintraub, 1993).

An interesting variant of the *homo economicus* is what Jensen and Meckling call the 'resourceful, evaluative, maximizing model' (REMM) (Jensen and Meckling, 1994). Regardless of the work they perform, be they politicians, managers, academics, professionals, philanthropists or factory workers, individuals in organizations always behave as resourceful, evaluative maximizers. Initially, Jensen and Meckling admit that individuals are open to almost any kind of good – knowledge, the plight of others, culture, wealth, water, and so forth – but none of these represents an absolute need. They are always subject to trade-offs and subsitutions according to the rule of transitivity. They illustrate this principle through an anecdote attributed to George Bernard Shaw during an ocean voyage (Jensen and Meckling, 1994: 9). The playwright purportedly asked an actress on deck whether she would be willing to sleep with him for a million dollars, and she agreed. He then followed up by asking, 'How about for ten dollars?' And she replied, indignant, 'What do you think I am?' To which he responded, 'We've already established that. We're now just haggling over price.' That is, 'like it or not, individuals are willing to sacrifice a little of almost anything we care to name, even reputation or morality, for a sufficiently large quantity of other desired things' (Jensen and Meckling, 1994: 9).

Furthermore, each individual's wants are unlimited; he can never be satiated, for him there is no such thing as enough. Therein lies his nature as a maximizer, in that he is constantly working to loosen the constraints that prevent him from doing what he in every given moment wishes. Another way of putting it is that individuals are forever scheming to widen or improve their opportunity sets (Jensen and Meckling, 1994: 4–5). Thus REMM behaviour is a highly mechanical one that basically consists in assigning probabilities and values to various actions and choosing that which yields the highest expected value. In this same line, the 'pain avoidance model' (PAM) is complementary to REMM as a descriptor of conduct or behaviour (Jensen and Meckling, 1994: 9).

Perhaps the time has come to turn these bits of conventional business wisdom on their head.

Among the fiercest critics of the neoclassical economic theory of the firm currently dominating management thinking we find those who stress its irrelevance to practice (Mintzberg, 2004) and those who emphasize the outright harm it causes. Belonging to this latter group was the late Sumantra Ghoshal of the London Business School. Making a play on what Lewin had affirmed, that 'nothing is as practical as a good theory' (Lewin, 1945: 129), Ghoshal, in turn, proposed the obverse, that 'nothing is as dangerous as a bad theory. [. . .] bad management theories are, at present, destroying good management practices' (Ghoshal, 2005: 86). Writing in the aftermath of the spate of corporate scandals just when the dot-com boom went bust, Ghoshal unequivocally declared that 'many of the worst excesses of recent management practices have their roots in a set of ideas that have emerged from business school academics in the last 30 years' (Ghoshal, 2005: 75).

Ghoshal includes in this bag of pernicious ideas Jensen and Meckling's agency theory in first place: 'we have taught our students that managers cannot be trusted to do their jobs – which, of course, is to maximize shareholder value – and that to overcome "agency problems", managers' interests and incentives must be aligned with those of the shareholders by, for example, making stock options a significant part of their pay' (Ghoshal, 2005: 75). Next comes Coase's transaction cost economics and its development by Williamson (1975) as the ultimate explanation for the existence of the firm *vis-à-vis* the market: 'we have preached the need for tight monitoring and control of people to prevent "opportunistic behavior"' (Ghoshal, 2005: 75). When we add into this tandem of agency theory and transaction cost economics elements of game theory and negotiation analysis, 'the picture that emerges is one that is now very familiar in practice: the ruthlessly hard-driving, strictly top-down, command-and-control focused, shareholder-value-obsessed, win-at-any-cost business leader of which Scott Paper's "Chainsaw" Al Dunlap and Tyco's Dennis Kozlowski are only the most extreme examples' (Ghoshal, 2005: 85). Ghoshal also makes a special mention of Friedman's dictum against the acceptance by corporate officials of any social responsibility apart from making as much money as possible for shareholders (Ghoshal, 2005: 79). For the late London Business School professor this represents 'the explicit denial of any role of moral or ethical considerations in the practice of management' (Ghoshal, 2005: 79).

Given the peculiarities of the social sciences, it might be more difficult to demonstrate the falsehood behind these assumptions of radical individualism and the exaltation of self-interest in the neoclassical economic theory of the firm. There is no denying, however, that, under the guise of asceptic, value-neutral, amoral and 'scientific' theory, immoral business and management practices have in fact been promoted. The academic discipline governing business and management has been reduced to some kind of physics wherein people's actions are determined by economic, social and psychological laws and causes (Ghoshal, 2005: 77). Free human intentionality and agency have been eliminated as a result, and together with them all relevant ethical considerations.

Perhaps the neoclassical economic model has not been completely successful in eradicating the human factor, reducing the firm to nothing more than a money-making machine, despite its efforts. After all, as Nobel laureate in economics Herbert Simon presciently advised, 'nothing is more fundamental in setting our research agenda and informing our research methods than our view of the nature of human beings whose behaviors we are studying' (Simon, 1985: 293). The vision of human nature forwarded, nonetheless, is a horrendously pessimistic and 'gloomy' one, based more on ideology than on scientific inquiry (Ghoshal, 2005: 82). The ensuing role of the social sciences, particularly of economics, is to devise and design institutions in such a way as to prevent bad people from doing more harm. Hence all the insistence on checks, monitoring and controls in organizations.

This premise on the radical imperfection or corruption of the human being is then compounded by the self-fulfilling mechanism proper to social science theories (Pfeffer, 2004). Unlike the case of the physical sciences, where the trajectories of the earth and the sun are totally unaffected regardless of whether one adopts a geocentric or a heliocentric view of the cosmos, in the humanities this is not the case. Among the social sciences, prophecies tend to be self-fulfilling, not because of any intrinsic truth on their part but simply because the knower cannot be fully separated from the object of his knowledge, which is he himself and his actions.

Applied to business and management, this means that, if you start out by suspecting that a worker in the firm is a crook, you will consequently treat him as one, subjecting him to all forms of surveillance since that would be the reasonable thing to do. And chances are that the worker, for his part, in the end will behave as a crook, if only not to disappoint you and your expectations of him. This is what is bound to happen independently of whether the worker really was a crook in the first place. A more open-minded and ultimately more realistic view should, of course, equally accept the possibility that at first the worker could have been honest.

For Williamson (1975), who advances Coase's transaction cost theory of the firm, it is not even necessary to believe from the outset that everyone or that the majority of people are opportunistic, lying and cheating when the benefits of doing so exceed the costs of keeping promises. It is sufficient to know that some people are, and that there is no foolproof method of determining ex ante those who are from those who are not. Hence, 'the manager's task is to use hierarchical authority to prevent the opportunists from benefiting at the cost of others. To ensure effective coordination, managers must know what everyone ought to be doing, give them strict instructions to do those things, and use their ability to monitor and control and to reward and punish to ensure that everyone does what he or she is told to do' (Ghoshal, 2005: 85).

Unfortunately, though, for Williamson, his theory is not only self-fulfilling, but also self-defeating. Surveillance and control systems, instead of curbing opportunistic behaviours, create and enhance them instead (Ghoshal, 2005: 85). Perceived management distrust through excessive monitoring erodes employee morale, self-worth and intrinsic motivation, giving rise to mere perfunctory compliance. It only leads to a spiral of ever-increasing surveillance and need for surveillance.

Given such a toxic combination of assumptions and theories, and given such unsavoury results, why do we put up with them? 'The answer – the only answer that is really valid – is that this assumption helps in structuring and solving nice mathematical models. [. . .] the elegant mathematics of principal–agent models can be applied to the enormously complex economic, social, and moral issues related to the governance of giant public corporations that have such enormous influence on the lives of thousands – often millions – of people', Ghoshal retorts (2005: 80). So behind this gross oversimplification of the structure and dynamics of the firm is an unenlightened subservience to mathematical models as the only vehicles worthy of the name of science. Maths is neat, real life is messy. Real life and its messiness, therefore, have to be sacrificed on the altar of science and mathematics. We may have gained enormously in neatness, then, but we would have also woefully lost out on the truth, which should really be the precise point.

So far we have surveyed different responses to the question of what a firm is. We began by considering the dominant, conventional account based on neoclassical economic theory and its assumptions. Then we reviewed an entirely different and contrary set of answers generated by the experience of a firm called Tasubinsa. Certainly, the Tasubinsa story alone and by itself cannot give rise to a full-fledged alternative theory of the firm, but it certainly poses some heavyweight objections to the received wisdom. These objections and whatever insights the Tasubinsa experience could have afforded us were later on supported by a tightly woven web of criticisms regarding how 'bad management theories are destroying good management practices'. This now leaves us better equipped in our intent to gain not only an improved understanding of the firm but, more importantly, a fuller, firmer grasp of its leadership and governance. To this we shall now direct our attention in the following chapters.

IV   IN BRIEF

- Neoclassical economic theory of the firm disguised as business common sense rests on the following assumptions: (1) shareholders own the firm, (2) shareholders seek to maximize their utilities, (3) the firm is a nexus of contractual relationships; and (4) the purpose of the firm is to maximize shareholder value. Theoretical support for these premises is provided mainly, though not exclusively, by transaction cost economics (Coase), agency theory (Jensen and Meckling) and shareholder theory (Friedman).
- In an advanced service economy where human capital has become the most valuable resource of a firm, a widespread slogan for success consists in 'attracting, motivating, developing and retaining the best talent'. In a sense, this is not an option open to Tasubinsa, a Spanish special employment centre where more than 90 per cent of the workers are mentally handicapped.
- Nonetheless, Tasubinsa's positive experience seems to imply that (1) it would be more proper to speak of 'members' of the firm rather than 'owners', (2) firm members pursue both economic and non-economic goals, and that self-interest is neither exclusive nor over-riding, (3) the firm is better understood as a community of persons working together; and (4) the purpose of the firm is to contribute to the common good, that is, the material and moral development of members through their work.
- To the extent that social science theories tend to be self-fulfilling (Pfeffer), there is a need to formulate a new theory of the firm to ground the practice of management and governance (Ghoshal). This calls for a realistic and ethical view of human nature (Simon) that acknowledges the person's capacity to work with others in institutions towards a common goal, perfecting himself in the process.

REFERENCES

B.O. del Parlamento de Navarra, n. 112/ 28 December 2004.

Coase, Ronald (1937), 'The nature of the firm', *Economica*, **4**(16), 386–405.

Coase, Ronald (1991a), 'The nature of the firm: meaning', in Oliver E. Williamson and Sidney G. Winter (eds), *The Nature of the Firm: Origins, Evolution and Development*, New York: Oxford University Press, pp. 48–60.

Coase, Ronald (1991b), 'The nature of the firm: influence', in Oliver E. Williamson and Sidney G. Winter (eds), *The Nature of the Firm: Origins, Evolution, and Development*, New York: Oxford University Press, pp. 61–74.

Diario de Navarra (2004), 'Empresas Navarras', Diario de Navarra, 8 June.

Eisenhardt, Kathleen M. (1989), 'Agency theory: an assessment and review', *Academy of Management Review*, **14**(1), 57–74.

Ernst & Young (2002), *Informe de auditoria. Talleres auxiliares de subcontratación Industria Navarra, S.A. (Tasubinsa)*.

Ernst & Young (2003), *Informe de auditoria. Talleres auxiliares de subcontratación Industria Navarra, S.A. (Tasubinsa)*.

Ernst & Young (2004), *Informe de auditoria. Talleres auxiliares de subcontratación Industria Navarra, S.A. (Tasubinsa)*.

Expediente 69/1999, Boletín Oficial de Navarra, n° 16, 4 February 2000.

Expediente 91/2004, Boletín Oficial de Navarra, n° 32, 16 March 2005.

Freeman, R. Edward (1984), *Strategic Management: A Stakeholder Approach*, Boston, MA: Pitman.

Friedman, Milton (1970), 'The social responsibility of business is to increase its profits', *The New York Times Magazine*, 13 September.

Ghoshal, Sumantra (2005), 'Bad management theories are destroying good management practices', *Academy of Management Learning & Education*, **4**(1), 75–91.

González, Óscar (2006), 'La cultura corporativa de una empresa de discapacitados', *Nuevas Tendencias*, January, **61**, 63–84.

Jensen, Michael C. and William H. Meckling (1976), 'The theory of the firm: managerial behaviour, agency costs and ownership structure', *Journal of Financial Economics*, **3**(4), 305–60.

Jensen, Michael C. and William H. Meckling (1994), 'The nature of man', *Journal of Applied Corporate Finance*, Summer, **7**(2), 4–19.

Lewin, Kurt (1945), 'The research centre for group dynamics at Massachusetts Institute of Technology', *Sociometry*, **8**, 126–35.

Ley 13/1982, 7 April (B.O.E. 30-05-1982).

Mintzberg, Henry (2004), *Managers Not MBAs. A Hard Look at the Soft Practice of Managing and Management Development*, San Francisco, CA: Berret-Koehler Publishers, Inc.

Orden 16 October 1998 (B.O.E. 21-11-1998).

Pfeffer, Jeffrey (2004), 'How economic language and assumptions undermine ethics: rediscovering human values', *TECNUN Journal*, **1**, May, 9–22.

Real Decreto 1368/1985, 17 July (B.O.E. 8-08-1985).

Real Decreto 27/2000, 14 January (B.O.E. n. 22, 26-01-2000).

Real Decreto 290/2004, 20 February (B.O.E. n. 45, 21-02-2004).

Roncal, Pablo (2004), 'Comparecencia en el Parlamento Foral', *Diario de Noticias*, 9 June.

Shankman, Neil A. (1999), 'Reframing the debate between agency and stakeholder theories of the firm', *Journal of Business Ethics*, **19**(4), 319–34.

Simon, Herbert (1985), 'Human nature in politics: the dialogue of psychology with political science', *American Political Science Review*, **79**, 293–304.

Tasubinsa (2005), *Informe: Centro Especial de Empleo*, 25 January.

Tasuvida (2005), 'Clave empresarial. Plan estratégico', *Revista de Tasubinsa*, December, **1**, 6–7.

Weintraub, E. Roy (1993), *General Equilibrium Analysis: Studies in Appraisal*, Ann Arbor, MI: University of Michigan Press.

Williamson, Oliver E. (1975), *Markets and Hierarchies: Analysis and Antitrust Implications*, New York: Free Press.

2. Corporate governance by box ticking

I SARBANES–OXLEY AND ENRON: IS THE REMEDY WORSE THAN THE DISEASE?

The Sarbanes–Oxley Act, also known as the Public Company Accounting Reform and Investor Protection Act (Pub.L.No. 107-204, 116 Stat. 745), became effective as United States federal law on 30 July 2002. This law was meant primarily to protect investors by improving the accuracy and reliability of corporate disclosures. At the law's signing, President George W. Bush affirmed that it contained 'the most far-reaching reforms of American business practices since the time of Franklin Delano Roosevelt' (Bush, 2002), in clear allusion to the New Deal of the 1930s. 'This law says to every dishonest corporate leader: you will be exposed and punished, the era of low standards and false profits is over; no boardroom in America is above or beyond the law' (Bush, 2002), continued the President with rhetorical flourish.

Sarbanes–Oxley consists of 11 sections or titles: one establishes the Public Company Accounting Oversight Board (PCAOB), two specifically create tough criminal penalties for executives committing fraud or issuing misleading information and several more cover areas such as auditor independence, corporate responsibility, financial disclosures, analyst conflicts of interest, and corporate and criminal fraud accountability. Sarbanes–Oxley also updates and amends provisions from the Securities Exchange Act of 1934, the Employee Retirement Income Security Act of 1974 and the Federal Corporate Sentencing Guidelines. Among Sarbanes–Oxley's major provisions we find the certification of financial reports by chief executive officers and chief financial officers as well as the disclosure of their compensation and benefits, a ban on personal loans to executive officers and directors, an accelerated reporting of insider trades and their prohibition during pension fund blackout periods, a demand for strict auditor independence through the exclusion of all other non-audit work (actuarial and legal services and management consultancies, for instance) and the requirement of independent annual audit reports regarding internal controls on financial reporting (Fried, Frank, Harris et al., 2003; Hogan, 2003, 2004; Rockness and Rockness, 2005: 43–4).

The background story to Sarbanes–Oxley is, of course, the series of corporate scandals triggered off by Enron that rocked the financial market in the United States beginning in the third quarter of 2001. In fact, most of the new rules and regulations that Sarbanes–Oxley mandated seemed to have been designed specifically to prevent a new Enron-like scandal from occurring. How did the Enron nightmare come to be?

With a market capitalization of $63 billion in 2001, Enron ranked seventh in the Fortune Top 500 list. It had also been voted America's Most Innovative Company for several consecutive years. Since the mid-1990s, the firm had reported an eight-fold increase in sales, to more than $100 billion, with income reaching a record-breaking $1.3 billion in 2000. No doubt these merits had contributed to Enron's board of directors being chosen as the third best in the US by *Chief Executive* magazine in 2001 (Sison, 2002: 24). Unfortunately, however, most of these purported achievements turned out in the end to be based on half-truths, if not on blatant lies.

On appearance, Enron's board scrupulously complied with most best practice recommendations for corporate governance, such as those issued by The Business Roundtable (2005), for example. Beginning with the board's composition and structure, we find that the post of Chairman, held by Kenneth Lay, was separate from that of President and CEO, occupied by Jeffrey Skilling. From a total of 15 directors – by most accounts, the ideal number – only Lay and Skilling came from management, the overwhelming majority being external and independent directors. This roster was composed of successful businesspersons, experts in finance and accounting, several of whom had served for more than 20 years in Enron and other companies. Four had polished academic backgrounds. Coming from countries such as the US, Hong Kong, Brazil and Great Britain, Enron directors arguably provided a truly global business outlook. The board itself was divided into five committees (Executive, Audit, Finance, Compensation, Nominations) each headed by an external director. Among them was Dr Robert Jaedicke, professor of accounting emeritus and former dean of the Graduate School of Business, Stanford University, in audit, and Sir John Wakeham, former UK secretary for energy and member of the House of Lords, in nominations (*The Guardian*, 2002).

From the viewpoint of operations, we discover that the board held five meetings yearly, with additional ones convoked whenever needed (The Permanent Subcommittee on Investigations of the Committee on Governmental Affairs, 2002: 8–9). These meetings usually lasted for two days: one, dedicated to committee meetings and another, to the full board. During committee meetings, directors received presentations on company performance, internal controls, new business ventures and other special transactions. The compensation committee regularly received inputs from the firm's external consultant, Towers Perrin, and the audit committee, from the external auditor, Arthur Andersen. At full board meetings the company's outside legal counsel, Vinson & Elkins, normally intervened as well. The working relationship between top management and the board and among the directors themselves was generally characterized as efficient and harmonious.

Yet on 3 December 2001, Enron filed what was until then the biggest bankruptcy case in American courts, seeking protection for assets worth $49.8 billion and debts of $31.2 billion. About half a year later, on 8 July 2002, a US Senate Investigations Committee released its findings accusing the Enron board of the company's collapse (The Permanent Subcommittee on Investigations of the Committee on Governmental Affairs, 2002: 3, 52–3, 55–6, 57–8). The board had egregiously failed to exercise its fiduciary duty, ignoring numerous questionable practices by Enron management. Among these practices were the continued use of high-risk accounting and extensive off-the-books activity which did not comply with generally accepted accounting principles. The board left conflicts of interest in senior officials to go unchecked, allowing its Chief Financial Officer, Andrew Fastow, to establish the LJM private equity fund and to profit at Enron's expense, for example. Directors too were overly generous with executive compensation, failing to monitor the Chairman, Kenneth Lay's pay. At over $140M in 2000, it was more than ten times the average for CEOs of US publicly-traded companies. Neither did the board stop Lay's abuse of a personal credit line, permitting him to avail himself of more than $77M in cash.

The board had not properly overseen the independence of its members, many of whom were compromised by business relations with Enron. Herbert Winokur, for instance, also served on the board of the National Tank Company, which sold oilfield equipment and services surpassing $2.5M to Enron subsidiaries between 1997 and 2000. Robert Belfer, former Chairman and CEO of Belco Oil and Gas, had been engaged with Enron in hedging arrangements worth tens of millions of dollars since 1996. Directors from not-for-profit institutions were equally mired in unseemly conflicts of interest. Two Enron directors, Dr LeMaistre and Dr Mendelsohn, were former presidents of M.D. Andersen. In 1991, Enron pledged $1.5M to the M.D. Andersen Cancer Center in Texas, and, since 1997, the Center had received nearly $600 000 in donations from Enron and Chairman Lay. Similarly, Enron and Lay had donated more than $50 000 since 1996 to the George Mason University, which employed Enron director, Dr Wendy Gramm. Most outrageous of all, perhaps, was the case of Lord John Wakeham. Besides his board compensation of $350 000 in 2000 (more than twice the average for directors of US publicly-traded companies), he had been receiving a monthly retainer of $6000 since 1996. And on the institutional level, both Enron and Andersen had made a mockery of the standards of professional independence. Andersen was earning more by providing consultancy services to Enron, the company it was, in principle, 'impartially' auditing. In 2000 alone, the combined audit and consultancy fees Andersen charged Enron ran up to $52M.

A well governed company, with a properly functioning board, requires far more things than just producing stellar financial results (since these could be faked) or an apparent strict compliance with codes of good corporate governance, since these focus on the letter rather than the spirit. For this reason one may welcome increased government regulation such as the Sarbanes–Oxley stipulations which seem to be tailor-made remedies for Enron's ills. Or are they, really? How effective could Sarbanes–Oxley have been in preventing the Enron meltdown? Is it sufficient to ensure good corporate governance? What else, if anything, is necessary?

It is disheartening indeed to hear an authority such as Harvey Pitt, former US Securities and Exchange Commission (SEC) chairman, remark, 'Everything that went wrong at Enron was already illegal before SOX [Sarbanes–Oxley] passage' (Boerner, 2004: 41). In other words, the Enron board could have perfectly ticked all the boxes of Sarbanes–Oxley compliance and still the scam would have gone on undeterred. Perhaps there is no such thing as a law that could singlehandedly eradicate corporate fraud once and for all, but the least one could expect is that a new law represents an improvement over the previous situation. Yet even on this very basic premise there seems to be serious doubts.

A huge number of Sarbanes–Oxley critics are simply of the belief that legislation is not the answer to the problem of corporate malfeasance. Honesty and integrity in business cannot be mandated, much less by government, so they say. A lot of attention has been focused on Sarbanes–Oxley section 406, promoting the adoption of a code of ethics for senior financial officers. Companies now have the obligation to disclose whether they have such a code and, if not, explain why. However, there are no indications as to the language or procedures the code must include. Instead, each company is free to decide for itself what the compliance procedures and disciplinary measures for ethical breaches will be.

Enron had a code explicitly prohibiting conduct which 'directly or indirectly would be detrimental to the best interests of the Company or [. . .] which would bring to the employee financial gain separately derived as a direct consequence of his or her employment with the Company' (The Permanent Subcommittee on Investigations of the Committee on Governmental Affairs, 2002: 25). The code also forbade employees from owning an interest or participating, directly or indirectly, 'in the profits of any other entity which does business with or is a competitor of the Company, unless such ownership or participation has been previously disclosed in writing to the Chairman of the Board and Chief Executive Officer of Enron Corporation and such officer has determined that such interest or participation does not adversely affect the best interests of the Company' (Powers et al., 2002: 44). Obviously, these provisos were repeatedly ignored or waived and, in the end, they proved useless. Codes could only be as good as the people who enforce them.

Furthermore, as a *Harvard Law Review* note suggests, 'Sarbanes–Oxley's attempt to improve the transparency of corporate codes by requiring enhanced disclosure is a good example of a legislative effort whose spirit may evaporate through compliance. Those executives who abused codes [. . .] before Sarbanes–Oxley are unlikely to be deterred now because codes can be craftily written and those honest executives who were using codes effectively prior to the Act will have perverse incentives to rewrite them for fear of the litigation and negative market signals that may stem from the heightened disclosure that Sarbanes–Oxley requires' (*Harvard Law Review*, 2003: 2141). That is, codes are not only oftentimes ineffective, but, depending on the intention with which they are used, they could even turn out to be pernicious.

Definitely, there has been no lack of laws in the US attempting to impose ethical behaviour on securities markets, the auditing profession or the corporate world in general, even before Sarbanes–Oxley entered the scene (Rockness and Rockness, 2005: 33–4). After the stockmarket crash of 1929, the Glass–Stegall Act was passed, prohibiting banks from selling securities to pay off loans to failing entities and creating an institutional barrier between commercial banks and investment banks. Succeedingly, the Securities and Exchange Acts of 1933 and 1934 were approved, regulating securities trading through the newly-created Securities and Exchange Commission (SEC), mandating common accounting standards and requiring the audit of publicly traded companies by certified public accountants (CPAs). By then, misrepresentation in the sale of securities, insider trading, manipulation of financial markets and fraudulent financial reporting already became included among the punishable behaviours. Way back in 1940, the Investment Company Act was legislated, recognizing the fiduciary responsibilities of company directors and calling for periodic disclosures of a company's structure, operations, financial conditions and investment policies. And after a spate of irregularities affecting the Savings and Loan industry in the late 1980s, the Federal Deposit Insurance Corporation Improvement Act came into being in 1991, requiring independent auditor attestation on management reports on internal control. Finally, in 1995, the Private Securities Litigation Reform Act went even a step further by obliging auditors to report fraud directly to the SEC. To say, therefore, that corporate finance is one of the most heavily regulated areas in modern American society could very well pass as a mild under-statement.

More regulation such as Sarbanes–Oxley cannot be the remedy, especially since markets themselves do a better job at self-correcting abuses and restoring investor confidence, some would hasten to add almost counterintuitively (Ribstein, 2002). Sarbanes–Oxley measures rely heavily on independent directors as watchdogs, auditors as detectives, increased disclosure and the dissuasive effect of heightened criminal liabilities, yet these are only marginally effective (Ribstein, 2002: 29–40). Outside directors face insurmountable limitations in terms of time, information and inclination to immerse themselves in management. They only have time to review, rather than make business decisions; they depend on insiders for crucial information; and understandably they would be very hesitant to second-guess the decisions of the same executives who nominated them to the board in the first place. Auditors, for their part, do not usually engage in forensic audits to uncover wrongdoing, but only in sampling audits. How more regulation would improve their ability to spot the instances of corporate fraud that managers are determined to hide is difficult to imagine. Furthermore, Enron's failings could be attributed more to the ambiguity of what it already disclosed than on its silence. Obliging firms to reveal off-balance sheet transactions, pro forma earnings and material changes in financial conditions could just be today's solutions to yesterday's problems. As for more stringent penalties, these could very well underestimate the overwhelming impulses of greed: 'The substantial existing regulatory framework was breached by aggressive outsiders who seemed determined to ignore the risks of their actions, including their personal exposure to punishment' (Ribstein, 2002: 68).

What is worse, Sarbanes–Oxley seems to have inadvertently ignored its attendant costs: 'increasing agency costs by skewing executives' incentives to engage in value-maximizing transactions; encouraging executives to move to less monitored firms and activities; increasing firms' costs of obtaining information about executives' fraudulent activities; and increasing friction in the organization by reducing trust' (Ribstein, 2002: 40). In fact, according to a 2003 survey conducted by LexisNexis and the International Bar Association (IBA), one in four US lawyers think that the most significant effect of Sarbanes–Oxley would be higher legal costs (LexisNexis and IBA, 2003: 3). Corporate legal expenses would balloon because, among other things, executives would hire their own attorneys to advise them on corporate decision making and communications.

For the above-mentioned reasons, market-based responses such as intensified scrutiny and alertness, signalling by honest firms to differentiate themselves from other competitors for capital, expanded shareholder monitoring including the possibility of takeovers and competition among multiple regulators would all make a better alternative to regulation (Ribstein, 2002: 52–68). In this connection, Gordon criticizes specific Sarbanes–Oxley provisions of being over-eager to mandate the immediate disclosure of material business developments (the so-called 'price-perfecting diclosure') even when this premature disclosure sacrifices shareholder value for very little gain in capital market efficiency (Gordon, 2003).

Another group of critics is not against legislation in itself, but only against Sarbanes–Oxley in particular. These individuals base their argument on Sarbanes–Oxley too quickly separating facts, processes and actions, on the one hand, from values, intentions and culture, on the other, hardly paying any attention to the latter. As a result, it enervates ethics, which should be instead the main driving force towards reform (Rothchild, 2005). To be sure, law occupies an important place, together with a study of the economic incentives of agents, but neither of them makes ethics superfluous. Without ethics, rules on transparency and disclosure would be like a net with holes too large to catch corporate miscreants. Similarly, an excessive emphasis on legal responsibilities could distract actors from their wider social and moral commitments. Less procedural and formalistic legislation and more ethics seems to encapsulate their message.

A third group welcomes Sarbanes–Oxley on the whole, although individually they find it out of focus, for different reasons. Cullinan believes that Sarbanes–Oxley merely addresses symptoms, proposing a superficial understanding of auditor independence, rather than attacking 'the underlying disease of a lack of sense of public duty, and inadequate emphasis on audit competence in the audit profession's culture' (Cullinan, 2004: 862). At the root of the issue was the auditor's lack of resolve in standing up to a client on misstatements. Deakin and Konzelmann object that the Enron affair was not so much the result of the board's failure in monitoring, as Sarbanes–Oxley implies, but its miscalculation of the risks inherent in the firm's otherwise legitimate business plan of 'intelligent gambling' (Deakin and Konzelmann, 2004). Only as a consequence of this error in managing corporate risk did the board flounder in implementing an effective system of internal control. Commenting on the whistleblower protections advocated by Sarbanes–Oxley from a criminal law perspective, Brickey states that they would not have been sufficient to induce Sherron Watkins, an Enron vice-president, to bypass the corporate chain of command and report the anomalies directly to the SEC (Brickey, 2003: 368). Therefore, despite the introduction of explicit prohibitions on retaliation against witnesses, it is far from clear that Watkins could have taken such a course of action.

Along the same lines of acknowledging the need for Sarbanes–Oxley while at the same time pointing out its deficiencies, Columbia professor

John C. Coffee, Jr offers us what is, perhaps, the most comprehensive view. Coffee identifies three different accounts, each featuring a separate actor, as plausible explanations of the Enron fiasco (Coffee, 2003). The first, the 'Gatekeeper Story', focuses on 'reputational intermediaries' such as auditors, analysts, debt rating agencies and attorneys on whom investors rely for verification and certification of information. Legislation and court decisions in the 1990s resulted in reduced legal exposure for gatekeepers. This development, combined with increased income opportunities from consulting services, led gatekeepers to acquiesce to their clients' financial irregularities. Next comes the 'Misaligned Incentives Story', focusing on managers and the shift in their compensation from cash to equities during that same decade. Stock options created perverse incentives among executives to inflate earnings reports and thus provoke dramatic spikes in share prices. In third place is the 'Herding Story', in which investment fund managers are the protagonists. Given their obsession with short-term quarterly performance, they had an enormous incentive to 'ride the bubble' or 'run with the bulls' in the market of the 1990s. Even if they sensed the danger of overvalued stocks, they preferred to take safety in the herd and be collectively wrong instead of sticking out and playing the role of the prophet of bad news.

Coffee concludes that Sarbanes–Oxley subscribes exclusively to the first account, the 'Gatekeeper Story' of how company executives seduced auditors with consulting income. Sarbanes–Oxley therefore loses out on the complementary explaining power of the other two stories. What is completely amazing, though, is the manner in which the board is all but exonerated for its role in the corporate breakdown by Coffee's account. For him, blame should justly be spread elsewhere, among both senior executives and outside gatekeepers. He thinks there is little reason to believe that board behaviour has deteriorated over recent decades and he even entertains the idea that it has probably improved (Coffee, 2003: 6).

This optimism not only over Sarbanes–Oxley in particular, but also over US corporate governance in general is, of course, shared by other authors, the spiral of scandals notwithstanding. Holmstrom and Kaplan underscore the fact that, over the past two decades, the US economy and stockmarket have performed well both on an absolute basis as well as relative to those of countries such as Great Britain, France, Germany and Japan (Holmstrom and Kaplan, 2003). Even after the scandals broke out into full public view, the US stockmarket continued to outperform other broad indices. No doubt certain parts of US corporate governance needed some fixing, such as the area of market and government oversight, but there has been a quick regulatory response since then. Sarbanes–Oxley could definitely help in making a good system better; however, one should be cautious of overreacting. Firstly, some provisions of Sarbanes–Oxley are ambiguous and even contradict specific aspects of state corporate law, such that they may very well invite aggressive litigation; and secondly, Sarbanes–Oxley brings about an abrupt shift from a more flexible state regulation such as that of Delaware, for instance, to a more rigid federal one (Holmstrom and Kaplan, 2003: 22). Sarbanes–Oxley therefore leaves the board with very little room for manoeuvring.

In response to this, perhaps, excessively rosy picture of US corporate governance, it may be helpful to refer to the attempt of some economists from the Brookings Institution to calculate the overall cost of the crisis. They estimated the combined Enron and WorldCom bankruptcies to have cost the US GDP around $35 billion, mainly through losses in stockmarket wealth (Graham, Litan and Sukhtankar, 2002). That is the equivalent of a $10 increase in the price per barrel of crude oil over a year or to the annual federal government spending on homeland security. It may be taken for granted that the bankruptcies were not enough to sink the ship of the US economy as a whole; nevertheless, the dent they made on its hull was far from inconsequential.

Taking a step backwards, one finds that the very effect of corporate governance on firm performance is in itself put in doubt. Some authors say that better-governed firms, at least according to eight categories including audit, board of directors, charter/bylaws, director education, executive and director compensation, ownership, progressive practices and state of incorporation, are more profitable, more valuable and pay greater dividends to shareholders (Brown and Caylor, 2004). But others suggest that structural indicators of corporate governance typically used in academic research and institutional rating services have very limited ability to explain organizational performance and managerial behaviour (Larcker, Richardson and Tuna, 2004). After a comparative study of corporate governance rating systems both at the level of individual companies and at country-level, some scholars could only infer that 'the link between corporate governance and performance is still open for discussion and requires further research' (Van den Berghe and Levrau, 2003: 73). From a more limited perspective, we are also told that several key governance characteristics, such as the independence of boards and audit committees or the provision of non-audit services by external auditors, are unrelated to the probability of a company restating earnings, which is often taken to be among the first signs of probable irregularities (Agrawal and Chadha, 2005). What if, in the end, corporate governance does not even matter to a firm's performance?

It is time for a recap before proceeding. The Enron débâcle and the barrage of corporate scandals it provoked was, at the very least, indicative that something was seriously wrong in the boardroom. The financial losses, the loss of jobs and the overall loss of investor confidence attest to this. Sarbanes–Oxley was a kneejerk reaction by the US government bent on demonstrating that it was taking steps to remedy the problem. Apparently, the law has not been as effective as everyone had hoped, and there is no lack of explanations for this. Beyond criticisms of the law itself, however, it has been unusual to find comments directed against the corporate governance model on which the law was based.

A closer scrutiny reveals that, once more, we are before a model of corporate governance premised on shareholder theory, agency theory and transaction cost theory of the firm. As Deakin and Konzelmann have lucidly remarked, 'The true lesson of Enron is that until the power of the shareholder value norm is broken, effective reform of corporate governance will be on hold' (Deakin and Konzelmann, 2004: 141). Apart from the obsession with shareholder value, there has also been an overbearing focus on monitoring, incentivizing and sanctioning manager-agents basically through the solitary instrument of money. And the final justification for the existence of the firm implicit in most discussions has been, simply, its cost-effectiveness in creating shareholder wealth. Perhaps the moment has arrived to seek an alternative model for corporate governance, one in which directors see themselves, not as mere representatives of shareholders, but as stewards ensuring the sustainability of a company's assets and guardians of a common good.

II   A CHANGE OF TACK IN CORPORATE GOVERNANCE

The overhauling of the corporate governance model requires a parallel revision in the understanding of the human being as an economic agent. As previously mentioned, the dominant theory of corporate governance is premised on the neoclassical economic view of the human being as an individual who manifests his rationality in choosing outcomes which maximize his utility function. The 'behaviour' of firms is nothing else but the result of the aggregate behaviours of such individuals. Individualism and utilitarianism, therefore, are the two pillars on which the neoclassical economic man rests.

By 'individualism' we understand the doctrine according to which human beings have fully constituted identities as individuals, independently of their social relations or belonging to any group, such as civil society or the state. From a physical or logical perspective, insofar as 'individual' means subsisting undivided in oneself and divided or separated from others, individualism is often conflated with social atomism. It denies that human beings have an essential social or relational dimension; or in any case, this relatedness is always secondary or posterior to one's individuality. Traces of individualism could be found in all schools of ethics and political philosophy which foster an individual's release from traditional ties of the social order and propound the corresponding elevation of his rights to a paramount position *vis-à-vis* those of any collective, primarily the state.

Apparently, the term 'individualism' was coined by the French conservative thinker, Joseph de Maistre, who associated it with the philosophy of the Enlightenment, particularly, its defence of self-interest and belief in the power of reason (Swart, 1962). In Henry Reeve's 1840 English translation of Alexis de Tocqueville's 'Democracy in America', individualism is defined as a 'mature and calm emotion, which disposes each member of the community to sever himself from the mass of his fellows and to draw apart with his family and his friends, so that after he has thus formed a little circle of his own, he willingly leaves society at large to itself' (Raico, 1997: 329). Since then, individualism has been very closely linked to *laissez-faire* liberalism in opposition to the different forms of state control, ranging from socialist interventionism to outright totalitarianism.

Utilitarianism, on the other hand, is an ethical, economic and political theory that regards utility as the ultimate good and standard by which actions are to be judged. In his 'Introduction to the Principles of Morals and Legislation' (1789), Jeremy Bentham refers to utility as an action's capacity to produce pleasure or 'happiness', and, conversely, to prevent pain (Bentham, 1996). To this extent utilitarianism ultimately leads to hedonism. Bentham also understood utility to be synonymous with 'welfare'. John Stuart Mill, for his part, developed the theory further by affirming in *Utilitarianism* (1863) that we ought to aim at maximizing the welfare of all sentient creatures (Mill, 1998). Thence the injunction to seek 'the greatest happiness of the greatest number'. Because actions have no inherent ethical value in themselves and instead depend entirely on the hedonic value of their consequences, utilitarianism has come to be known more generally as 'consequentialism' since the 1960s. The neoclassical economic man or *homo oeconomicus*, therefore, weds individualism with utilitarianism to yield a distinct form of enlightened egoism.

Now, then, both individualism and utilitarianism, which the dominant model of corporate governance presupposes through its dependence on neoclassical economic man, are considered by a long-standing moral tradition to be vices, that is, character defects of human beings. According to the school of virtue ethics, best represented by Aristotle and Thomas Aquinas, neither individualism nor utilitarianism contributes to true human perfection; on the contrary, each one detracts from real happiness.

Because individualism deliberately ignores the relational or social aspect of human nature, it impedes the full flourishing of man which can only be achieved in society. After all, man is, by nature, a political or social animal.

Utilitarianism likewise errs in proposing utility and pleasure as the supreme and absolute human good. As its very concept reveals, utility is but an instrumental good and never a good in itself. Something useful may be considered as a good only relatively, that is, insofar as it is a means to another good. Since this causal chain of goods cannot go on forever, at some point it would have to stop at something which is a good in and by itself, from which all other goods and goodness derive. At least in the case of human beings, characterized by reason and free will which distinguish them from other living creatures, pleasure, too, seems to be an unlikely candidate for this supreme and absolute good, among other reasons, because pleasure is an experience that human beings share with other animals, and it is only fitting that the highest human good be exclusive to men alone. Furthermore, the greatest human good should also require the proper functioning of reason and will, our most noble capacities, apart from our sense organs exclusively. Therefore, although pleasure is a good in and by itself, and here it proves superior to utility, it cannot be the supreme and absolute good for human beings. A life dedicated to the pursuit of pleasure is neither the happiest nor the one in which human beings would attain greatest perfection.

Hence, it should come as no surprise that the practice of corporate governance fails, precisely because it has been built on the wrong pillars, atop the vices of individualism and utilitarianism. What we have had so far is corporate governance designed for crooks; it is time to devise one that makes corporate virtue possible (Osterloh and Frey, 2003).

For Osterloh and Frey, an unequivocal sign that the corporate governance orthodoxy based on agency theory has run out of steam is that its three main methods of counteracting management misuse of power have not only proven ineffective, but also, sometimes, even counterproductive (Osterloh and Frey, 2003: 16–18). Firstly, intensive monitoring and sanctioning has led to the paradoxical effect of an ever-expanding need for stricter control. More laws and regulations have resulted in less order in the firm because they discouraged employee loyalty and trustworthiness. Secondly, pay linked to company performance through stock options did not align management interests with those of shareholders, with executive compensation continuing to increase despite plummeting share prices. Managers have just gained greater control over their own compensation and they have produced short-term increases in share prices by resorting (on occasions) even to misrepresentation or fraud. At other times, they simply reprice their options. Agency theory has unrealistically and wrongly assumed that earnings and share prices cannot be manipulated. And thirdly, as for corporate control through hostile takeovers, these mechanisms have been seldom used in the US or the UK, much less in other countries. Besides, when all else fails, management could always have recourse to anti-takeover defences such as poison pills or supermajority amendments.

At the end of the day, agency theory cannot satisfactorily respond to the fundamental question of corporate governance ('Who's watching the watchers?') because it takes for granted that actors are inherently self-seeking individuals unworthy of trust. We would just have to look elsewhere for a solution.

The basic problem hounding corporate governance is framed by Osterloh and Frey in terms of a 'social dilemma' (Osterloh and Frey, 2003: 5). A social dilemma occurs when the actions of self-interested individuals – those overcome by the vices of neoclassical economic man – lead to socially undesirable outcomes. From an economic perspective, this happens because self-interested individuals do not consider the externalities of their actions, falling either into the overuse or the undersupply of collective goods. This describes a classic case of the so-called 'tragedy of the commons' (Hardin, 1968). The twist that Osterloh and Frey introduce lies in including corporate virtue among the crucial elements of the business commons, apart from organizational knowledge, corporate culture and routines (Osterloh and Frey, 2003: 5).

A chief example of corporate virtue is integrity, which entails behaving honestly even when not being watched. Again from an economic perspective, integrity as an instance of corporate virtue is what one may call a public good: its benefits do not diminish as the number of people dealing with a firm increase (non-rivalry) nor is it easy to prevent others from having access to or taking advantage of it (non-excludability). Like all public goods, however, corporate integrity tends to be in short supply. There are two ways of remedying this shortage: one, through the institution of formal sanctions embedded in contracts or informal mechanisms of peer pressure, another, by introducing the common good into the preference set of workers. The latter solution based on the common good was first broached by Sen (1974) and further developed by Osterloh and Frey.

Referring to recent corporate disasters such as that of Enron, characterized by faulty governance, Osterloh and Frey detect 'a general deterioration of intrinsic motivation to contribute to the corporate virtue' (Osterloh and Frey, 2003: 6). By 'intrinsic motivation' they understand an activity that is valued for its own sake and is thus self-sustaining, work that in itself is satisfying or whose performance produces its own utility. In the background is the contrast with extrinsic motivation, or the indirect satisfaction of needs, mostly through money, to which conventional economists have limited their attention. Intrinsic motivation comes in two forms. It can be 'enjoyment-based', such as when one engages in a game or reads a novel; or it can be 'obligation-based', also called 'pro-social' intrinsic motivation, as in open source software (for example, Linux) programming, which is carried out like a gift-giving activity and without any monetary compensation, a voluntary contribution to the common good. 'If the love of work and the good of the community enter into the preference of actors, the social dilemma is transformed into a coordination game in which there is no social dilemma' (Osterloh and Frey, 2003: 8). Furthermore, thanks to the magic wrought by intrinsic motivation in the workplace, corporate virtue is increased.

The relationship between intrinsic and extrinsic motivations has been described by Osterloh and Frey through 'crowding effects' (Osterloh and Frey, 2003: 9–16). Given an initial amount of intrinsic motivation among actors for the performance of certain activities, the introduction of extrinsic motivators such as monetary rewards ends up 'crowding out' the former. For instance, paying donors for giving blood undermines their intrinsic motivation to do so and most likely reduces total blood supply. Similarly, when a community in central Switzerland was offered money to host a nuclear waste depot, the acceptance level among its members dropped by almost 25 per cent. Another study reveals that fining parents for picking their children up late from a daycare centre resulted in lower levels of punctuality, or that, when school children were offered commissions on the funds they collected for worthy causes such as cancer research, they reduced their efforts by 36 per cent.

Therefore there is empirical evidence that individuals voluntarily contribute to public goods as long as a sufficient number of people also contribute. They are what one may call 'conditional cooperators' or, conversely, 'conditional defectors'. Transposed to the corporate environment, we find that employee honesty is seriously undermined by the self-seeking behaviour of bosses who reward themselves with exorbitant pay and profit at the company's expense. Workers begin to feel exploited and are discouraged from contributing to the common good of corporate integrity. Once this has occurred, no amount of money slipped into their pockets can by itself reverse the situation. The firm then quickly degenerates into a downward spiral of fraud and corruption. This was, in broad strokes, the basic plot of the Enron story.

On the upside of things, Osterloh and Frey have likewise discovered certain conditions that 'crowd in' intrinsic motivation (Osterloh and Frey, 2003: 15–16). The greater the autonomy, competence and recognition an employee perceives in his work, the stronger his intrinsic motivation grows. Individuals have deep-rooted desires to see themselves as causal agents rather than pawns, and to be acknowledged for their positive contributions to group efforts by peers. All of this elevates their sense of self-worth and, with it, their intrinsic motivation at work.

From the observations above, Osterloh and Frey draw some concrete proposals for the improvement of corporate governance (Osterloh and Frey, 2003: 18–21). In the first place, selection processes should favour individuals with pro-social intrinsic motivations rather than focus exclusively on perceived efficiencies at work. A greater number of honest, intrinsically motivated workers raises the level of corporate virtue, conditionalities notwithstanding. Secondly, they advocate a return to fixed salaries, because pay for short-term performance, by means of bonuses and stock options, induces workers to switch to a selfish and calculating mode, casting their intrinsic motivation aside. And thirdly, self-governance and participation should be promoted, instead of provoking an inflation of rules. Miscreants are more easily identified by colleagues and could be admonished more effectively by them, albeit informally, than by superiors. Unlike purely rational egoists who do not experience any shame, people who at least feel ashamed of their wrongdoings have a minimum of intrinsic motivation to follow rules and contribute to the common good. Osterloh and Frey recognize that these suggestions buck the trend of traditional corporate governance; however, they believe that, by banking on corporate virtue, there are better chances of achieving improvements in the long term.

While we may agree with the distinction between extrinsic and intrinsic motivations and the importance of the latter for the development of corporate virtue, perhaps it would be better to call 'pro-social' or 'obligation-based' motivations 'transcendent' motivations instead (Pérez López, 1996: 55). Unlike 'enjoyment-based' intrinsic motivations, where the emphasis lies on the pleasure the actor experiences while realizing his task, in 'pro-social' or 'obligation-based' transcendent motivations, the stress is on what other parties benefit as a result of one's action or on one's net contribution to the common good. For Pérez López, this net positive result usually translates into different forms of learning. By 'learning' he means the acquisition of new knowledge and skills which perfect human beings on a superior level compared to money (extrinsic motivation) and pleasure (intrinsic motivation). And, lest we forget, the knowledge into which learning issues has always been the paradigm of virtue, ever since it was first discussed by Socrates. So corporate virtue, which develops with corporate learning, could very well be corporate common good which governance should seek to foster.

Seeking the good of learning for other people in the performance of one's work is a clear example of transcendent motivation because it goes beyond an actor's solipsistic satisfaction. Not that transcendent motivation necessarily excludes either extrinsic or intrinsic goods; it is just that the pursuit of both extrinsic and intrinsic goods is now subject to a higher good, which is precisely the transcendent motive. Here we encounter a foreshadowing of the true nature of the common good. For the common good, too – just like transcendent motivation – goes beyond the dialectic between extrinsic and intrinsic goods. Furthermore, the common good displays that peculiar characteristic of public goods, allowing itself to be shared by many without diminishment. In fact, it is justly called 'common good' because everyone in the community ought to be able to participate in it, not only individually, but also as a group.

In our attempt to elucidate the causes of Enron's egregious corporate governance failure and the reasons why the expectations of reform based on Sarbanes–Oxley tended to be overoptimistic we have discovered a root cause common to both: a corporate governance model resting on the flawed assumptions of neoclassical economics. The most damning critiques we have reviewed have centred on the obsession with maximizing shareholder value, on the individualism and utilitarian thinking of actors, and on the credulity in the power of contracts effectively to solve agent–principal problems. These same studies have expressed a greater need for ethics, not so much as the dead letter in codes but as part of institutional practice.

Thus understood, virtue becomes not only an individual trait but a corporate one as well. To see how virtue can be fostered in the workplace we have had to examine the nature of motivations. While acknowledging the presence of different kinds of motivations, we have also established the need for a hierarchy among them. We have renamed obligation-based or pro-social motivations as 'transcendent' motivations and have given them top priority over enjoyment-based intrinsic motivations and extrinsic motivations such as monetary rewards. Transcendent motivations refer to goods that can be shared or participated in by many. Insofar as a transcendent motive or good belongs to everyone in a given firm, organization or community, it may be aptly called a 'common good'. And nothing enhances the corporate common good or virtue as much as the participation of all actors in governance. If the goal of corporate governance is a good that is truly common and as such is assumed by each and every actor, then corporate governance becomes, in a very real sense, self-governance. Once this has been attained, social dilemmas and principal–agent problems are most likely to disappear.

Having assimilated these changes it now becomes clear that the way forward in corporate governance passes through the adoption of an ethical–political viewpoint, with an understanding of the human agent different from that advanced by neoclassical economic theory thus far.

III IN BRIEF

- That Enron's board of directors was voted among the United States' best one day and that the whole company collapse in a cloud of financial scandals shortly thereafter indicates the serious inadequacy of corporate governance criteria based almost exclusively on structural and procedural characteristics, such as the separation between the posts of Chair and CEO, a majority of external and independent directors, the division of the board into operating committees, the holding of regular meetings with audit, compensation and legal consultants, and so forth.

- It is even more surprising indeed that the American society's main reaction consisted in the passing of the Sarbanes–Oxley Law, which once more insisted largely on the same structural and procedural measures that had already proven ineffective. As former SEC Chairman Harvey Pitt remarked, everything that went wrong with Enron was already illegal even before Sarbanes–Oxley was enacted.

- A legal response alone, such as Sarbanes–Oxley, is radically insufficient to deter corporate governance abuses for a variety of reasons: there has been no dearth of laws covering corporate finance and many of the regulations even seem contradictory with each other; the disclosure of corporate codes of ethics may produce perverse incentives among executives; new legislation introduces further costs which the lawmakers apparently ignored; and markets may do a better job at regulating corporate activity than government.

- Sarbanes–Oxley exemplifies a typical solution based on neoclassical economic theory to corporate governance problems. It is premised on an individualistic and utilitarian view of human nature in general and of economic agents in particular. To this extent, it aggravates rather than solves a host of conflicts between individual short-term gains and the overall long-term good of the group. It takes for granted features of human conduct that have been heretofore considered by other traditions to be 'vices' or mental and moral traits harmful both to oneself and to others.

- Effective remedies to corporate governance problems have to do more with having the proper motivation than with the box-ticking compliance with a long list of legal requirements. Efforts have to be taken to make individual and corporate virtue possible. This requires institutional practices which curb selfishness, greed and immediate material satisfaction. Furthermore, an operational concern for the common good will have to be rewarded and promoted in company policies.

- Insofar as notions such as transcendent motives, personal and corporate virtues, self-governance and participation in the common good come to play in dealing with these issues, we are led from a technical, predominantly economic and legal understanding of the task of corporate governance to a wider, ethical and political perspective. Could it be, therefore, that corporate governance is, in essence, the same as the governance of other human institutions?

REFERENCES

Agrawal, Anup and Sahiba Chadha (2005), 'Corporate governance and accounting scandals', *Journal of Law and Economics*, **XLVIII** (October), 371–406.

Bentham, Jeremy (1996), *Introduction to the Principles of Morals and Legislation* (J.H. Burns and H.L.A. Hart (eds); F. Rosen, introduction), Oxford: Clarendon Press.

Boerner, Hank (2004), 'The Sarbanes–Oxley 'Revolution': two years and counting', *Corporate Finance Review*, September/October, 37–41.

Brickey, Kathleen F. (2003), 'From Enron to Worldcom and beyond: life and crime after Sarbanes–Oxley', *Washington University Law Quarterly*, **81**, 357–401.

Brown, Lawrence D. and Marcus L. Caylor (2004), 'Corporate governance and firm performance', http://papers.ssrn.com/sol3/papers.cfm?abstract_id=586423, 7 December.

Bush, George W. (2002), 'President Bush signs corporate corruption bill', *White House Press Release*, www.whitehouse.gov/news/releases/2002/07/20020730.html, 30 July.

The Business Roundtable (2005), Principles of Corporate Governance www.businessroundtable.org/pdf/CorporateGovPrinciples.pdf.

Coffee, John C. Jr (2003), 'What caused Enron? A capsule social and economic history of the 1990s', *The Center for Law and Economic Studies, Columbia Law School, Working Paper No. 214*, http://ssrn.com/abstract_id=373581.

Cullinan, Charlie (2004), 'Enron as a symptom of audit process breakdown: can the Sarbanes–Oxley Act cure the disease?', *Critical Perspectives on Accounting*, **15**, 853–64.

Deakin, Simon and Suzanne J. Konzelmann (2004), 'Learning from Enron', *Corporate Governance*, **12**(2), April, 134–42.

Fried, Frank, Harris, Shriver & Jacobson (2003), 'The post-Enron corporate governance environment: where are we now?', *Memorandum*, www.ffhsj.com/cmemos/031017_post_enron.pdf.

Gordon, Jeffrey N. (2003), 'Governance failures of the Enron board and the new information order of Sarbanes–Oxley', *The Center for Law and Economic Studies, Columbia Law School, Working Paper No. 216*, http://ssrn.com/abstract_id=391363.

Graham, Carol, Robert Litan and Sandip Sukhtankar (2002), 'The bigger they are, the harder they fall: an estimate of the costs of the crisis in corporate governance', *Working Paper Economic Studies/Governance Studies Programs*, The Brookings Institution, 30 August.

The Guardian (2002), 'Enron's board of directors', *The Guardian Digital Edition*, www.guardian.co.uk/enron/story/0,11337,643429,00.html, 1 February.

Hardin, Garrett (1968), 'The tragedy of the commons', *Science*, **162**, 1243–8.

Harvard Law Review (2003), 'The good, the bad, and their corporate codes of ethics: Enron, Sarbanes–Oxley, and the problems with legislating good behavior', *Harvard Law Review*, **116**, 2123–41.

Hogan, Joris M. (2003), 'The Enron legacy: corporate governance requirements for a new era', *Securities Regulation Law Journal*, **31**, 142–73.

Hogan, Joris M. (2004), 'Corporate governance update: changes in the boardroom after Enron', *Securities Regulation Law Journal*, **32**, 4–55.

Holmstrom, Bengt and Steve N. Kaplan (2003), 'The state of US corporate governance: what's right and what's wrong', *NBER Working Paper Series*, No. 9613, www.nber.org/papers/w9613, April.

Larcker, David F., Scott A. Richardson and Irem Tuna (2004), 'Does corporate governance really matter?', *Knowledge at Wharton*, http://knowledge.wharton. upenn.edu/papers/1281.pdf, 9 June.

LexisNexis and IBA (2003), 'Sarbanes–Oxley. Disclosure and confidentiality', *Executive Summary. The 2003 LexisNexis-IBA Legal Survey*, Section Two, www.lexisnexis.com/about/whitepaper/LexisNexis_ExecSummary.pdf.

Mill, John Stuart (1998), *Utilitarianism* (ed. Roger Crisp), Oxford/New York: Oxford University Press.

Osterloh, Margit and Bruno S. Frey (2003), 'Corporate governance for crooks? The case for corporate virtue', *Institute for Empirical Research in Economics/University of Zurich, Working Paper Series, no. 164*, July.

Pérez López, José Antonio (1996), *Fundamentos de la Dirección de Empresas*, 3rd edn, Madrid: Rialp.

The Permanent Subcommittee on Investigations of the Committee on Governmental Affairs, United States Senate (2002), *The Role of the Board of Directors in Enron's Collapse*, (8 June).

Powers, William C. Jr et al. (2002), *Report of Investigation by the Special Investigative Committee of the Board of Directors of Enron Corp.*, http://news. findlaw.com/hdocs/docs/enron/sicreport/sicreport020102.pdf, 8 June.

Raico, Ralph (1997), 'Individualism', *Blackwell Encyclopedic Dictionary of Business Ethics*, Malden, MA/Oxford: Blackwell Publishers, pp. 328–30.

Ribstein, Larry E. (2002), 'Market vs. regulatory responses to corporate fraud: a critique of the Sarbanes–Oxley Act of 2002', *Illinois Law and Economics Working Papers*, September, LE02-008, http://ssrn.com/abstract_id=332681, 1–74.

Rockness, Howard and Joanne Rockness (2005), 'Legislated ethics: from Enron to Sarbanes–Oxley, the impact on Corporate America', *Journal of Business Ethics*, **57**, 31–54.

Rothchild, Jonathan (2005), 'Ethics, law, and economics: legal regulation of corporate responsibility', *Journal of the Society of Christian Ethics*, **25**(1), 123–46.

Sen, Amartya K. (1974), 'Choice, orderings and morality', in Stephan Körner (ed.), *Practical Reason: Papers and Discussions*, Oxford: Blackwell, pp. 54–67.

Sison, Alejo José G. (2002), *The Moral Capital of Leaders. Why Virtue Matters*, Cheltenham, UK and Northampton, MA, USA: Edward Elgar.

Swart, Koenraad W. (1962), 'Individualism in the mid-nineteenth century (1826–1860)', *Journal of the History of Ideas*, **23**(1), 77–90.

Van den Berghe, L.A.A. and Abigail Levrau (2003), 'Measuring the quality of corporate governance: in search of a tailormade approach?', *Journal of General Management*, **28**(3), Spring, 71–86.

3. Governance and government from an Aristotelian perspective

Whenever one hears the word 'govern' and its cognates, such as 'governance' and 'government', the notions of 'authority' and the exercise of power and control immediately come to mind. Normally, one also thinks of a political unit such as the state in its dual role as both the subject and the object of the act of governing. The state governs the lives of those found under its authority, although at the same time – and in the best of cases – those who live under the state's authority are precisely the ones who determine how the state should go about this task. In other words, the state is ideally an instrument through which the very same people who are subject to its authority do in fact govern themselves.

It is indeed surprising that none of these associations takes place upon a simple reading of the definition of a corporate governance system: the complex set of constraints that shape the ex-post bargaining over the quasi-rents in the course of a relationship (Williamson, 1985). Not even after it is explained that the definition refers to a contractual relationship of an incomplete kind, such that no previous agreement on how to divide the spoils (so to speak) arising from the relationship can be made. A governance system seems to indicate rules of bargaining over contigent future goods that escape contractual agreements. This distance between the common understanding of what it means to govern and the formula afforded us by a corporate governance system further increases when the latter is linked to the market. Given the context of an economy where the free market is responsible for the efficient allocation of resources, what need is there for authority and control, as governing implicitly demands (Zingales, 1997: 2)?

As it cannot be otherwise, the concrete notion of corporate governance is dependent on the theory of the firm adopted (Zingales, 1997: 4). Based on the dominant neoclassical economic premises, three main models have been put forward. The first is the definition of the firm as a 'nexus of contracts' (Alchian and Demsetz, 1972), an idea with which we are already quite familiar.

The second, called a 'property rights' view, conceives the firm essentially as a collection of physical assets that are jointly owned (Grossman and

Hart, 1986; Hart and Moore, 1990). Ownership of the physical assets then becomes the key to corporate governance issues because it confers the right to decide over what the initial contract has left unspecified. Hence, a duly modified explanation of corporate governance then becomes 'the complex set of constraints that shape the ex post bargaining over the quasi-rents generated by a firm' (Zingales 1997: 4). From a narrow but less technical view, Shleifer and Vishny state that corporate governance 'deals with the ways in which suppliers of finance to corporations assure themselves of getting a return on their investment' (Shleifer and Vishny, 1997: 737). In effect, 'the fundamental concern of corporate governance is to ensure the means by which a firm's managers are held accountable to capital providers for the use of assets' (Gregory, 2001: 438). Compared to the first definition, this holds the advantage of distinguishing the firm from ordinary contractual relationships. However, it also has the fault of limiting considerations exclusively to the rights of the owner of the physical assets. As suppliers of capital, shareholders alone would have the power and authority to decide over governance issues.

Arguing that, in the 'new enterprise', the importance of human capital relative to physical or inanimate assets has considerably increased, a third model currently construes the firm as a 'network of specific investments', a combination of reciprocally specialized assets and people that cannot be reproduced by the market (Rajan and Zingales, 2000). Unlike in the second definition, all mutually specialized parties such as workers, suppliers and customers can now be considered as belonging to the firm. We now have an explicit recognition of the other stakeholders – apart from shareholders or owners of physical capital themselves – as parties to corporate governance. From this wider perspective corporate governance may be understood as the relationship among shareholders, management and the board as it determines the direction and performance of corporations (Monks and Minow, 2001: 1). More specifically, it refers to the processes surrounding the election of board members, their compensation and the evaluation of their task of supervising management. Although this explanation outlines the board's major functions, it may however obscure other dimensions of governance. As Koehn observes, 'corporate governance is better understood as the art of governing – in a principled fashion – so as to maximize the welfare of the company and of its relevant stakeholders' (Koehn, 1999: 1). Agency problems involved in corporate governance would be better addressed not only with legal safeguards and economic incentives, but also with trust-building institutional practices: 'Governing well ultimately means acting in a trustworthy fashion. No company will ever succeed in the long run if it is not trusted by its customers, employees, suppliers, advisors, shareholders, and other important stakeholders' (Koehn, 1999: 13).

After determining who should 'control the firm', that is, who should possess the 'residual rights' to make bargaining decisions, most corporate governance literature goes on to explain how these interests are to be safeguarded in light of the incentives of each of the parties involved. This is usually done under two different scenarios: ex ante, that is, before specific investments are sunk by means of a contract, and ex post, when the contingent quasi-rents are to be divided (Zingales, 1997: 7–11). In other words, corporate governance issues undergo careful scrutiny *before* one takes the leap and commits oneself and one's resources to a business venture and again *afterwards*, when profits are to be distributed. It is within these contexts that issues concerning the allocation of ownership, capital structure, managerial incentives, corporate takeovers and the structure and dynamics of boards of directors, among others, are commonly discussed.

At its very core, therefore, corporate governance may be interpreted as the manner in which quasi-rents are *best* to be produced or generated (in terms of efficiency, granted the available resources) and *best* to be distributed among relevant parties (within the context of a particular sense of justice) in a business firm. These two tasks are to be carried out under contingency conditions that make it impossible to make ex ante decisions or to devise fixed rules beforehand about how future quasi-rents are to be partitioned and seal them through a contractual agreement. Contigency and the absence of rules are of the essence of corporate governance in this respect.

When it comes to politics, we often hear that, just like governance, it is basically a matter of deciding 'who gets what, when, where, how and at what price'. This is the essence of the 'social contract' on which most modern political theories are founded. For, indeed, cynicism aside, politics concerns itself with how certain 'goods' are generated or produced – that is, things that purportedly satisfy human needs, desires or interests – and how these 'goods' are later on distributed among various claimants. Efficiency and justice, undeniably, also play important roles. And these political decisions are necessarily made in the absence of previously set rules and under conditions of uncertainty. In other words, they are not the mere execution of directives that have already been agreed upon beforehand, and prudence, the knack for making correct decisions on the fly, becomes utterly crucial.

Aristotle's *Politics* is generally recognized as an obligatory reference for the study of government, particularly, of the government of states: 'Government . . . is the subject of a single science, which has to consider what government is best and what sort must it be, to be in accordance with our aspirations' (*Politics*, henceforth Pltcs, 1288b). If corporate governance is essentially a form of government, albeit applied to the firm and not to the state, could we not find in Aristotle's *Politics* any useful considerations?

Probably yes, but first we have to develop the analogy between Greek city-states and modern business firms. At present, corporations have evolved into primordially economic entities characterized by limited investor liability, transferability of investor interests, legal personality and professional management (Monks and Minow, 2001: 8–10). For obvious historical reasons Aristotle could not have imagined any such institution. For their part, Greek city-states have been transformed largely into the image of Westphalian nation-states; that is, self-contained territories inhabited by people related to each other by blood, having the same birth-place and culture (Krasner, 1999: 20–25). Given these fundamental differences, would it still be possible to find meaningful similarities between states and corporation?

We honestly think so, if only because at their very root both happen to be social institutions with clearly defined objectives. Firstly, both states and corporations are composed of a large number of people divided into multiple social classes that are hierarchically ordered. Secondly, both states and corporations admit a plurality of regimes, depending on their particular structures of authority and power. And finally, in both states and corporations, these different groups of people are organized in such a way that a common purpose or end is optimally pursued: a political one in the case of the state and one of an economic nature in the case of the firm. We can therefore work out the analogy between states and corporations, that is, focus on their similarities and differences as social institutions, on the basis of three main points: the kinds of people who comprise them, the types of organizations or regimes they assume, and the particular ends they seek. Let us begin with this last one.

I STATES AND FIRMS, MEANS AND ENDS

That the governance of corporations is inspired by the government of states is evidenced by the very choice of similar terms, eschewing other likely candidates such as 'corporate management', 'corporate administration' or even 'corporate leadership'. This striking parallelism has led certain prescient authors to think that 'theories of government offer a way of fully understanding the behavior of [. . .] large corporations' and that 'management can only be properly studied as a branch of government' (Kitson and Campbell, 1996: 111). The problem with this, however, lies in that 'unfortunately, corporate governance is often misconstrued, and interpreted as if its task were not governing corporations but making them more like governments' (Sternberg, 1994: 199). Notwithstanding the similarities between the two institutions, good corporate governance should not boil down to transforming corporations into the oftentimes bloated, rigid and inefficient bureaucracies that characterize many state governments.

On account of their end or purpose, states are considered by Aristotle in the *Politics* to be 'natural' and 'perfect' societies, whereas present-day corporations by contrast would figure as examples of 'artificial' and 'imperfect' associations.

The state, like the family and the village, is a 'natural' society, because it stems from an innate tendency in human beings (Pltcs, 1252b). The family, which issues from the union of man and woman as husband and wife, is 'natural' because it arises in response to a deeply felt need in all human beings to leave behind living images of themselves in and through their children. The village, too, is 'natural' because the human instinct for self-preservation requires that one look beyond the daily needs which can be satisfied within the limits of the household to the requirements of a longer term of existence. The village – which includes children, grandchildren and other relatives by blood or marriage – is, in this sense, like a prolongation or extension of one's original family. Next down this line of 'natural' institutions comes the state, which results from several villages being united in a single, complete community.

From among these three 'natural' institutions, however, only the state is 'perfect' because it alone is 'self-sufficing' for the good life. This means that not only day-to-day needs, but also those of a life whole and entire can be expected to be met within the bounds of the state. Only in the state, that is, beyond the family and the village, can human beings truly aspire to live a completely good life. The state thus represents the 'end' or 'final cause', the fully developed stage of human existence (Pltcs, 1252b). For this reason, although the state may be considered chronologically posterior to both the family and the village, it is in reality prior to them: 'The proof that the state is a creation of nature and prior to the individual is that the individual, when isolated, is not self-sufficing; and therefore he is like a part in relation to the whole' (Pltcs, 1253a). Individuals, then, just like the families and the villages they form, are like parts with respect to the whole represented by the state. Moreover, although nature has implanted in all human beings a social instinct, only in the state can this innate tendency be fully developed and perfected through the institutions of law and justice. Otherwise, that is, outside of the state, human beings become the most savage and worst of animals (Pltcs, 1253a).

What does a good, perfect and self-sufficing, happy and honourable life consist in? Aristotle offers several complementary accounts in the *Politics*. One lists down basic ingredients and conditions – food, arts, arms, revenue, religion and a power of deciding the public interest and what is just – explaining that they could only be fulfilled in adequate proportions within the state (Pltcs, 1328b). A good human life could only be achieved in the state, and in order to be viable, a state would require all of the above-mentioned functions, goods and services. Another passage enumerates the necessary ingredients for a flourishing life: external goods, goods of the body and goods of the soul, also known as excellences or virtues (Pltcs, 1323a). Furthermore, it establishes the proper order or hierarchy among these indispensable elements, such that external and bodily goods are set, above all, as conditions for the performance of excellent actions, the goods of the soul or the virtues: 'the best life, both for individuals and states, is the life of excellence, when excellence has external goods enough for the performance of good actions' (Pltcs, 1324a).

It seems like happiness, a good and flourishing life, is more common among those of a cultivated mind and character, as long as they are assisted by a moderate share of external goods, than among those who have a surplus of external goods but lack the goods of the soul and the virtues. In this latter case, external goods sometimes bring their possessors no real benefit, but may even cause them harm. These observations indicate the true nature of all material goods as nothing more than means or instruments, that is, their possession and use should attend to a limit established by their purpose, which is the performance of the virtues: 'it is for the sake of the soul that goods external and goods of the body are desirable at all' (Pltcs, 1323b).

Within the context of Aristotle's political theory, just how does the firm fit in? First of all, although Aristotle does not mention business firms and corporations in the *Politics*, we could find allusions to them in the 'family connections, brotherhoods, common sacrifices and amusements' (Pltcs, 1280b) that draw human beings together. In contrast to the family and the village, and most importantly to the state, the firm may be considered an 'artificial' society because it arises neither directly nor organically from human nature. Rather, the firm is based on voluntary bonds of 'friendship' – a foreshadowing of contracts – primarily among citizens of the same state. It is also called an 'imperfect' society because it is not self-sufficing for the good life. A business corporation is an example of an 'intermediate body or association' situated between individuals and their families, on the one hand, and the state, on the other. As such, it is not meant to replace the family in the provision of the daily needs for survival, nor the state as the proper locus of a full and flourishing human life. Rather, like all other intermediate bodies, its purpose is to supply some of the necessary means (in this particular case, goods and services) for the good life in the state (Pltcs, 1280b).

Let us dwell a little more on the differences and the relationship between the state and the intermediate groups among which we count firms and corporations. That citizens of the same or different states band together for the purpose of defending themselves against an internal aggressor, thus safeguarding justice, or from a common external enemy, as in the case of war, does not by itself constitute them into a state, no matter how urgent and necessary this action may be. At most, it would only constitute them into a security or military alliance resulting from a treaty among states. Neither is it enough, in order to constitute a state, that human beings meet and associate solely for the production and exchange of goods and an increase in wealth; that would only give rise to contracts, trade agreements or commercial treaties. As Aristotle unequivocally affirms, 'suppose that one man is a carpenter, another a farmer, another a shoemaker, and so on, and that their number is ten thousand: nevertheless if they have nothing in common but exchange, alliance, and the like, that would not constitute a state' (Pltcs, 1280b). That a great number of men dedicated to different crafts and trades come together to pursue their mutual economic benefit is certainly convenient, but even that is insufficient for the founding of a state.

Beyond security and wealth, a state is concerned pre-eminently with the good life, that is, a life shared among all its citizens. For this reason, the state has to take care that its citizens be as they ought, that they display political excellence or justice, something which in turn depends on the practice of other supporting excellences or virtues. Security and wealth are mere conditions with a view to this aim or objective of a good life in the state or *polis*, that is, 'a community of families and aggregations of families in well-being, for the sake of a perfect and self-sufficing life' (Pltcs, 1280b).

How do intermediate groups such as corporations and business firms relate to the state? Although intermediate groups are founded on voluntary – and to that extent, contingent – associations and are neither 'natural' nor necessary in the sense of families and states, they are nevertheless vital to achieving the overall political purpose of a good life. A flourishing life for citizens would not be possible without properly functioning intermediate groups or by counting on families and the state alone. A tight web of these intermediate associations is essential, if the state in its entirety is ever to achieve its goal. This is not to say that the existence of any concrete or particular example of an intermediate group – take for granted, 'Acme & Co.' – is in and by itself absolutely necessary. The point is that the bread-making function, for instance, that the bakery Acme & Co. performs, may be deemed indispensable for a good life in a state in general. It is not any specific intermediate body or representative of an intermediate body (Acme & Co.) that matters, but the presence of intermediate bodies as a whole in the state.

The appropriate reciprocal relationship between the state and intermediate groups has come to be called, in certain traditions, one of 'subsidiarity' (Pontifical Council for Justice and Peace, 2005, *Compendium of the*

Social Doctrine of the Church, nn.186–7). Given that both the state and the intermediate groups have their own legitimate objectives and spheres of action, they owe each other mutual respect, notwithstanding the proper hierarchy beween them which acknowledges the superiority of the state. There is a double dimension to the state's role with regard to intermediate associations. It is incumbent upon the state as the superior-order society to *positively* help, support and assist – even to promote and develop – lesser-order intermediate bodies. Put *negatively* or in the converse, the state should refrain from replacing or absorbing these intermediate associations and misappropriating their functions. By encouraging the growth of these intermediate associations as private initiatives, the state contributes to a healthy pluralism and diversity in society. The state should delegate to these intermediate groups tasks that these would carry out better by themselves, since they are in closer contact with the needs and desires of citizens and the rest of the people. Furthermore, by fostering the legitimate initiatives of intermediate groups, the state makes a more rational and efficient use of its limited resources, focusing instead on matters such as defence, foreign relations or the administration of justice that are of its exclusive competence. Subsidiarity guards against statism in its many forms, from excessive centralization or the usurpation of decision-making powers from the people most concerned, involved and affected, through bureaucratization or the shirking of personal responsibility by government personnel over their own actions, to welfarism or a paternalist demeanour on the part of the state regarding the welfare of its citizens. The principle of subsidiarity provides the most effective protection against a self-serving state, ensuring instead that the state serves its citizens and people as it rightly should.

In the welter of intermediate bodies normally found in a healthy state, a special place is reserved for those that broadly seek economic ends, and it is among these that we include firms and business corporations. This primarily economic focus distinguishes businesses from other possible intermediate groups such as churches, professional colleges, sports associations, neighbourhood councils, cultural clubs and the like. It is not that these other intermediate bodies lack any economic dimension or significance; it is just that such an economic dimension or significance is not their main concern, unlike the case of firms and business corporations.

Business firms and corporations, then, are intermediate bodies that pursue economic goals. Returning once more to Aristotle's *Politics*, we are told that the economy was born within the family, as 'household management' (Pltcs, 1253b). His treatment of the economy in its original, etymological meaning of 'household management' begins with a survey of the different parts and of the relationships among these parts that are necessary for a complete household: 'the first and fewest possible parts of a family are master and slave, husband and wife, father and children. We have therefore to consider what each of these three relations is and ought to be: – I mean the relation of master and servant, the marriage relation (the conjunction of man and wife has no name of its own), and thirdly, the paternal relation (this also has no proper name)' (Pltcs, 1253b).

The need for a husband and a wife bound to each other in marriage is pretty obvious for the state, because there is no other way in accordance with nature for children – the state's potential citizens – to be born, raised and educated to a responsible adulthood. Moreover, a stable and exclusive marriage relation best assures mutual help to both husband and wife for the daily necessities of life: care in the case of illness, comfort in moments of distress, and even the simple joys of companionship.

The other two relations required for a complete household or a properly functioning economy in the original Aristotelian sense demand a little more explaining. In Aristotle's historical and social milieu, in fourth century BC Athens, it was peacefully accepted that, within the family, the children belonged to the father or the husband, not to the mother or wife. Of course no child could have been conceived and born without the woman's cooperation, but she merely represents the passive principle. In a paternalistic and patriarchal society such as Aristotle's, the offspring, like all property, as we shall see later on, belong to the male, who contributes the active principle, the seed or 'form' to the female's soil or 'matter'. There was no equality between the male and the female spouse in this sense.

How about the institution of slavery? Why are slaves essential to the economy in Aristotle's mind? The reason behind this is that slaves are a form of property: 'Property is a part of the household, and the art of acquiring property is a part of the art of managing the household; for no man can live well, or indeed live at all, unless he is provided with necessaries' (Pltcs, 1253b). Aristotle then understands property in a broad sense, encompassing all the material things, objects, instruments and means that are indispensable for the good life. Yet there are different kinds of property, some living, others lifeless: 'And so, in the arrangement of the family, a slave is a living possession, [. . .] and the servant is himself an instrument for instruments' (Pltcs, 1253b). Slaves, therefore, are like livestock, a form of living property no family could do without for its subsistence. But they are living property of a special kind, because they are useful insofar as they obey or anticipate the will of others, who are their masters. Strictly speaking, the work of a slave, its function, is to accomplish the will of its master, whatever this may be. 'Hence we see what is the nature and office of a slave; he who is by nature not his own but another's man, is by nature a slave; and he may be said to be another's man who, being a slave, is also a possession' (Pltcs, 1254a).

Apart from the living and the lifeless, an ulterior division in property is between 'instruments of production' and 'instruments of action' (Pltcs, 1254a). Instruments of production are those the use of which yields something else, just as the weaving loom or shuttle yields cloth; while instruments of action are those that yield nothing more than their use, as when a garment is worn or a bed is slept on. A few lines onward, by way of reference to life which is a kind of action, Aristotle suggests the superiority of action over production, and consequently, of instruments of action over instruments of production.

Early in his discussion of the economy as household management, Aristotle distinguishes between the art of household management in itself and the art of getting wealth or chrematistics, which some consider identical and others, a principal part of the former (Pltcs, 1253b). In both arts, however, Aristotle acknowledges the difference between a natural and a non-natural form.

Natural chrematistics pertains to the provision of 'such things necessary to life, and useful for the community of the family or state, as can be stored' (Pltcs, 1256b), whereas non-natural chrematistics of 'riches and property [which] have no limit' (Pltcs, 1267a). Natural wealth getting is based on the premise that true riches, the kind and amount of property needed for a good life, is not without limit, but has fixed boundaries. There is a level beyond which the mere accumulation of material things, whatever these may be, becomes more of a nuisance or a liability with a view to human flourishing than an advantage or help. Nowadays, one could think of having more cars than those that could reasonably fit in the garage, or more foodstuffs than those that the refrigerator could store, for example.

Non-natural wealth getting, on the other hand, believes that 'more is always better' and that for the good of the economy there should be no halt in piling up possessions. Although the example may be rather dated, proper to an underdeveloped economy, as was prevalent during Aristotle's time, by non-natural wealth getting he referred primarily to retail trade and exchange, which allowed one to accumulate riches in the form of money or coin, practically without limit. But 'coined money is a mere sham, a thing not natural, but conventional only, because, if users substitute another commodity for it, it is worthless, and because it is not useful as a means to any of the necessities of life, and, indeed, he who is rich in coin may often be in want of necessary food. But how can that be wealth of which a man may have great abundance and yet perish with hunger?' (Pltcs, 1257b). Somehow we can still relate to the situation Aristotle describes if we imagine ourselves in a foreign country without the proper currency or where our credit cards are not honoured. Whatever wealth or money we think we have is rendered useless, unable to buy us even a miserly piece of bread.

In itself, however, the art of household management or economy properly speaking seems to refer more to the use of property than to its mere acquisition, Aristotle implies. Once again, in the use of property or its corresponding art we ought to differentiate between the natural or proper and the non-natural or improper. Take the case of a shoe: if it is used for wear, one makes a proper use, while if it is used for exchange, one makes an improper use, 'for a shoe is not made to be an object of barter' (Pltcs, 1257a). The proper use of any material possession acknowledges a limit or a further end that makes the activity honourable, whereas its improper use is void of limit and thus becomes justly censurable. To illustrate this unnatural and hateful use of wealth – once more, within the context of a primitive economy – Aristotle points out 'usury, which makes a gain out of money itself [. . .] For money was intended to be used in exchange, but not to increase at interest' (Pltcs, 1258b).

Beyond these significant distinctions in the acquisition and the use of wealth which the economy entails, it is important that we realize that the difference between the natural and the non-natural depends more on the dispositions of human beings, on their sometimes unlimited desires, than on the very essence of the material things in themselves (Pltcs, 1257b–1258a). Unbridled desires, the want of wealth and pleasure or enjoyment untutored by virtue, lead human beings to non-natural forms of getting and using material possessions. This way, unbeknownst to them, their search for happiness or a flourishing life becomes self-defeating. It is not the fault of the material things but exclusively of their own vices.

Recapitulating within the framework of Aristotle's *Politics*, we may say that firms and business corporations are artificial and imperfect societies, examples of intermediate bodies found between families and the state. Among the variety of possible intermediate associations, business firms are singled out as those dedicated to the pursuit of economic ends, in particular, the production of goods and services or the acquisition of the material means necessary for a good and flourishing life. This 'happy life' is a social life, and although it finds complete fulfilment only within the bounds of the state, it inexorably begins in the intimacy of the family home. Thus it becomes easy to understand that the first corporations arise from the family's struggle to cope with its basic needs through the division of labour and specialization.

Speaking about the non-natural art of chrematistics or wealth getting in which business firms and corporations ultimately engage, Aristotle states that 'in the first community, indeed, which is the family, this art is obviously of no use, but it begins to be useful when the society increases. For the members of the family originally had all things in common' (Pltcs, 1257b). The next stage, characterized by a still natural form of chrematistics, begins when the family grows and becomes big enough to be 'divided into parts, the parts shared in many things, and different parts in different things, which they had to give in exchange for what they wanted, a kind of barter [. . .]; giving and receiving wine, for example, in exchange for corn, and the like' (Pltcs, 1257a). Finally, non-natural chrematistics inevitably takes place when a society's needs becomes more complex. Together with it comes the widespread use of money and the establishment of the first businesses or firms. As Aristotle relates, 'when the inhabitants of one country became more dependent on those of another, and they imported what they needed, and exported what they had too much of, money necessarily came into use' (Pltcs, 1257a). These new functions resulting from the development of the economy and society can only be carried out effectively by larger organizations such as corporations or firms, understood as extensions of the family or 'economic friendships' (Pltcs, 1280b).

For similar reasons that natural chrematistics or wealth acquisition is superior to non-natural chrematistics, Aristotle also considers that the economy or household management has got more to do with wealth use or administration than with mere wealth getting or acquisition. That is, the only rational purpose for acquiring wealth or material possessions is that one have a use for them, that they contribute in the end to the good life. Otherwise, there would be no sense in accumulating wealth just for its own sake. Therefore, the economy should concern itself more with the proper use or administration of wealth and property than its production or acquisition.

Certainly, without the adequate resources, there would be nothing for the economy to use and administer. Hence the importance of chrematistics, which is concerned with the production or provision of the necessary material means. Yet, strictly speaking, wealth getting is only a subordinate function, and not the one proper for him who manages the household, or 'economist'. The economy presupposes the availability of these means and the task of providing them in the long run falls upon nature. As Aristotle explains, the duty of the manager of a household is 'to order the things which nature supplies – he may be compared to the weaver who has not to make but to use wool, and to know, too, what sort of wool is good and serviceable or bad and unserviceable' (Pltcs, 1258a). Economic knowledge, therefore, deals more directly with the proper use and administration of material resources than with their procurement and production. These latter activities Aristotle entrusts to nature: 'the means of life must be provided beforehand by nature; for the business of nature is to furnish food to that which is born, and the food of the offspring is always what remains over that from which it is produced' (Pltcs, 1258a).

In this regard, insofar as business firms and corporations play a role specifically in the production of goods and services understood as a means to the good life in general, they operate within the realm of wealth getting or chrematistics. And, inasmuch as business firms and corporations are artificial societies, they are meant as a mere help or complement to the material resources that nature, in principle, ought to provide. In other words, the activity of business firms and corporations forms part of the so-called 'non-natural' chrematistics. What is clear by Aristotle's reckoning, in any case, is that business firms and corporations only fulfil a subordinate or secondary function in the economy, which 'attends more to men than to the acquisition of inanimate things, and to human excellence more than to the excellence of property which we call wealth, and to the excellence of freemen more than to the excellence of slaves' (Pltcs, 1259b). That is to say, the main purpose of the economy is to facilitate the development of human excellence or virtue by guaranteeing, to the extent possible, the material conditions for its practice. And virtue, in turn, is sought primarily because it affords us happiness, or a good, flourishing life.

What, then, is the relationship between the economy and politics? And how does ethics relate to both of them? An Aristotelian response would focus, in the first place, on the object proper to each branch of knowledge. As we already know, the end of politics is none other than happiness (*eudaimonia*) or human flourishing, the good life in the state. This could only be achieved, however, if one had the material means and the human excellences or virtues at the same time. Hence the importance of the economy, which is concerned precisely with the material resources, the 'external goods' and 'goods of the body', and ethics, which in turn refers to the virtues or the 'goods of the soul' as the non-material elements of human flourishing (Aristotle, *Nicomachean Ethics*, henceforth NE, 1098b; Pltcs, 1323a). Both the economy and ethics, therefore, are subordinated to politics, which is the 'controlling' or 'ruling science' (NE, 1094a), because it is directed towards the supreme or highest good represented by human flourishing. Happiness is the supreme or highest good because it is the end that we desire for itself with a view to no other, and whatever other good we desire or do, ultimately, we desire or do it because of happiness, which is the best good.

However, none of the supremacy or dominance of politics should detract from the importance of the economy and ethics, both of which remain equally indispensable. As Aristotle himself reminds us, 'happiness evidently also needs external goods [. . .] since we cannot, or cannot easily, do fine actions if we lack resources' (NE, 1099a). Among the external resources we use to do fine actions, immediately after friends, Aristotle counts wealth, even before political power. Elsewhere, Aristotle adds, 'the happy person is a human being, and so will need external prosperity also; for his nature is not self-sufficient for study, but he needs a healthy body, and needs to have food and the other services provided' (NE, 1178b). Although it is true that no one can achieve happiness without external resources, that is, without the economy, it is likewise true that we do not need excessive external goods to be happy: 'we can do fine actions even if we do not rule earth and sea; for even from moderate resources we can do the actions expressing virtue. [. . .] It is enough if moderate resources are provided; for the life of someone whose activity expresses virtue will be happy' (NE, 1179a). Virtue, then, should be a cause of greater concern than the abundance of material goods in achieving happiness. Hence the need for ethics.

Ethics, for its part, deals with the whole range of manifestations of virtue, from 'fine actions' to 'character', which enable a state's citizens to aspire to the good life (NE, 1099b). However necessary, virtue alone is insufficient for happiness, hence the requirement of external or material goods, which belongs to the province of the economy. At this point, nonetheless, one could affirm that virtue and ethics is more important than material goods and the economy, not only because virtue has 'greater being' than material goods, but also because virtue, unlike material goods, can never be used for evil purposes. That is why the immediate objective of the economy or the management and use of material goods is to provide the conditions that make acts of virtue possible and, better still, easier (Pltcs, 1324a). (This does not mean that virtue is impossible without material resources, only that it becomes more difficult.) The economy seeks its correct orientation from ethics, then. And together, the economy and ethics look forward to the supreme good of happiness, which politics affords.

Getting back to our initial query of how business firms and corporations fit in the state, we can now say, in accordance with Aristotle's teachings, the following. As a class of artificial intermediate bodies, business firms and corporations belong to the realm of the economy. In particular, their purpose is the non-natural acquisition or provision of material goods beyond the capabilities of the family. Resulting from a variant of the art of wealth getting or chrematistics, business firms and corporations should be subject to the superior art of the economy itself, which consists in the administration and use of material goods. All economic activity in turn, and the institutions it gives rise to, such as business firms or corporations and the market, should function under the guidance of ethics, which is the 'practical science' or art of virtue, the supreme human excellence. The economy has as its mission to facilitate the practice of virtue or ethics by establishing favourable material conditions among the citizens of a state. And virtue and ethics, in the final analysis, are sought after insofar as they help us attain happiness or a flourishing life in the state, our ultimate goal under the tutelage of politics.

Only within this hierarchy of disciplines and institutions, each one with its own proper object, can the true role of business firms and corporations within society be ascertained, because 'the end of the state is the good life, and these [i.e., family connections, brotherhoods, common sacrifices and amusements, and by extension, firms] are the means towards it' (Pltcs, 1280b). The economic ends that corporations seek are simply means to the political end that city-states for their part propose. The production of goods and services which is the purpose of business corporations and firms is not at all self-justifying. It is desirable and acquires meaning only insofar as it contributes to a flourishing life in the state. Later on we shall have the occasion to draw from here implications for the proper governance of business corporations and firms.

II   MULTINATIONAL CORPORATIONS AND STATES IN THE AGE OF GLOBALIZATION: AN EXCHANGE OF ROLES

Over the millennia, a number of significant changes have occurred in the structure and purpose of both business corporations and states that would have made them quite difficult to recognize in their current forms for anyone among Aristotle's contemporaries. The bearing of these changes on the task of governance, be it over a company or a state, is certainly hard to overestimate.

Most of these changes affecting businesses and states have taken place against the backdrop of what we now call 'contemporary globalization'. Contemporary globalization may be defined as both the process and the end-result of an ever closer integration of what heretofore have been known as 'national economies'. Note that globalization does not refer to the progressive coming together of 'states', or even of 'nation-states', as could have previously been expected. This is so not only because a handful of globalization's major players are not full-fledged states – for instance, the 'Special Autonomous Region' of Hong Kong – but also because globalization in itself seems to imply a waning protagonism of the state. When economies get more and more integrated in a truly global market, states end up mattering less and less, the dominant line of thinking goes. To a large extent, business firms and, more specifically, multinational corporations (MNCs), end up filling in the leadership role left by states in present-day globalization.

Some economists and historians trace the roots of contemporary globalization to half a century before World War I, when there was a very high level of interdependence among the capital, goods and labour markets of the major European powers. This was evidenced by the high proportion of foreign direct investment (FDI) in each country's gross domestic product. FDI refers to long-term investments made by foreigners in a host country's enterprises. This is usually done by setting up manufacturing facilities in a greenfield site or by injecting new capital through mergers and acquisitions. In either case the long-term foreign direct investor creates new production capacities and jobs, transfers technology and management know-how, and provides the host country with valuable linkages to the global marketplace.

Strictly speaking, however, modern globalization as we know it could not have taken off until after the end of the Cold War and the fall of the Berlin Wall in November 1989. Until then, the planet was divided into three worlds that sailed past each other like ships in the night: the First World or the 'Free World', consisting largely of the Unites States and its Western European allies; the Second World or the communist world, comprising the Soviet Union and its satellite states; and finally, the Third World, composed by a majority of non-aligned developing countries. Apart from these crucial political and ideological factors, other enabling conditions for the growth of globalization include the advances in the 'net' technologies and the liberalization of commerce. 'Net' technologies, those used in transportation, telecommunications, computer systems and, above all, the Internet, are special in that their value increases exponentially with the addition of every unique individual user. In other words, although a single telephone would be useless because there would not be anyone to call or talk to, the more subscribers there are linked to the telephone network, the greater a telephone's potential use or benefit. The liberalization of commerce, on the other hand, has been greatly enhanced by the establishment of multilateral institutions such as the World Trade Organization (WTO), the European Union (EU), the North American Free Trade Agreement (NAFTA), the Asia Pacific Economic Conference (APEC) and Mercosur in Latin America, to name a few. They provide a marked contrast to the tendencies in the previous decades of nationalizing companies and whole industries deemed strategic, as well as of implementing policies of central planning and import substitution. Generally, every change that has favoured modern globalization has in the end produced a similar effect in MNCs.

There are three main schools of thought regarding the end, meaning, purpose or future of today's globalization (Held et al., 1999: 3–10). The first is composed of the 'hyperglobalists', for whom globalization would inevitably result in the definitive triumph of the market over the state, as the ultimate framework or reference of human action (Guéhenno, 1985; Ohmae, 1995; Wriston, 1997). Our identities would no longer be shaped mainly by the country whose citizenship we claim, but by the corporation for which we opted to work or the business firm whose products and services we have chosen to patronize. In a cosmopolitan and market-driven civilization, it is as if the market has taken over the state in its function of producing and distributing well-being.

Markets obliterate states. The second school consists of the 'sceptics' for whom globalization is, in truth, only a myth, an empty mask. Behind it three regional blocks, the American, the European and the Asian, each one backed by powerful nation states, continue to determine the course of world events (Hirst and Thompson, 1996). What we have, at most, is a heightened form of 'internationalization', where national governments continue to initiate, regulate and still very much control global exchange. The 'clash of cultures or civilizations' perspective may be considered chiefly as a variant of this view (Huntington, 1996). Through each of these blocks, powerful nation states in fact increase their reach and strength of influence, albeit covertly. Lastly, we have the 'transformationalist' school with its current debate over what in reality is transformed by globalization, into what other things, and on whether there are matters that still remain the same (Castells, 1996; Giddens, 1990; Scholte, 1993). Within this context one hears of 'reinventing' both the state and the market – including MNCs, of course – and of 'restructuring' world politics and the world economy at the same time in order to fashion a truly global civil society.

The transformationalist interpretation of globalization comes like glove in hand in explaining the changes undergone by both states and business corporations, since we first described them in Aristotelian categories. States and nation states have ceased to have the good life or human flourishing within their borders as their purpose or objective. Beginning with the 17th-century British philosopher Thomas Hobbes, the state has come to be understood as the result of a 'social contract' among individuals, meant to remedy a life that, outside it, that is, in the 'state of nature', is condemned to be 'solitary, poor, nasty, brutish and short' (Hobbes, 1660, *The Leviathan*, chapter XIII). The state is now conceived to exist pre-eminently to protect individual citizens from suffering a violent death; and in order to fulfil this mandate it needs to concentrate all power and authority unto itself. Individuals surrender their 'natural rights' or rights in the 'state of nature' to an absolute, sovereign state in exchange for peace and security as citizens. However minimalist it may seem, this is the new sole objective the state proposes for itself: to be the guarantor of internal peace and common defence in case of war. All the rest – however citizens may choose to conduct their lives and their economic affairs, the ethical principles by which they determine to live, and so forth – are left to their free individual volition. The only condition, in principle, is that these do not enter into conflict with the state's objective. However, it is for the state alone to decide when this, in fact, occurs.

Tracing the evolution of the absolutist, Hobbesian state into the present-day democracies we now hold up as models would force us to go far beyond the scope of this work. Suffice it to say, however, that this evolution has been accompanied by a few significant constants (MacIntyre, 1988). First is an increasingly radical scepticism about the nature (particularly the social nature) of the good life for human beings and an ever-deepening disbelief over the possibility of carrying this ideal out. Human beings are seen essentially as individuals bereft of any necessary social dimension who cannot get themselves to agree about what a flourishing life is, despite the fact that they seem condemned to pursue it. Second is the relegation of ethics to the realm of private discourse: its manifestation in the public square is tolerated exclusively in the form of a relative 'consumer choice' which is neither to be questioned nor to be imposed. And third is the growing prominence of the economy, especially in what refers to the accumulation of wealth, among vital human concerns. All human relations are now cut after the model of market exchange, where individuals are preoccupied above all with making the most, in terms of utility and pleasure, of their money and resources.

There is hardly anything of substance that could characterize modern democratic regimes, despite the incredible amount of lip-service that they pay to a purported defence of 'universal human rights'. At most, the only feature they have in common is something purely procedural: the regular holding of elections that are, hopefully, free and fair, and in which all citizens, in principle, have an equal right to participate. This is true not only of the more socially inclined democratic regimes but also of the more liberal capitalist ones. Social democracies are those that take an active part in the redistribution of wealth or the 'social product' among its citizens through policies which promote equality. However, this inevitably comes at the cost of curtailing economic freedoms. Liberal capitalist democracies are not so inclined and favour a lighter touch in economic regulation, confident that no one knows better than the citizens themselves where to employ their resources to draw the greatest benefit. Yet both social and liberal capitalist democracies see themselves at the core as purveyors of resources – political, civil and socioeconomic rights – that their citizen-clients could then use to promote their own individual welfare, however understood (Holmes and Sunstein, 1999).

Here we can see how modern democratic states have not only abandoned the idea of 'a good life in the *polis*' (Aristotle), but have also changed their goals from the guaranteeing of security (Hobbes) to simply providing means for each citizen's welfare or well-being. In other words, they have ended up assuming roles that in the previous order of things were assigned to businesses and corporations. They have cast aside meaningful deliberations about the end or purpose of human life and have limited themselves to purveying the means that any one of their citizens should feel free to use, however they deem fit.

States behave like business firms and corporations in several ways. Perhaps the most obvious manner is when they put up their own corporations in sectors of the economy they consider strategic, such as in oil and gas or in energy production and supply in general. Unfortunately, however, most national oil companies are prone to overstaffing, underinvestment and various forms of political meddling and corruption: what occurs in PDVSA of Venezuela under the mandate of President Hugo Chávez is a clear example (*The Economist*, 2006). State governments also masquerade as businesses when they more or less covertly support a 'national champion' while pretending to abide by and uphold the principles of the free market. Take, for instance, the case when the government prevents a local bank which dominates the domestic market from being bought by a foreign investor, or conversely, when it helps a strong local bank in its bid to acquire a significant player in a foreign market. This was exactly what occurred in the proposed alliance between the Banco Santander Central Hispano (BSCH) and the Champalimaud Group, in the end vetoed by the Portuguese Government in 1999 (Sison, 2002). In either case, the state engages, albeit vicariously, in an activity that is proper to a business organization.

In conducting themselves like business firms, state governments may compete against each other in attracting foreign direct investment. For example, they may offer favourable tax breaks to foreign investors, effectively granting them some form of government subsidy. From the viewpoint of the state's coffers, it really does not matter whether a government voluntarily gives up a certain amount of money it is due or hands that same amount over to an investor as a grant. Oftentimes, there is also a 'race to the bottom' among competing states in the matter of taxes so as to attract foreign investment. The same thing occurs with respect to environmental regulations, which tend to be less stringent, and salaries and labour policies, which tend to be lower and more lax. Together with adequate transportation and communication facilities – once more, infrastructure that is in the state's hands to provide – these are the main reasons that usually incline foreign investment favourably to one country instead of another. In some developing countries, the business strategy to attract foreign investment even goes to the point of partially surrendering state sovereignty over certain parts of its territory, through 'export processing zones', for example. These regions – free trade zones, special economic zones, bonded warehouses, free ports, customs zones and maquiladoras – are governed by special laws that act as a sweetener or incentive for foreign investors.

On the other side of the equation, globalization has simultaneously resulted in business firms and corporations taking over some of the normal attributions of the state. This becomes especially clear in the case of the multinational corporations (MNCs), particularly those operating in developing countries. Also known as 'multinational enterprises', these are defined in documents from the Organization for Economic Cooperation and Development as 'companies or other entities whose ownership is private, state or mixed, established in different countries and so linked that one or more of them may be able to exercise a significant influence over the activities of others and, in particular, to share the resources with the others' (OECD, 1997: 9).

Briefly, an MNC is a company that has production and sales operations in more than one country. Why are economic activities organized around an MNC? A quick response would be because MNCs, at least in theory, make more efficient use of capital, technology and human resources, thus making greater contributions to the economic growth and social development of home and host countries alike. Oftentimes, the main reason host countries are less developed is that they lack financial capital. Certainly, funds could be sourced through foreign aid or private bank loans, but the first is seldom sufficient while the second is too expensive. Hence, the only remaining option is for developing countries to welcome in MNCs from industrialized countries as purveyors of foreign direct investment. As we already know, apart from money, MNCs also bring into their host countries technical know-how and management expertise; they build factories and maintain offices; they provide jobs and offer training to locals. MNCs thus represent the concrete channels through which the comparative advantages of different countries are exploited in the global market.

In accordance with technological, economic and political changes, MNCs have evolved through three distinct phases in recent history (Dunning, 1993a, 1993b; Elfstrom, 1991; Vernon, 1998). The first phase, which began after World War II and ran up to the early 1970s, was characterized by the dominance of American MNCs. This was because of the United States' victory in the War and the fact that it was practically the only country that had kept its production facilities intact and in full throttle. In general, American MNCs carried out their manufacturing at home and only set up subsidiaries abroad to acquire raw materials or to oversee export markets. In due time, European and Japanese MNCs began to follow the American strategy and they, too, consolidated their own 'national champions'. The only countries practically excluded from the influence of MNCs were the communist ones, because of an ideological mix of nationalism, isolationism and hostility to foreign capital that pushed them to pursue policies of economic self-reliance. This initial phase of MNCs ended in the early 1970s, with the wave of nationalizations of foreign-owned assets in Third World host countries.

The second phase in the development of MNCs began with the careful renegotiations between home and host countries over the ownership and control of production assets. Pressure on all sides was increased as a result of the oil crisis, the proliferation of petro-dollars from the Gulf countries, and the ballooning Third World debt. East Asian nations, by agreeing to lift most controls on trade and investment, became the first ones to emerge from the doldrums. In due course, these countries came to be known as the 'Asian Tigers'. Later on, multilateral agencies such as the General Agreement on Tariffs and Trade (GATT) – precursor of the present-day World Trade Organization (WTO) – spearheaded more intense efforts towards trade liberalization in other nations. The thawing of the Cold War in 1989 may be said to have signalled the end of this second phase in the evolution of MNCs.

The third phase in the development of MNCs began with the introduc-tion of the 'transnational' variants. Unlike traditional MNCs, the opera-tions of which are run independently and are loosely coordinated from headquarters, transnational corporations (TNCs) carry out operations in a manner inextricably linked to each other. In it clearest manifestation, a TNC would consist of vertically integrated units located in two or more countries that turn out goods and services at different stages of production. For example, a garments label headquartered in the Netherlands could source financial capital from the US, do its design in Italy or France, get its raw materials from Egypt or Morocco, assemble parts in China, and sell its products all over the world. By contrast, a conventional MNC would be composed of free-standing units that are replicated in different countries. Think of popular softdrink brands that are sold by different bottlers and distributors, depending on the region or country, for example.

Because of globalization, some MNCs have gone beyond their tradi-tional roles of offering goods and services for the benefit of the general public to assume functions more proper to governments and states. An example of this was Mobil Oil, now known as ExxonMobil Corporation (Sison, 2001). For several decades, Eket, an oil-producing region in Nigeria, was actually known as 'Mobiland', because Mobil Corporation had all but formally replaced the Nigerian government as the main provider of 'public goods' in the area. 'Public goods' are those that tend to be in short supply owing to lack of economic incentives and thus normally end up becoming the responsibility of governments.

Prodded by economic interests in the first place, Mobil had put up and maintained most of the roads, bridges and other important bits of infra-structure in the region. It had also built hospitals and schools, apart from offering employment, directly or indirectly, to a huge number of Eket's inhabitants. It even had its own security force, although organized to protect its own installations and employees primarily. Mobil could arguably claim that, in a sense, it was doing more for Eket and its people than the Nigerian government itself. As with other oil companies operating in the area, Mobil had considerable clout in the environmental, employment and industrial relations policies of Nigeria. Albeit hesitantly, it also became a significant player in domestic politics, in the manner of dealing with some minorities the government considered as rebels and secessionists, and in international relations, because of its foreign origin. By exercising its corporate social responsibility, that is, by engaging in economic, environmental and social initiatives beyond those legally required by different stakeholder groups, business organizations such as Mobil inadvertently get dragged into playing the role of a quasi-state or government.

Modern globalization, therefore, has turned into an occasion for a crossing-over of roles between state governments and MNCs. Increasingly, states behave in the manner of firms, providing its citizen-clients with the means – political, civil and socioeconomic rights, basically – so that each of them could in turn pursue his own ideal life. Conversely, in the exercise of 'corporate social responsibility', business firms conduct themselves in the manner of state governments, providing people with all sorts of public goods, at times, even with defence and security. Certainly business corporations hold a significant advantage in wealth creation, thanks to greater organizational discipline and a more efficient use of resources. Businesses could even hold greater assets than some states. But, on the other hand, they lack democratic legitimacy in their decision making, something to which, by contrast, state governments could readily stake a claim. State governments, therefore, stand to learn much from business corporations in matters of organization and efficiency, although, at the same time, corporate governance also has a lot to learn from state governments in issues pertaining to stakeholder rights, representation and participation.

III IN BRIEF

- A parallel could be drawn between politics, or the study of the government of states, and the study of corporate governance. Both states and corporations are social institutions composed of different kinds of people organized in a particular way in order to pursue common ends.
- In accordance with the categories of Aristotle's *Politics*, states are natural and perfect societies for the purpose of living a flourishing human life. Business organizations and firms, on the other hand, are examples of artificial and imperfect societies. They are a kind of intermediate body between families and the state seeking economic ends.

- The proper relationship between the state and intermediate bodies such as corporations is one of subsidiarity. The state has the positive duty of helping intermediate bodies to contribute in their particular, limited, way to the good life; it also has the negative duty of refraining from absorbing intermediate bodies or taking over their corresponding functions.
- Within the context of the Aristotelian economy, the business organization may be understood as an institution entrusted with the task of producing or acquiring wealth or property (chrematistics) in a non-natural manner. As such, the business organization is subject to the superior art of administering or using wealth and other material resources.
- For Aristotle, politics represents the ruling science by virtue of its object, happiness, which is the highest good. Subordinate to politics is ethics, which is the science of virtue, the 'internal good' or the 'good of the soul'; and subordinate to ethics is the economy, which is the science of 'external' or 'material goods' and the 'goods of the body'. From this we infer that, insofar as they belong to the realm of the economy, business organizations should be subject to ethics and ultimately to politics.
- Modern globalization has made possible a redefinition of the goals of states, under the guise of nation states, and of business organizations, in the form of multinational corporations (MNCs). States have assumed the roles of corporations, and corporations, those of states. These changes have important implications not only in the government of states or politics, but also in the governance of corporations.

REFERENCES

Alchian, Armen and Harold Demsetz (1972), 'Production, information costs and economic organization', *American Economic Review*, **62**, 777–95.
Aristotle (1985), *Nicomachean Ethics*, trans. Terence Irwin, Indianapolis, IN: Hackett Publishing Company.
Aristotle (1990), *The Politics*, ed. Stephen Everson, Cambridge: Cambridge University Press.
Castells, Manuel (1996), *The Rise of the Network Society*, Oxford: Basil Blackwell.
Dunning, John (1993a), *The Globalization of Business: The Challenge of the 1990s*, London/New York: Routledge.
Dunning, John (1993b), *Globalization: The Challenge for National Economic Regimes*, Dublin: The Economic and Social Research Institute.
The Economist (2006), 'Oil's dark secret', 12 August, 58–60.
Elfstrom, Gerald (1991), *Moral Issues and Multinational Corporations*, London: Macmillan.

Giddens, Anthony (1990), *The Consequences of Modernity*, Cambridge: Polity Press.

Gregory, Holly (2001), 'Overview of corporate governance guidelines and codes of best practice in developing and emerging markets', in Robert Monks and Nell Minow (eds), *Corporate Governance*, Oxford/Malden, MA: Blackwell Publishing.

Grossman, Sanford and Oliver Hart (1986), 'The costs and benefits of ownership: a theory of vertical and lateral integration', *Journal of Political Economy*, **94**, 691–719.

Guéhenno, Jean Marie (1985), *The End of the Nation State*, Minneapolis: University of Minnesota Press.

Hart, Oliver and John Moore (1990), 'Property rights and the nature of the firm', *Journal of Political Economy*, **98**, 1119–58.

Held, David, Anthony McGrew, David Goldblatt and Jonathan Perraton (1999), *Global Transformations: Politics, Economics and Culture*, Cambridge: Polity Press.

Hirst, Paul and Grahame Thompson (1996), *Globalization in Question: The International Economy and the Possibilities of Governance*, Cambridge: Polity Press.

Hobbes, Thomas (1660), *The Leviathan*, http://oregonstate.edu/instruct/phl302/texts/hobbes/leviathan-contents.html.

Holmes, Stephen and Cass Sunstein (1999), *The Cost of Rights. Why Liberty Depends on Taxes*, New York/London: W.W. Norton & Company.

Huntington, Samuel (1996), *The Clash of Civilizations and the Remaking of World Order*, New York: Simon & Schuster.

Kitson, Alan and Robert Campbell (1996), *The Ethical Organization: Ethical Theory and Corporate Behavior*, London: Houndmills.

Koehn, Daryl (1999), *An Overview of Issues in Corporate Governance*, www.stthom.edu/cbes/conferences/daryl_koehn.html (accessed 16 October 2002).

Krasner, Stephen (1999), *Sovereignty: Organized Hypocrisy*, Princeton, NJ: Princeton University Press.

MacIntyre, Alasdair (1988), *Whose Justice? Which Rationality?*, London: Duckworth.

Monks, Robert and Nell Minow (2001), *Corporate Governance*, Oxford/Malden, MA: Blackwell Publishing.

Ohmae, Kenichi (1995), *The End of the Nation State*, New York: The Free Press.

Organization for Economic Cooperation and Development (OECD) (1997), *The OECD Guidelines for Multinational Enterprises*, www.oecd.org/document/28/0,2340,en_2649_34889_2397532_1_1_1_1,00.html.

Pontifical Council for Justice and Peace (2005), *Compendium of the Social Doctrine of the Church*, Rome: Librería Editrice Vaticana.

Rajan, Raghuram G. and Luigi Zingales (2000), 'The governance of the new enterprise', *NBER Working Paper Series*, 7958, www.nber.org/papers/w7958, October.

Scholte, Jan Aart (1993), *International Relations of Social Change*, Buckingham, UK: Open University Press.

Shleifer, Andrei and Robert Vishny (1997), 'A survey of corporate governance', *Journal of Finance*, **52**, 737–83.

Sison, Alejo José G. (2001), 'When multinational corporations act as governments: the Mobil corporation experience', in Jörg Andriof and Malcolm McIntosh (eds), *Perspectives on Corporate Citizenship*, Sheffield, UK: Greenleaf Publishing Ltd.

Sison, Alejo José G. (2002), 'National champions in a unified market: the BSCH-Champalimaud case', in Heidi von Weltzien Hoivik (ed.), *Moral Leadership in Action. Building and Sustaining Moral Competence in European Organizations*, Cheltenham, UK and Northampton, MA: Edward Elgar.

Sternberg, Elaine (1994), *Just Business: Business Ethics in Action*, London: Little, Brown and Co.

Vernon, Raymond (1998), *In the Hurricane's Eye: The Troubled Prospects of Multinational Enterprises*, Cambridge, MA/London: Harvard University Press.

Williamson, Oliver (1985), *The Economic Institutions of Capitalism*, New York: The Free Press.

Wriston, Walter (1997), *The Twilight of Sovereignty*, New York: Charles Scribers & Sons.

Zingales, Luigi (1997), 'Corporate governance', *NBER Working Paper Series*, No. 6309, www.nber.org/papers/w6309, December.

4. Shareholders, stakeholders and citizens

Having studied in the previous chapter the ends proper to states and to firms, the next step in developing the analogy between the two institutions consists in examining the different kinds of people that comprise each of them. This will provide us with a better understanding of the various parties involved in corporate governance and the role that each one is supposed to play.

I   WHO CONSTITUTES THE FIRM? FROM SHAREHOLDERS TO CORPORATE CITIZENS

To the question of who constitutes the corporation, many would find 'shareholders' a fitting initial response. After all, without their money or financial capital, the funds necessary to support any economic activity would be sorely lacking. Although there will always be firms managed by shareholder-owners – think of IKEA with Ingvar Kamprad, Virgin with Richard Branson and Benetton with Luciano Benetton, for example – among bigger corporations, however, this is more of an exception than the rule. The sheer size of the corporation requires that other people work for it, apart from the owner and the members of the owner's family. And these people normally work in exchange for a salary or a wage. Hence, while shareholders receive interest on their capital, workers receive salaries for their labour. All those who work for a corporation without owning shares in it may be said to belong (broadly) to the professional or managerial class.

The division between shareholders and managers has also been provoked, apart from company size, by the necessary specialization of tasks (Berle and Means, 1932). Increased organizational size brings greater functional complexity. The division and specialization of labour thus becomes the corporation's response to this new complexity and to market demands for greater productivity. Oftentimes, the separation of tasks is the only way for a company to produce goods on a certain scale: think of cars or airplanes, for instance. In those cases, within the same firm, some workers would have to concentrate on design, others on financing, and still others on sales or on post-sale service, and so forth.

After shareholders, therefore, managers and professionals form the next important group of people within the corporation. And between shareholders and managers there exists an 'agency relation', wherein managers play the role of 'agents' of shareholders or 'principals'. At the beginning of this volume, much had already been said about the 'agency relation', its strengths and difficulties. In this regard, and citing Friedman (1970), we have also referred to what is purportedly the primary duty of managers, that is, to make as much money as possible for shareholders within the bounds of the law.

However, since the publication of Friedman's essay, parallel developments in corporate social responsibility (CSR) and stakeholder theory have pushed for a critical re-evaluation of the dominant view of the firm, heretofore based on agency relations and shareholder theory. Let us now turn to the first of these notions.

Within the Anglo-American tradition, the modern discussion of CSR may be traced to Bowen (1953), who first proposed that managers pursue policies, make decisions and follow lines of action in keeping with the values and objectives of society. A few years later, Eells and Walton (1961) developed the concept further by referring to CSR, among other things, as the ethical principles that should govern the relationship between corporations and society. It was McGuire (1963), however, who gave a sharper focus to the understanding of CSR as the set of company obligations beyond the economic and legal realms.

In large measure, the idea that corporations possess obligations outside of those defined by law could only have been considered a novelty within the Anglo-American tradition. Anglo-American culture has always been characterized by a deep streak of individualism. Because of this, Anglo-American business thinking was conflicted since the very beginning with the acceptance of such a thing as 'corporate responsibility', different from the responsibilities of individual workers (Sison, 2000: 288). After all, unlike individual persons, corporations are mere creatures of law 'without bodies to be jailed nor souls to be damned'. In consequence, many people thought, 'Would not attributing collective responsibilities to corporations – which are mere legal fictions – be foolish?' Only in 1819 did the US Supreme Court explicitly recognize the corporation as a legal person in its *Dartmouth College* v. *Woodward* decision. Since then it was established that, although the corporation is not an individual, physical person, before the law it, too, is a subject, albeit a collective one, of rights and responsibilities. Because of its legal status, for example, corporations are entitled to acquire or to sell property and to hire or to fire workers. Likewise, corporations are expected to pay taxes and to honour contracts. The ultimate rationale for these rights and responsibilities is, of course, to allow corporations to produce goods and services for the benefit directly of shareholders and indirectly of society at large.

Apart from individualism, the other obstacle in Anglo-American business thinking's adoption of CSR is legalism. Having established that the corporation is a legal person and, as such, the subject of rights and duties, the issue is now to determine their nature and scope. The tendency within the Anglo-American tradition has always been to reduce these rights and duties strictly to the minimum set by law (Sison, 2000: 288–9). Consider that, when a collective 'corporate responsibility' was first defined in the US, it was understood to be exclusively of a civil nature, as an obligation to pay fines and damages. It took almost a century, in the *New York Central Railroad* v. *United States* verdict of 1909, for the US Supreme Court to take a broader view and recognize a 'criminal responsibility' in corporations besides. This then opened up the possibility of a corporate criminal intent and likelihood that employees be imprisoned for involvement in corporate criminal actions.

By contrast, Continental European perspectives of business have been aware from the very beginning that, insofar as firms are institutions necessarily embedded in society, they have duties apart from those enshrined in law towards society's other members. In fact, CSR has even been the object of definition by a European Commission document: 'Corporate social responsibility is a concept whereby companies integrate social and environmental concerns in their business operations and in their interaction with their stakeholders on a voluntary basis. It is about enterprises deciding to go beyond minimum legal requirements and obligations stemming from collective agreements in order to address societal needs. Through CSR, enterprises of all sizes, in cooperation with their stakeholders, can help to reconcile economic, social and environmental ambitions. [. . .] In Europe, the promotion of CSR reflects the need to defend common values and increase the sense of solidarity and cohesion' (European Commission, 2006).

In this respect, Continental European views are more in keeping with the Aristotelian conception of corporations as contingent intermediate associations, located between families and states, for the purpose of producing economic goods and services, as we have already seen.

In the mid-seventies, two sets of authors made significant contributions to the development of CSR within the Anglo-American context. First, Davis and Blomstrom asserted that 'social responsibility is the obligation of decision makers to take actions which protect and improve the welfare of society as a whole along with their own interests' (Davis and Blomstrom,

1975: 23). There are a couple of things we would like to point out: Davis and Blomstrom's belief that social responsibility is something that accompanies corporate interests and the observation that corporate action may affect society in two ways. CSR may now be understood negatively, as the duty to avoid harm to society, and positively, as the obligation to promote social well-being. In that same decade, Sethi advanced a standard against which corporate behaviour is to be judged: its congruence with prevailing social norms, values and expectations (Sethi, 1975). Not only does this standard transcend the legal sphere, but it also enters into the domain of social expectations.

These two streams fed directly into Carroll's definition, 'The social responsibility of business encompasses the economic, legal, ethical and discretionary expectations that society has of an organization at a given point in time' (Carroll, 1979: 500). In a sense, this statement merely reflected a change of attitude in American courts and government agencies which began to accept cases against companies on social and ethical grounds, despite the absence of a legal basis. Such was the celebrated bribery case involving Lockheed and the Japanese Liberal Democratic Party, which led to the ouster of Prime Minister Kakuei Tanaka and the belated passing of the Foreign Corrupt Practices Act by US Congress in 1977 (Sison, 2000: 288–9). It was an acknowledgement that corporations indeed had responsibilities apart from those contained in law and there was a corresponding public clamour for corporations to own up to these.

Carroll divided CSR into four different categories – economic, legal, ethical and discretionary – which he conceived as distinct levels of a pyramid-like structure (Carroll, 1991). At the very base are a business's economic obligations, its duty to produce goods and services that society wants at a profit. In keeping with its economic obligations, business must be effective, efficient and follow the right strategy. When a company does not turn out a profit, not only does it fail to meet economic responsibilities, it will not be able to fulfil other responsibilities either. Next come a corporation's legal responsibilities, its obligation to obey the laws of the land. These laws may be local, regional, national or even transnational, as in the case of some treaties and agreements. Upholding the law is the 'price' a company has to pay for its 'licence to operate' given by the state. In third place we find a company's ethical obligations, its duty to comply with social customs even if these were not contained in law. Ethical responsibilities look more to achieving the spirit of the law than mere compliance with its letter. When it comes to keeping social standards, ethical responsibility requires that corporate behaviour be unquestionably above board, rather than just struggling or scraping to make the cut. Lastly, at the very top of the pyramid, we have a corporation's discretionary or philanthropic responsibilities. Strictly speaking, these are not duties or obligations; they are simply expectations, more or less well-founded, of what society deems desirable. It is taken for granted that companies make donations to charitable causes, fund schools or sponsor community events and programmes. No legal action can be taken against a company for failing to do any of these and, furthermore, not even everyone will agree that they belong to a corporation's ethical remit, but, in themselves, they are certainly choice-worthy actions to be undertaken. From Carroll's perspective, therefore, the CSR ideal is for a company – while producing a society's desired goods and services – to turn up a profit, obey the law, live up to ethical expectations and contribute to philanthropic activities.

To be sure, Carroll makes an invaluable contribution in mapping out the different areas which together comprise CSR. However, neither the limits between the categories nor the relations among them are as clear as he initially described. To begin with, perhaps profit should not be understood in purely economic terms; otherwise, non-profits or not-for-profits, such as Caritas Internationalis, Oxfam or Save the Children, would be paradigms of socially irresponsible organizations on that account. Also, there may be compelling reasons to put legal obligations at the base of the pyramid. After all, corporations come into existence as creatures of law, so it would make every sense for them to comply with legal requirements first before assuming any other kind of social responsibility, including economic ones. Moreover, an excessively narrow concept of the ethical seems to be at work, pertaining to social expectations that have not been codified in law, when ethics, in fact, covers the whole range of social responsibilities.

Responsibility is primarily an ethical concept, even before its adoption by law. No amount of insistence by law on the existence of any kind of responsibility would hold, if it lacked an ethical basis. Ethics is where the law ultimately draws its strength, although, conversely, good law above all serves to lend muscle to ethics. Responsibility is a consequence of free action. A free and rational agent, in this case, the collective represented by the corporation, must respond to society for its actions and their consequences, good and bad. Thus the consideration of ethical responsibilities on the part of the corporation should not be postponed only until economic and legal obligations have been met, as Carroll seems to imply. Finally, philanthropic or discretionary responsibilities may be better explained as a subclass of ethical responsibilities. They refer to the aspirational goals of excellence or virtue that, in all rigour, cannot be demanded, but only encouraged. They represent the perfection of freedom precisely because they are carried out under no obligation from law. Inasmuch as there is no legal coercion involved, philanthropic or discretionary actions carry greater responsibility. Far from being the least important component of CSR, the last one to be examined, that which occupies the least room at the apex of the pyramid, it should probably be given the place of honour. They should be the first thing in the minds of corporate decision-makers at the level of intentions, although they may actually be the last item in implementation.

In addition to these theoretical objections, CSR has also been receiving a lot of flak from the practical side, during this past decade or so. In response to criticisms regarding its lack of practicality, the notions of 'corporate accountability', 'corporate social responsiveness' and 'corporate social performance' have been developed as offshoots of CSR. 'Corporate accountability' refers to the explicit recognition of the firm as a sociopolitical actor, just like government, with responsibilities not only to shareholders but also to the wider society (Crane and Matten, 2004: 55). Granted that corporations, willy nilly, assume functions previously attributed to government, in effect privatizing certain tasks such as security and welfare provision, new mechanisms have to be introduced to hold them accountable to the public. Among these initiatives we find 'triple bottom line' audits, which delve into a corporation's impacts on people, the planet and profits; stakeholder dialogues, which create a venue for discussion among social actors; public–private partnerships, which allow companies to work hand-in-hand with government agencies on particular issues; and transparency policies, through which firms make their relevant decisions known to society at large. In other words, since corporate activities have social as well as economic impacts, there is also a need, together with corporate social accountability, for 'corporate social accounting', the measurement and reporting, both internal and external, of information concerning an organization's activities and impacts on society (Estes, 1976).

'Corporate social responsiveness' concentrates on the strategic and processual dimensions of CSR, manifested in a company's ability to respond to social pressures (Crane and Matten, 2004: 48). Social pressures elicit four types of responses from a corporation, ranging from the least to the most desirable: reaction, defence, accommodation or proaction. Reaction means that the organization has been caught flat-footed and is hardly able to control events. Defence connotes an element of denial in assuming responsibility over a situation. Accommodation, on the other hand, implies acceptance and assimilation of responsibility, a kind of 'rolling with the punches'. And lastly, proaction signifies foresight and a capacity to maximize benefits and minimize damage over corporate behaviour. Nike, which at first denied or presented itself as a helpless client, almost a victim of unfair labour practices at its contractors' factories, ended up spearheading the drive to upgrade working conditions in the sector at the behest (on occasions, in the form of a boycott) of consumers and the general public (Bernstein, 2004; Vietnam Labor Watch, 1997). This clearly illustrates a migration from reaction to proaction in corporate social responsiveness.

'Corporate social performance' combines the principles of CSR with the processes of corporate social responsiveness and the outcomes of corporate behaviour (Wood, 1991). Outcomes are broken down into social policies (statements regarding the corporate mission, its values, beliefs and goals), social programmes (activities that materialize those policies) and social impacts (measurable changes brought about by those programmes). For example, a company may include the protection of the environment in its mission statement. In consequence, it may enroll in the corresponding ISO certification programme. After a given period, the company could then cite positive pollution data that would lend substance to its claims. Recently, 'corporate social performance' has evolved into what is now known as 'global corporate citizenship' (Wood et al., 2006). We shall return to this later.

Aside from CSR and its derivatives, the other concept that has contributed hugely to an altogether different understanding of the firm is 'stakeholder theory'. The term 'stakeholder' was first coined in a Stanford Research Institute document on corporate planning in 1963, designating 'those groups without whose support the organization would cease to exist' (Freeman, 1998: 602). The intention of the paper was to broaden the group of people to whom management could be held responsible. A stakeholder would then refer to 'any group or individual which can affect or is affected by an organization' (Freeman, 1998: 602). Thus, included among a company's stakeholders are its employees, customers, suppliers, competitors, the government and the community, apart, of course, from its shareholders. Each of them is characterized by 'legitimate interests in procedural and/or substantive aspects of corporate activity' (Donaldson and Preston, 1995: 67).

Rather than being a mere pun on 'shareholder' or 'stockholder', the purpose of stakeholder theory is something which is deadly serious. Stakeholder theory rejects the notion that the sole criterion in management decisions should be its fiduciary duty towards shareholders, and suggests instead that the stakes of all interested parties be likewise considered. In particular, demands on corporate decision makers to maximize share price and shareholder wealth ought to be tempered by an effective concern for the welfare of other stakeholders.

To some extent, management's striving to protect the interests of all stakeholders clashes with the American legal tradition, which heavily favours shareholders (Boatright, 1999: 172). However, granting priority to the financial interests of shareholders does not mean granting them exclusivity, for even these could best be served (arguably) when framed in the long-term. Therefore, although shareholder interests dominate, adopting a long-term perspective would require that managers include inputs from all the other stakeholder groups in their decision-making processes. After all, business transactions do not occur in a void and their success would always depend, to a greater or lesser degree, on the amount of cooperation obtained from the relevant social actors or stakeholders. As the American Bar Association Committee on Corporate Laws once clarified, 'directors have fiduciary responsibilities to shareholders which, while allowing directors to give consideration to the interests of others, could compel them to find a reasonable relationship to the long-term interests of shareholders' (Monks and Minow, 2001: 37).

Continental European business thinking, more cognizant of the social embeddedness of business institutions, has always taken the interests of other social agents into account, regardless of whether they were actually called 'stakeholders' or not. This is especially true in the case of German-speaking countries, with their tradition of codetermination (*Mitbestimmung*) in which labour representatives are granted the right to participate in high-level corporate deliberations (Charkham, 1995), as well as in Scandinavia, where industrial democracy has enjoyed a long and successful history (Nasi, 1995).

In comparison with shareholder theory or a purely financial theory of the firm, stakeholder theory enjoys the clear advantage of presenting a broader and more realistic view of the corporation as a socially embedded institution. It identifies, at the same time, all the relevant social actors or stakeholders with whom the firm interacts and describes their reciprocal relations. Unsurprisingly, stakeholder theory has exerted a strong influence not only in business ethics (Freeman, 1984, 1994; Donaldson and Preston, 1995), but also in organization theory (Thompson, 1967; Dill, 1958) and in finance and strategic management (Mason and Mitroff, 1982). Implicitly, at the very least, stakeholder theory encourages managers to strike a balance between long-term shareholder interests and the interests of all the other stakeholders in their corporate decisions and behaviour. However, such an equilibrium is not always possible, nor should shareholder interests always have the priority.

Take, for example, the Tylenol case, where Johnson & Johnson ordered the massive recall of potentially tampered products, protecting consumers at the expense of shareholders, albeit in the shortest terms (Mallenbaker.net, 2006). In 1982, Tylenol commanded 35 per cent of the analgesic market in the US and represented something like 15 per cent of Johnson & Johnson's profits. As a result of the scare, the company took a $100 million charge against earnings and its market value fell by one billion dollars. The rationale behind Johnson & Johnson's corporate behaviour may be ultimately found in its credo: 'We believe our first responsibility is to the doctors, nurses and patients, to mothers and fathers and all others who use our products and services' (Johnson & Johnson, 2006). Although stakeholder theory could have contributed to raising an awareness of the other parties aside from shareholders that are affected by the company's activities, nothing in it indicated that customer interests should prevail in that particular situation. That would require something more than a mere 'balancing of interests' and points, instead, to what may be called a theory of the firm premised on the 'common good'.

Little by little, we have witnessed an ever-broadening comprehension of the people who constitute a corporation and their particular relationships with it. At first we began with owner-managers, then continued with the inclusion of the professional class of workers and managers, and ended with the admittance of the whole range of stakeholder groups. In parallel we have also observed a change in the grasp of corporate responsibility, from a purely economic and legal one, directed exclusively towards shareholders, to one that encompasses social and ethical duties as well to other stakeholders. What we have gained in breadth we seem to have lost in clarity with regard to managerial decision making, however. Simply 'balancing out' different and oftentimes conflicting stakeholder interests does not guarantee good corporate decisions. Instead, these seem to require a more enlightened understanding of the 'common good' and the business organization's specific contribution to it. Yet to speak of the 'common good' means to enter into the province proper of politics, and this leads us right into the discussion of 'corporate citizenship'.

'Corporate citizenship' (CC) is a term first used by practitioners, by people working in corporations, and later popularized by American business press writers in the 1980s (Crane, Matten and Moon, 2003). It was originally meant to emphasize, broaden and redirect specific dimensions of CSR, and as such was adopted in recent years by members of the academy. Obviously, the expression CC cannot be taken in its literal sense, meaning that corporations are real citizens vested with the corresponding rights and duties in the state. For that to be true, the corporation would have to be an individual, physical person, which it clearly is not. At most, it could only be a fictional, legal person, as we already know. The term seems to indicate, rather, that the being or identity and the activities of corporations within society could somehow be studied through the lens of citizenship. CC therefore borrows heavily from political theory, the academic discipline in which the notion of citizenship is native, with the hope that it will shed light on the constitution and dynamics of corporations as human and therefore social institutions.

At first blush, CC is a simple metaphor where citizenship is applied to something to which, in fact, it cannot be applied – that is, the corporation – in order to suggest a strong resemblance. CC connotes primarily that corporations, just like physical persons, may somehow be considered as 'citizens' of the state. This is what almost all CC theorists explore. After examining the content and limits of this line of research for corporate governance, nonetheless, we would also like to have a look at another different angle of CC: we would like to propose that CC could likewise be interpreted in terms of the corporation itself as the state and the various stakeholder groups – shareholders, workers, consumers, suppliers, competitors and so forth – as possible citizens of that 'corporate state'. We believe that this second line of interpretation would yield results no less illuminating than the first one, once more for our main purpose of understanding the practice of good corporate governance.

II BEYOND THE METAPHOR OF CORPORATE CITIZENSHIP

Business theory has borrowed the notion of citizenship from politics, for several reasons. The major one is to highlight the social dimension of business organizations and, consequently, to analyse the role of power, under its different disguises, in resolving the inevitable conflicts of interests that arise therein. Through the concept of citizenship, politics also lends to business firms a sense of identity, by way of membership in the community, and a justification for their rights and responsibilities as artificial or legal persons, being a channel for participating in community life. Wood and associates even go as far as affirming that business organizations, in comparison to individual or physical persons, are 'secondary citizens' (Wood et al., 2006: 35–6). Although we normally treat business organizations as independent legal entities carrying out their own activities in pursuit of particular goals, the truth is that they only exist thanks to the objectives and the resources furnished by their human incorporators. In this respect, corporations are collective instruments created by individual citizens to achieve ends which, otherwise, they will not be able to attain as effectively. Given the nature of these individual citizens, those ends are most likely to have a sociopolitical dimension and reflect the values of the community to which they belong.

But the notion of citizenship itself has had a long history and, to discover its full potential in clarifying the status of corporations and the issues concerning how corporations ought to be governed, it would be convenient to have a look into its origins and evolution.

In the *Politics*, Aristotle delves into the question of citizenship upon observing that the 'state is composite, [and] like any other whole [is] made up of many parts – these are the citizens, who compose it' (Pltcs, 1274b). He then proceeds to identify who is the citizen, and what is the meaning of the term, essentially by determining what the citizen does. Next, Aristotle tries to differentiate citizens from all other classes of people resident in the state, explaining the process by which one acquires citizenship on the side. Finally, he seeks to distinguish the various kinds of citizens depending on the form of government adopted by the state. Only within this context could the query 'what makes a citizen a good citizen?' receive an appropriate response.

According to Aristotle, 'a citizen in the strictest sense, against whom no such exception can be taken' is he who 'shares in the administration of justice, and in offices' (Pltcs, 1275a). The essential task of the citizen is to participate in deciding what is good and just in the state and in putting this into effect. A few lines later he specifies that a citizen is a 'juryman and member of the assembly', to whom 'is reserved the right of deliberating or judging about some things or about all things' (Pltcs, 1275b). Although many people in a state may actually participate in the process of deliberating and deciding on the public good, only citizens have the right to do so. What characterizes a citizen, therefore, is 'the power to take part in the deliberative or judicial administration of any state' (Pltcs, 1275b). This does not mean, however, that a citizen always has to hold state office. It would suffice that he at least have the power to occupy such a post, for citizenship requires 'sharing in governing and being governed' (Pltcs, 1283b). In other words, one does not lose citizenship when being governed and out of office, as long as one can also govern and hold office in turn at some other time.

Aristotle was aware that the state needed other kinds of people apart from citizens in order to be viable (Pltcs, 1278a). Mere necessity for the state's survival or even for the state's flourishing did not automatically qualify one for citizenship. Consider children who, not being grown-up, still cannot exercise sufficient deliberation and judgment in state matters. They may only be called citizens on the basis of certain assumptions. Neither are the members of the artisan class citizens, properly speaking. In ancient times and among many nations, the artisan class was composed by a majority of slaves and foreigners: 'The necessary people are either slaves who minister to the wants of individuals, or mechanics and laborers who are servants of the community' (Pltcs, 1278a). In the best of states, citizens do not refer to free men as such – in which case foreign workers would be citizens – but only to free men who are the same time freed from providing necessary menial services. Citizenship requires a certain distance from the tyranny of having to satisfy daily needs; participating in the discussion about the public good and how to put it into practice demands leisure and time to spare. Because of this, citizenship seems to imply having reached relative affluence or an acceptable level of material wealth and comfort; it is not something everyone can afford at the outset.

Elsewhere, Aristotle enumerates the many different classes that constitute the state and are needed for its existence: the food-producing class or farmers, artisans, traders, labourers, the military and so forth (Pltcs, 1291a). Nonetheless, 'as the soul may be said to be more truly part of an animal than the body, so the higher parts of the states, that is to say, the warrior class, the class engaged in the administration of justice, and that engaged in deliberation, which is the special business of political understanding – these are more essential to the state than the parts which minister to the necessaries of life' (Pltcs, 1291a). To the extent that citizens are involved in deciding the public good and in dispensing justice, they are like the soul, the most important part of the state, although by themselves they do not suffice to constitute the state, in the same way that the soul still needs the body. Just the same, citizens occupy the topmost place in the hierarchy of the many different classes comprising the state.

Not all residents of a state nor even all the necessary ones, therefore, are citizens. Resident aliens and slaves share with citizens the same living space, although not the same rights (Pltcs, 1274a). To be a citizen, it is not enough to have the right to sue or be sued before a state's tribunals; this could also be obtained by resident aliens through treaties between home and host states. Citizens have more and farther-reaching rights. Insofar as resident aliens are normally obliged to have a citizen–patron, they could only participate in the community very imperfectly, never in their own name and always under this citizen–patron's tutelage. In this respect, they are much like children, the very old or the feeble. None of these could rightfully be considered citizens, except in a limited and qualified sense.

How, then, does one become a citizen? Excluding special cases, where one is made or becomes a citizen accidentally, 'in practice a citizen is defined to be one of whom both the parents are citizens (and not just one, i.e., father or mother)' (Pltcs, 1275b), Aristotle responds. As we have seen, to become a citizen it is not sufficient for one to reside in a particular state, nor to enjoy just some rights there; one would also have to be an adult possessing more than adequate wealth and, above all, be the offspring of people who themselves are citizens. It was generally believed during Aristotle's time that these are the conditions for exercising the prerogatives of citizenship, namely, deliberating on the public good and administering justice. In short, citizens are the only ones qualified to rule or govern the state by virtue of the above-mentioned characteristics.

Notice that, for Aristotle, nature matters more than nurture for the purpose of citizenship: 'For that some should rule and others be ruled is a thing not only necessary, but expedient; from the hour of their birth, some are marked out for subjection, others for rule' (Pltcs, 1254a), he maintains. He apparently presumes that, by being the child of citizen-parents, one would be able to perform the tasks of citizenship competently. He may be right in part, because parents usually guarantee children a favourable position, in terms of wealth and education, to start with in life. So requiring that both parents be citizens for oneself to become a citizen is some form of shorthand for all the other prerequisites. Yet the absoluteness of this condition is appropriately tempered when he acknowledges the difficulty of determining how far back in generations one should go, to establish a pedigree worthy of citizenship. Moreover, Aristotle admits that "born of a father or mother who is a citizen", cannot possibly apply to the first inhabitants or founders of a state' (Pltcs, 1275b). In citizenship, as in most other human things, nature may matter more than nurture, but it could only account for as much, never for everything.

Having defined citizenship and established the process by which it is acquired, Aristotle insists that there are as many kinds of citizenship as states or forms of government, such that 'he who is a citizen in democracy will often not be a citizen in an oligarchy' (Pltcs 1275a). Given that citizens differ according to forms of government, he cautions that his definition is best suited to a democracy, but not to other states. It does not apply, for example, to states where people (the demes) are not acknowledged, do not hold regular assemblies, or decide on lawsuits (Pltcs, 1275b). Neither does it apply to aristocracies, where citizenship is granted on the basis of excellence and merit, nor in oligarchies, where it is given on the basis of wealth (Pltcs, 1278a). It could happen, however, that a state begins to lack population and starts admitting aliens, illegitimate children, children of a single citizen-parent (father or mother) and even children of slaves as citizens; but that process would most likely be reversed as soon as the dearth was remedied (Pltcs, 1278a).

Even allowing for the variances in citizenship in accordance with the different kinds of states, Aristotle nonetheless affirms that the excellence of the good citizen may, in some instance, coincide with the excellence of the good man. That would occur in the best of states, so long as the good man and citizen takes part in the conduct of public affairs (Pltcs, 1278b).

Twenty-four centuries later, several models and typologies of citizenship, still based on differences in the kinds of states, have been offered (Stokes, 2002; Crane and Matten, 2004; Wood et al., 2006). Closer scrutiny reveals that these categories could ultimately be collapsed into two, with their respective variants: liberal–minimalist citizenship, on the one hand, and civic republican or communitarian citizenship, on the other.

The liberal–minimalist ideal conceives citizenship fundamentally as freedom from oppression and protection against the arbitrary rule of an absolutist government or state (Crane, Matten and Moon, 2003: 7–9). For this reason, citizens are vested with political rights which enable them to choose their rulers, to vote and to be voted into public office. The duty of government is to secure these individual political rights together with a few others which form the core or minimum of citizenship. For some, this minimum is composed of the rights to life, to liberty and to property (Locke); for others, the right to a just share of the social product or utility (Smith, Bentham); while, for still others, it consists in the universal rights to equality before the law and to free rational agency or autonomy (Kant). What is important is that this minimum of rights and freedoms be guaranteed. With a certain amount of latitude we can include in this group the libertarians (Wood et al., 2006: 41–2, 44), who support a very limited state, and those who uphold a deliberative democracy (Crane, Matten and Moon, 2003: 15–16), who may want a more robust form of government to safeguard conditions of equality in political discourse. Both persuasions are particularly concerned with rights.

For its part, civic republican or communitarian citizenship emphasizes participation in the public good through the fostering of community ties and the practice of civic virtues (Crane, Matten and Moon, 2003: 9; Wood et al., 2006: 42–3). While liberal–minimalist citizenship is marked off by 'negative freedoms' or 'freedoms from' state oppression and interference, for example, civic republican or communitarian citizenship is set apart by 'positive freedoms' or 'freedoms to' actively seek and work together with others for the common good. Liberal–minimalist citizenship stresses individual rights or state-guaranteed powers against all collectives including itself; civic republican or communitarian citizenship underscores belonging to the group as the factor consitutive of identity and the element that lends meaning to action. It is the group or collective with its hierarchically ordered set of goods, rules and practices that makes virtue or human excellence possible.

Within the civic republican or communitarian mind-set, the role of government or the state is to strengthen already existing institutions such as families, neighbourhoods, schools, churches and so forth, such that the good is rewarded, rules upheld and practices allowed to flourish. Only when these institutions are lacking should government intervene to help set them up, without losing sight of its subsidiary function, however. By the same token, state coercive power should be used so that evil is minimized, sanctioned and punished. Thus there is greater insistence on fulfilling obligations – to protect the family, obey the law, pay taxes and comply with jury or military service, and so forth – than on demanding rights, which somehow separate the individual from the group. Developmental democracy (J.S. Mill) may be said to favour civic republican or communitarian citizenship in the understanding that ties and obligations link one more to civil society than to the state or government (Crane, Matten and Moon, 2003: 14–15).

Liberal–minimalist citizenship guarantees one the right to stand up to the group; civic republican or communitarian citizenship admonishes one to participate in social affairs and contribute to the common good well beyond the periodic exercise of political rights or voting. Liberal–minimalist citizenship is very limited with regard to rights; civic republican or communitarian citizenship, maximalist in terms of duties, obligations and virtues. Insofar as Aristotle accentuates the embeddedness of citizenship in a particular sociocultural and historical context, as well as the mutual dependence between the human excellence of the citizen and the excellence of *polis* or the state, he unequivocally sides himself with the civic republican or communitarian model.

How do these different views of citizenship measure up with the notion of the corporation as a citizen, as a 'corporate citizen'? As a citizen in the liberal–minimalist mould, a corporation would be expected, first and foremost, to protect its 'right to exist' zealously, based on the freedom of association of its incorporators, and its 'licence to operate', resting on the freedom of enterprise. A corporation would very much prefer 'to stick to its own business' and embark on philanthropic activities only with utmost reluctance, in response to urgent or pressing social demands. In such instances, necessarily few and far between, corporations could justify their behaviour in the name of 'enlightened self-interest'; that is, corporate philanthropy is all right because it ultimately benefits the economic bottom line; it is just an additional 'cost of doing business'. In all the other social and political issues, the corporation as liberal–minimalist citizen would be quite content to remain passive. This description of liberal–minimalist corporate citizenship would correspond to a mix of what other authors call limited and equivalent views of CC (Crane and Matten, 2004: 63–7). Similarly, it would have great affinity with a shareholder view of the firm focused almost exclusively on increasing share price.

On the other hand, if a corporation were to follow the civic republican or communitarian type of citizenship, apart from exercising political, civil and social rights to the degree possible, it would also strive to fulfil what it understands to be political, civil and social obligations. Such a company would not hesitate to step in, harnessing resources and expertise, when it considers government or the state to be remiss in its duties. In particular, it

Corporate governance and ethics

could provide social rights (e.g. healthcare or housing), enable civil rights (e.g. be an 'equal opportunity employer') and serve as a channel for the exercise of political rights (e.g. hosting a forum for political debate on certain issues). This sort of company would not be troubled in justifying sociopolitical action, because it thinks that its mission transcends purely economic goals, to begin with. Active involvement in community affairs and uninhibited political activism characterizes the civic republican or communitarian corporate citizen. For the civic republican or communitarian corporate citizen, responsibility is not only of an economic nature, but sociopolitical as well; and it is owed not only to shareholders, but to other stakeholder groups also. A company of this type falls within the extended view of CC (Crane and Matten, 2004: 67–70).

III CITIZENS OF THE CORPORATE POLITY

Earlier we insinuated another possible interpretation of CC, different from the understanding of the corporation itself as a citizen of the state. It consists in the view of the corporation as an analogue of the state and of the various stakeholder groups as potential citizens. The approach and intent is similar to that carried out by Manville and Ober (2003) who tried to derive management lessons from classical Athenian democracy, although the outcomes will be somewhat different. Here we shall try to examine the different stakeholder groups and decide which of them best fits into the general definition of citizenship. Thus we will find out who among the different stakeholders of the corporation should be rightfully entrusted with the task of governance.

Drawing inspiration from the study by Wood and associates on the different approaches to CC, we may link the liberal–minimalist perspective of citizenship to a notion of the corporation as a mere 'civic association' and the civic republican or communitarian view to a more substantive idea of the firm as a corporate polity (Wood et al., 2006: 41–5). The liberal–minimalist theory of citizenship insists, above all, on the value of individual freedom – dressed in the language of rights – in order to pursue one's self-interests, whatever these may be. The only thing certain is that the satisfaction of these individual self-interests, insofar as they are divergent or rivalrous, cannot constitute a corporate common good. The corporation is then reduced to the status of a 'civic association', some sort of 'clearing house' where the minimum necessary restraints are applied to keep an individual exercising his rights from infringing on those of another. The different groups of people dealing with the corporation do not really behave as 'citizens' but as mere 'residents of a common jurisdiction', albeit with certain rights. They comply with the laws, but only as a means to reach individual goals, and not because this forms part of an excellence that is both personal and shared. In some respects, for the liberal–minimalist citizens of such a corporation, coercive laws are the only forces that keep them together. Outside of this, there is no attachment or loyalty among themselves or between them and the corporation. Hence, relationships are purely contractual, and the corporation, essentially, becomes nothing more than a 'nexus of contracts'. Shareholder-principals who provide capital are granted ownership rights and manager-agents are hired on the understanding that they will maximize the former's investment returns. The corporation is just an empty shell wherein investment, employment and sales contracts are negotiated and fulfilled: 'The language of citizenship might even be used, but the motivation is not to provide a collective good or to contribute to society's [or we may say in this case, the corporation's] well-being, but only to achieve a private end' (Wood et al., 2006: 42).

The demands of a civic republican or communitarian kind of citizenship on the stakeholders who comprise the corporate polity will be altogether different. On the premise that their personal flourishing is not independent of the flourishing of the corporate polity, they would take it upon themselves to participate actively in the deliberation and execution of the corporate good. This does not mean that there would be no regard for individual rights; it simply means that those rights are neither supreme nor absolute goods, as the liberal–minimalist ideal of citizenship seems to suggest. Rather, the recognition, enforcement and respect for those individual rights should always be conducted within the context of the corporate common good. As we have explained in previous sections, the common good is not inimical to individual goods such as rights, when properly understood. All that is needed is an order or hierarchy, such that 'goods in respect of another', for instance, rights, are subjected to 'goods in themselves', and the various 'goods in themselves' subjected in turn to the supreme and absolute good which is the 'common good' of the corporate polity. In all probability, the right to free enterprise would not include the right to buy and sell body parts, if only to safeguard the physical integrity of prospective suppliers, for instance.

A misconstrual of the common good and its relationship with individual goods may be at the root of the conflict that Wood and colleagues detect between communitarian and global citizenships (Wood et al., 2006: 42–6). At a superficial level, a strong attachment to one's local community may be at odds with an equally robust relationship with a multicultural global society. But global society and the local community do not exist on the same level, any more than the local community and the family. No doubt serious conflicts among these different levels and forms of organization may arise. However, we should not forget that the strength and success of the superior levels in terms of human flourishing ultimately depend on the strength and success of the inferior levels, through an interplay of the principles of subsidiarity and solidarity, as we have previously explained.

Let us try to clarify this relationship further by means of an example. A corporation that applies pollution control measures in its home community but neglects them in other communities where it is a mere guest is simply not a good corporate citizen, even by the communitarian standard. It need not follow a free-standing 'universalist' standard of global citizenship to recognize its duty to reduce pollution wherever it holds operations; it would be sufficient to become aware of the interdependence between its home and host communities, between its efforts to curb pollution locally and globally. Otherwise, the communitarian form of citizenship would fall into an incoherence. Only by identifying and fully integrating itself with the good of its home region – that is, by subscribing to the communitarian ideal of citizenship – can a corporation realistically contribute to the good of a wider global and multicultural society.

So far, the analysis of the different stakeholder groups as prospective citizens of the corporate polity have only been carried out (to our knowledge) from the viewpoint of liberal–minimalist citizenship, with a heavy emphasis on rights (Crane and Matten, 2004). In the succeeding pages, we shall use this as a starting point to draw a picture of the various stakeholders that comes closer to the civic republican or communitarian ideal: who among the different stakeholders best fulfils the requirements of the civic republican or communitarian citizenship within the corporate polity? Who among them is most deserving to govern?

Consonant with what has subsequently been called the civic republican or communitarian model, let us recall that, for Aristotle, a citizen is someone who 'shares in the administration of justice, and in offices' (Pltcs, 1275a). By 'administration of justice', he means taking part in the deliberative or judicial administration of the state (Pltcs, 1275b), and by 'sharing in offices', holding some kind of rule (Pltcs, 1276a). In substance, 'a citizen is one who shares in governing and being governed' (Pltcs, 1283b).

If citizenship consists in participating in government, who is best equipped to do so in the firm as a corporate polity? Shareholders are the first to come to mind from among the many different groups of stakeholders. After all, having provided the financial capital, they are normally acknowledged as the 'owners' of the company; and in accordance with the application of 'agency theory' to business firms, laws are generally designed to protect their interests as 'principals', in particular, against possible abuse by 'manager-agents'.

Yet this account is not entirely accurate. The shareholders' only real property is a piece of paper, the certificate that entitles them to a 'share' or a 'stock' of the firm's residual equity. Depending on whether management has been skilful in running the company and has thereby produced a profit, they may then have a right to receive dividends or sell their shares at a higher price. But none of these positive outcomes can be guaranteed. Other shareholder rights include choosing board members, participating in general meetings and voting on proposed changes in capital structure, as in the case of mergers and acquisitions. Nothing more, substantially. It would be erroneous, therefore, to consider shareholders as the real 'owners' of a company, when all they own are share certificates (Clarkson and Deck, 1998: 608). What is more, given the huge number of shareholders, their highly fragmented interests and their utter dependence on the decisions of management and of the other shareholders, it is quite understandable that they do not consider themselves as 'owners' of the company at all. Nor do they act as such, as a consequence.

Contrary to the general opinion, therefore, shareholders do not 'own' the company. They just cannot walk into the company premises and occupy a room or start selling the furniture, for example – something that they would be perfectly entitled to do with their own homes and furnishings, in contrast. They simply hold some rights over the company, particularly, the right to a share of its residual equity and, as a consequence of this, the right to vote in shareholders' meetings. Of course they could also always sell their shares for whatever reason they deem fit. The problem is, however, that shareholders hardly ever exercise their rights, and this is so for various motives.

In publicly traded companies, shareholders normally form a huge and diverse group with interminably splintered interests. It is easy, then, to imagine why a shareholder, with an infinitesimal holding, would not even bother himself with attending general shareholder meetings; his vote will not make a difference to the outcome, anyway. That is something for institutional shareholders (who in turn keep those large packets of shares for their own shareholders), major shareholders (who reserve for themselves special voting rights beyond those strictly corresponding to their number of shares) and, above all, management (who have their jobs and stock options on the block) to negotiate and manoeuvre. For his part, the 'regular Joe' shareholder does not hold on to his shares for very long and sells them as soon as he thinks he will make a reasonable profit. Beyond this, he feels no further commitment to the firm, certainly none that would deserve the name of ownership.

Because of their rights to residual equity and other prerogatives deriving from this, shareholders may claim liberal–minimalist citizenship within the corporate polity. But that is not sufficient for a civic republican or communitarian kind of citizenship, which would require, apart from the possession of such rights, their effective exercise with a view to the corporate common good. Certainly, this is something that liberal–minimalist citizenship cannot by itself guarantee in the case of simple shareholders. Unlike the case of liberal–minimalist corporate citizenship, shareholder status is not enough for one to qualify for civic republican or communitarian corporate citizenship, since this implies active involvement in management and governance.

We should then broaden the field to include other stakeholders, apart from shareholders, in our quest for civic republican or communitarian citizens of the corporate polity. Before we have identified as 'stakeholders' all those who may have 'legitimate interests' (Donaldson and Preston, 1995: 67) in the firm. This does not mean, however, that each and every one of those interests warrants formal legal protection, although a country's jurisprudence sometimes ends up according them such a recognition. The legitimacy of stakeholder interests could very well come, not from courts, but from a heightened awareness or ethical sensitivity among society's members. As for the requirement of active involvement in governance in order to qualify for civic republican or communitarian corporate citizenship beyond the mere possession of rights, we should guard against interpreting this in the sense that *all stakeholders* have to participate in *all corporate decisions*. Clearly, that was not the intention of Aristotle, or of the civic republican and communitarian authors, for that matter, when they expounded on the demands of citizenship. Neither should it be ours, then, in applying civic republican and communitarian citizenship to the members of the corporate polity. In truth, it would be enough that those with legitimate interests intervene in the issues that directly concern them.

The next stakeholder group we shall turn to in our search for the civic republican or communitarian corporate citizen is that of clients or consumers. They have always been a pampered lot. In recent decades, corporate strategy has often been formulated from their perspective, as a way for the firm to satisfy their needs and serve them better, as a means of coming up with the best 'value proposition' for them (Porter, 1980). Hence the far-reaching spread of business truisms such as 'The customer is always right' or 'The customer is king.' This alleged 'consumer sovereignty', however, has been better known in the breach than in the observance.

In fact, until recently, the prevailing legal framework in the market was based on the principle '*caveat emptor*' or 'buyer beware' (Boatright, 2000: 273). That is to say, responsibility for safeguarding the consumer's interest in a purchase lay almost exclusively with the consumer himself, not with the vendor. The consumer or client's only right consists in not buying a product, if he disagrees with any of the terms and conditions in whichever way. Nowadays, especially in the developed world, we have seen a vast expansion of consumer rights. Apart from the basic right to make free market choices, we also enjoy, in varying degrees, the right to fair market prices, to safe and efficacious products, to truthful advertising and honest communications, to privacy and so forth (Crane and Matten, 2004: 270). Moreover, tests have been designed to protect 'consumer sovereignty' in its different dimensions: from consumer capability (freedom from limitations in rational decision making) to information (availability of relevant data) and to choice (switching possibility) (Crane and Matten, 2004: 289). For example, by virtue of the first aspect of consumer sovereignty, neither tobacco nor alcohol should be sold to minors; by virtue of the second, foodstuffs should be properly labelled for common allergens; and, by virtue of the third, we should be able to change our telephone service providers while keeping our numbers. The guarantee of these rights in support of consumer sovereignty could be said to justify a liberal–minimalist corporate citizenship for clients and consumers.

How do consumers as liberal–minimalist corporate citizens make the transition to civic republican or communitarian ones? They would do so to the extent that they actually participate somehow in the governance of the corporation: for instance, when consumers decide to patronize and recommend wholeheartedly, or, on the contrary, boycott and urge others to do the same, a company and its entire range of products, because of ethical, social and environmental reasons. Consumers and clients could also flex their 'governance' muscle by actively participating in product design and promotion; for example, when passengers share their travel preferences with the airlines in whose frequent flier mileage programmes they have enrolled. Only consumers who have walked this extra mile of engagement would perhaps be worthy of being called civic republican or communitarian corporate citizens. But the issue would then be this: just how effective, really, are their initiatives in influencing corporate policy and strategy? Should the exercise of their rights go that far? That would be the ultimate test of civic republican or communitarian corporate citizenship for consumers and clients.

The turn now comes for the stakeholder group comprising competitors and suppliers. How do they qualify as citizens of the corporate polity? Firstly, in properly functioning market economies, the various rights of competitors and suppliers with regard to each other – often summarized as the 'right to fair play' – are all quite sufficiently laid down in competition law. These would include, to name a few, the freedom to enter and to leave the market, the right to set prices without coercion, the right to offer products to potential customers, and so forth (Crane and Matten, 2004: 305).

Once more, simply upholding these rights may suffice for competitors and suppliers to display liberal–minimalist corporate citizenship. However, corporate citizenship of a civic republican or communitarian kind would again demand a stronger commitment and a higher level of engagement.

For example, suppliers could organize themselves around an ethical supply chain management initiative, such that unfair labour practices (child labour), unhealthy working conditions (sweatshops) and environmental degradation are all greatly diminished if not entirely eliminated within their sector or industry. They could do this even before Third World governments – which are often seriously hampered by limited resources and corruption – are able to introduce their own regulations. Also, suppliers and erstwhile competitors could engage in 'fair trade' agreements similar to those in some coffee, tea and cocoa markets; they could then guarantee minimum prices and offer better conditions to small commodity growers in developing countries (Crane and Matten, 2004: 333). These are some of the activities that would push suppliers and competitors up the ranks to civic republican or communitarian grade corporate citizenship. Yet, unfortunately, these practices are still uncommon and their effects on corporate governance quite unknown.

Regarding government or the state, its role as a stakeholder of the corporation is affected by a serious ambivalence (Crane and Matten, 2004: 391). On the one hand, it seems more proper to think of the corporation – in itself and, ultimately, in the physical persons who constitute it – as a stakeholder of the state than the other way around. After all, in modern liberal democracies, governments are understood to be formed by the elected representatives of the citizenry and, indirectly, of the different intermediate associations and civil society organizations that these found and support. On the other hand, the state and government could by itself also constitute an important interest or stakeholder group within the corporation; and this not only by owning a significant, if not a controlling, tranche of shares, but in a host of other ways as well.

With their monopoly on force, governments and states could choose to play a dual role, either restricting or enabling corporate activity. States somehow restrict business activity by collecting taxes, which eat into the profits or, at the very least, represent a considerable cost; but they also enable business by allowing tax breaks or granting subsidies. At the same time, we could also see states and governments as either depending on or competing with corporations. We have already examined how governments and states compete with multinational companies in the provision of welfare and even of security, for example in a previous chapter. Yet we could also imagine that, were it not for independent business organizations, born of the freedom of enterprise and association of citizens, states and governments would fall into a paralysis or become terribly inefficient, as they were in the former communist countries.

Getting back to the analysis of the state and government as corporate stakeholders, we might say that they undoubtedly hold important rights, which would more than qualify them as a liberal–minimalist corporate citizen. Lest we forget, corporations only exist thanks to a legal charter, that is, an explicit recognition by the state. In this respect, there is no escaping state or government influence, both for good and for ill. The problem then arises when we try to apply the civic republican or communitarian standard of corporate citizenship to government or the state. What exactly is the level of government or state involvement in corporate governance that we would consider desirable?

Perhaps the most we could venture to say is that it lies on a golden mean or virtuous middle. We certainly would not like to succumb to statism, where private initiative, freedom of association and freedom of enterprise have all been annihilated and government or the state has completely taken over the economy. But neither would we find an absolutely *laissez-faire* regime appealing, where markets would have usurped functions such as internal and external security or the administration of justice, effectively getting rid of both government and the state. Therefore, apart from the degree of involvement of government or the state in corporate governance, there are also certain matters or issues that should be of one or the other's competence and not outsourced. Government should not be in the business of developing and peddling software, for example, no less than corporations setting up private tribunals of justice or private armies. The state or government could behave as a good civic republican or communitarian corporate citizen if it proceeds in accordance with the principle of subsidiarity in its relations with corporations, promoting privatization and self-regulation without renouncing areas of its exclusive competence.

This leaves us with just one remaining stakeholder group, that composed of a company's workers or employees, including management. It is no exaggeration to say that, among the different stakeholders, employees are the ones most closely integrated and identified with the corporation: 'employees, in many cases even physically "constitute" the corporation. They are perhaps the most important production factor or "resource" of the corporation, they represent the company towards most other stakeholders, and act in the name of the corporation towards them' (Crane and Matten, 2004: 224).

A liberal–minimalist analysis of employees as corporate citizens would limit itself almost exclusively to their rights and duties as spelled out in the employment contract: a right to fair wages, a right to healthy and safe working conditions, freedom from unjust discrimination, a duty to provide an acceptable level of work performance and quality, a duty to respect company property, and so forth (Crane and Matten, 2004: 228). The civic republican or communitarian standard would look into other areas besides, such as the economic externalities and the socioethical opportunities that escape formulation in those contracts. The company, for instance, is one of them. No employment contract could fully capture the demands of employee loyalty and, to that extent, most of them would hardly be actionable in the tribunals of law. Yet employee loyalty counts as an enormous positive externality for the company and, at the same time, a precious opportunity for growth in virtue for the employee. Of course, employee loyalty towards the company also makes demands on the part of the company itself: to begin with, it should never consider the employee merely as an expendable resource, the first one to jettison when the sailing gets rough. Instead, the corporation should try to reciprocate by apportioning resources and allowing for the continuous professional development and personal growth of the individuals in the workplace. Loyalty is not so much the economic result of locking-in assets as a mutual ethical concern for each other's flourishing and well-being.

Among employees, those who, at the same time, own shares in the company, and, in particular, shareholding-managers merit special consideration from the viewpoint of civic republican or communitarian corporate citizenship. Let us recall for an instant Aristotle's teaching that citizens carry out the task of government for no one else but themselves: they govern their own affairs, they practise self-governance. This means that, no matter how involved one may be in government, if one did so for the benefit of any other, excluding oneself (think of someone called upon to rule in a foreign land, for instance) that does not turn him into a citizen of that land, since citizenship requires self-rule. At most, he could be something like a 'professional governor'. In some measure, the demand for self-rule could also resolve agency problems, since the shareholding employee – and especially the shareholding manager – now becomes both agent and principal all at once. By owning shares through stock option plans, managers begin to exercise power and authority over the firm in their own name, as principals, albeit collectively.

That manager or employee and shareholder, agent and principal, governor and governed simultaneously coincide in one and the same person is precisely the biggest advantage of workers over other stakeholder groups in their bid for civic republican or communitarian corporate citizenship. Only here can the condition of actively taking part in corporate self-government be adequately fulfilled. Only here, too, can we find the objective dimension of work, that is, the external goods and services produced, united to its subjective dimension, that is, the improvements in knowledge, skills, habits and virtues that work causes in the worker. Alienation from the worker of the products of his labour is avoided. In this sense, cooperatives, or business organizations that are run and controlled by their owners, would fit the definition of a self-governing corporate polity to perfection. Its shareholding workers and managers would represent civic republican or communitarian corporate citizenship in the highest form.

For this reason, other non-shareholding employees have to be set apart. Surely the corporation cannot exist without them, yet they should not be considered corporate citizens because their tasks are carried out for others – that is, the shareholders – and not for themselves. To a large degree, the situation of non-shareholding employees is very similar to that of the artisan class composed of slaves and foreigners in the Greek city-states (Pltcs, 1278a). Without them, the city-state would not stand, yet their integration in the city-state was very limited and their participation in government practically nil. In like manner, all the other stakeholder groups we have examined – shareholders, clients, consumers, competitors, suppliers, governments, states and non-shareholding workers – through contracts and agreements hold a status comparable to those who enjoyed certain rights in the Greek city-states where they resided, owing to trade treaties or military alliances, without being citizens (Pltcs, 1274b). Possessing just some rights is not enough; the right to participate in government is necessary, as even a liberal–minimalist model of citizenship would require. Furthermore, neither is the mere possession of these rights sufficient; rather, they also have to be effectively exercised, if one is to qualify for civic republican or communitarian citizenship, be it political or corporate.

IV IN BRIEF

- The introduction of Corporate Social Responsibility (CSR) and stakeholder theory has triggered important modifications in response to the question of who constitutes the firm. CSR has widened the scope of the firm's obligations from the economic and legal spheres to the social and ethical ones. Stakeholder theory has broadened the groups to whom the firm is held accountable. Apart from the initial group of shareholders, among the firm's stakeholders we now include workers, customers, suppliers, competitors, government or the state, communities, and so forth.
- There are significant differences in the manner in which both CSR and stakeholder theory have been understood, developed and put into practice in the United States and in Europe. Because of its tradition of individualism and legalism, business culture in the United

States is more reluctant to accept the view of the firm as a socially embedded institution, unlike the situation in Continental Europe, where this notion is welcome and prevalent despite variations.

- Applying the political concept of citizenship to the corporation is useful in several ways. It highlights the social dimension of the corporation as an institution, it provides a source of identity or belonging, and it offers a justification of the different rights and responsibilities that the corporation possesses as an artificial or legal person.

- In its origins, as explained to us by Aristotle, 'citizen' pre-eminently applies to an adult, able-bodied male, himself the son of citizen-parents, who enjoys sufficient economic means to engage actively in the governance of his home city-state, by voting or being voted into office. Although a state may require other classes of people in order to be viable, citizens form the most important group among them all. The definition of a citizen may vary according to the regime or form of government: Aristotle's description best fits citizens in a democracy. However, in the best of states, the characteristics of a good citizen fully coincide with those of an excellent human being.

- In more recent times, the discussion of citizenship has revolved around two distinct models. Liberal–minimalist citizenship stresses the 'negative freedoms', such as freedom from oppression or arbitrary rule, especially by the state, and its discourse is based on the language of rights. The primary duty of the state or government is to secure these rights. Civic republican or communitarian citizenship, on the other hand, focuses on active participation in the common good by fostering community ties and promoting civic virtues. The emphasis lies in the fulfilment of duties and obligations towards the group. Government and the state are expected, above all, to act in a subsidiary manner and strengthen already existing institutions such as families, schools, churches, and so forth. Aristotelian doctrine undoubtedly comes closer to civic republican or communitarian citizenship than to the liberal–minimalist model.

- There are at least two possible readings of the expression 'corporate citizenship'. The more widely spread one consists in imagining the corporation as a citizen of the state where it operates. According to the liberal–minimalist perspective, such a corporate citizen will be primarily concerned with protecting its rights to pursue mainly economic interests; that is, those of its shareholders. This sort of company will be very reluctant to involve itself with broader social and political issues. From the civic republican or communitarian viewpoint, in contrast, the company as citizen should have no trouble engaging in sociopolitical actions because its mission transcends purely economic goals. The firm owes itself to many other people (the different stakeholder groups) besides its shareholders.

- The second – and, to our knowledge, unique – understanding of 'corporate citizenship' consists in taking the different stakeholder groups as potential citizens of the corporation, held to be an analogue of the state. The liberal–minimalist persuasion in citizenship then conceives the corporation as a 'civic association' formed by the 'nexus of contracts' among different agents exercising their rights. Each of these agents has its own individual goal with respect to which the corporation is just a means. The civic republican or communitarian model of citizenship, for its part, perceives the corporation as a 'corporate polity' whose flourishing is reciprocally dependent on the flourishing of its various stakeholder-constituents. In this regard, every stakeholder-constituent is admonished to take part actively in the deliberation and execution of the corporate common good.

- Within the framework of the corporation as a polity, we could examine how well each stakeholder group fulfils the requirements of 'corporate citizenship' from both a liberal–minimalist and a civic–republican or communitarian perspective. As long as they possess certain rights, practically all the different stakeholder groups would qualify for liberal–minimalist corporate citizenship. On the other hand, the demands of civic–republican or communitarian corporate citizenship are more stringent, and only shareholding managers are able to meet the standard of active participation in self-governance.

- From the viewpoint of corporate citizenship, therefore, shareholding managers represent the stakeholder group best equipped to govern the corporation. Only in their case are we able to avoid all the different forms of alienation or separation between ownership and control, capital and labour, principals and agents, the objective dimension and the subjective dimension of work, rulers and ruled.

REFERENCES

Aristotle (1990), *The Politics*, ed. Stephen Everson, Cambridge: Cambridge University Press.

Berle, Adolf and Gardiner Means (1932), *The Modern Corporation and Private Property*, New York: The Macmillan Company. [Reprint, 1991, Transaction Publishers, New Brunswick, NJ].

Bernstein, Aaron (2004), 'Online extra: Nike's new game plan for sweatshops', *BusinessWeek online*, September 20, www.businessweek.com/magazine/content/04_38/b3900011_mz001.htm (accessed 25 October 2006).

Boatright, John (1999), *Ethics in Finance*, Malden, MA/Oxford: Blackwell Publishers.

Boatright, John (2000), *Ethics and the Conduct of Business*, Upper Saddle River, NJ: Prentice-Hall.

Bowen, Howard R. (1953), *Social Responsibilities of the Businessman*, New York: Harper & Bros.

Carroll, Archie B. (1979), *Business and Society: Ethics and Stakeholder Management* 2nd edn, Cincinnati, OH: South-Western Publishing Co.

Carroll, Archie B. (1991), 'The pyramid of corporate social responsibility: toward the moral management of organizational stakeholders', *Business Horizons*, July–August, 39–48.

Charkham, Jonathan (1995), *Keeping Good Company: A Study of Corporate Governance in Five Countries*, Oxford/New York: Oxford University Press.

Clarkson, Max and Michael Deck (1998), 'Stockholder', in *The Blackwell Encyclopedic Dictionary of Business Ethics*, edited by Patricia Werhane and R. Edward Freeman, Malden, MA/Oxford: Blackwell Publishers.

Crane, Andrew and Dirk Matten (2004), *Business Ethics: A European Perspective*, Oxford: Oxford University Press.

Crane, Andrew, Dirk Matten and Jeremy Moon (2003), 'Can corporations be citizens? Corporate citizenship as a metaphor for business participation in society', *International Center for Corporate Social Resposibility (ICCSR) Research Paper Series*, no. 13, ISSN 1479–5116.

Davis, Keith and Robert Blomstrom (1975), *Business and Society: Environmental Responsibility*, New York: McGraw-Hill.

Dill, William (1958), 'Environment as an influence on managerial autonomy', *Administrative Science Quarterly*, **2**(4), 409–43.

Donaldson, Thomas and Lee Preston (1995), 'The stakeholder theory of the corporation: concepts, evidence and implications', *Academy of Management Review*, **20**, 65–91.

Eells, Richard and Clarence Walton (1961), *Conceptual Foundations of Business*, Homewood, IL: Richard D. Irwin.

Estes, Ralph (1976), *Corporate Social Accounting*, New York/London/Sydney/Toronto: John Wiley & Sons.

European Commission (2006), *Implementing the Partnership for Growth and Jobs: Making Europe a Pole of Excellence on Corporate Social Responsibility*, http://ec.europa.eu/employment_social/soc-dial/csr/index.htm (accessed 14 August 2006).

Freeman, R. Edward (1984), *Strategic Management: A Stakeholder Approach*, Boston, MA: Pitman.

Freeman, R. Edward (1994), 'The politics of stakeholder theory: some future directions', *Business Ethics Quarterly*, **4**(4), 409–21.

Freeman, R. Edward (1998), 'Stakeholder theory', in *The Blackwell Encyclopedic Dictionary of Business Ethics*, edited by Patricia Werhane and R. Edward Freeman, Malden, MA/Oxford: Blackwell Publishers.

Friedman, Milton (1970), 'The social responsibility of business is to increase its profits', *The New York Times Magazine*, 13 September.

Johnson & Johnson (2006), 'Our Credo', www.jnj.com/our_company/our_credo/index.htm (accessed 25 October 2006).

Mallenbaker.net (2006), 'Companies in crisis. What to do when it all goes wrong. Johnson & Johnson and Tylenol', www.mallenbaker.net/csr/CSRfiles/crisis 02.html (accessed 25 October 2006).

Manville, Brook and Josiah Ober (2003), *A Company of Citizens. What the World's First Democracy Teaches Leaders about Creating Great Organizations*, Boston, MA: Harvard Business School Press.

Mason, Richard O. and Ian I. Mitroff (1982), *Challenging Strategic Planning Assumptions*, New York: John Wiley and Sons.

McGuire, Joseph W. (1963), *Business and Society*, New York: McGraw-Hill.

Monks, Robert and Nell Minow (2001), *Corporate Governance*, Oxford/Malden, MA: Blackwell Publishers.

Nasi, Juha (1995), *Understanding Stakeholder Thinking*, Helsinki: LSR-Julkaisut Oy.

Porter, Michael E. (1980), *Competitive Strategy*, New York: Free Press.

Sethi, S. Prakash (1975), 'Dimensions of corporate social responsibility', *California Management Review*, **17**, 58–64.

Sison, Alejo José G. (2000), 'Integrated risk management and global business ethics', *Business Ethics. A European Review*, **9**(4), October, 288–95.

Stokes, Geoffrey (2002), 'Democracy and citizenship', in April Carter and Geoffrey Stokes (eds), *Democratic Theory Today*, Cambridge: Polity Press.

Thompson, James D. (1967), *Organization in Action*, New York: McGraw-Hill.

Vietnam Labor Watch (1997), 'Nike Labor Practices in Vietnam', www.saigon.com/~nike/reports/report1.html (accessed 25 October 2006).

Wood, Donna J. (1991), 'Corporate social performance revisited', *Academy of Management Review*, **16**, 691–718.

Wood, Donna J., Jeanne M. Logsdon, Patsy G. Lewellyn and Kim Davenport (2006), *Global Business Citizenship. A Transformative Framework for Ethics and Sustainable Capitalism*, Armonk, NY/ London: M.E. Sharpe.

5. Corporate despots and constitutional rulers

The third element of our analogy between states and firms refers to their organization. Both states and firms require a governing body with its rule or constitution. The major difference between them, however, is that, while states are sovereign (Pltcs, 1278b), corporations are not. Therefore, the governance of business organizations or firms is always subject to the governments of the states, which represent the supreme authority in the places where they reside and operate.

In the *Politics*, Aristotle explores a plurality of state regimes, depending on the number of people who govern and for the good of whom. The main division he establishes is between 'despotic' and 'constitutional' rules. A despotic rule is one exercised over subjects who are 'by nature slaves', and a constitutional rule is one over those who are 'by nature free' (Pltcs, 1255b). Previously we have seen the preponderant role that nature plays over nurture – that is, education and culture – in a person's fittingness for citizenship. The same is true for one's propensity to govern or rule, exercising authority and lordship, or to be governed or ruled, exercising obedience. With regard to a despotic rule or regime, although both slave and master may have coincident interests, a slave is ruled primarily for the master and only accidentally for himself (Pltcs, 1278b). Compare this with a father's government of his wife and children as an example of a constitutional rule, where the good of the governed or the common good of the household comes first (Pltcs, 1278b). Aristotle states, 'there is one rule which is for the sake of rulers and another rule which is for the sake of the ruled; the former is despotic, the latter a free [constitutional] government' (Pltcs, 1333a). Furthermore, to the extent that a despotic regime regards only the interests of rulers, it is 'perverted' and 'defective', whereas a constitutional rule, to the extent that it looks after the common interest in accordance with the principles of justice, is a 'true' one (Pltcs, 1279a).

Both 'true' and 'perverted' or 'defective' regimes are, in turn, subject to further subdivisions, depending on the number of rulers in each case. Among the true forms of government we have 'kingships' or 'monarchies', when there is but one ruler, 'aristocracies', when the best of men – who are always comparatively few – rule, and 'constitutional rules', when the many rule (Pltcs, 1279a–b). In all of the above, it is the good or the best interests of the state and the citizens which prevails. By contrast, among the defective forms of government, we find 'tyrannies', when the ruler is one, 'oligarchies', when the rulers are few, and 'democracies', when the rulers are many (Pltcs, 1279a–b). In tyrannies, the whole state is ruled with the sole interest of the monarch in mind, in oligarchies, in accordance with the interests of the wealthy, and in democracies, with the interests of the needy: in 'none of them the common good of all' matters (Pltcs, 1279b).

In the following pages we shall examine how relevant these classifications of state governments are to the governance structures and systems of business corporations or firms. At first blush, it seems that the division into despotic and constitutional rules is applicable, because apparently some firms are run for strictly private interests, while others have the wider common good in view. As a result, some companies may be said to be governed justly, with every one of the constituents receiving his due, and others unjustly, with most of the parties feeling short-changed. In addition, some corporations may appear to be despotically run, when the governed are treated almost like slaves, while others are managed constitutionally, when the governed are regarded as freemen and equals of the ruler or rulers.

As for the distinctions depending on the number of rulers; that is, among 'kingships' or 'tyrannies', when there is one, 'aristocracies' or 'oligarchies', when there are few, and 'constitutional regimes' or 'democracies', when there are many, they also would seem to apply in the case of corporations. An instance of a corporate 'kingship' would be a firm whose shareholding CEO is, at the same time, chairman of the board, an 'imperial CEO/Chairman' as this figure has come to be called. Perhaps such concentration of power in just one person is not by itself objectionable, for it could certainly bring heightened effectiveness to the 'imperial CEO/Chairman's' leadership; yet, simultaneously, we could not help but admit that the danger of abuse in such a corporation is rife. This same 'imperial CEO/Chairman' would be a tyrant if he were to put his own private interests before the common good of the firm as a whole.

On the other hand, we may consider as corporate 'aristocracies' those businesses whose governance lies in the hands of a few people, if the members of this small group happen to be the most qualified professionally – or simply, the 'best' (*aristoi* in Greek) – to manage the firm. In the Anglo-Saxon corporate culture, that could be the case, for example, of a perfectly 'balanced' unitary board, where the different powers and functions are equitably shared among a handful of shareholding executive directors and non-executive directors. An equivalent in the Central European tradition could be the dual supervisory and management board arrangement found in some companies, as long as the members of both boards held shares and exercised executive functions seeking the corporate common good above all. The issue of determining, from among the various corporate constituents, who are the ones 'best' equipped to govern the firm is a highly controversial matter. Despite the lack of an absolute consensus on what their positive traits should be, this much we know: at the very least, the qualifier 'best' refers to a limited group of people whose claim to corporate governance does not rest on wealth and property alone (that would correspond more to a corporate 'oligarchy'), but on a shared genuine concern for the good of all, including that of the governed.

Finally, we could also think of corporations where some sort of 'constitutional rule' holds. Such firms would have to fulfil the requirement that 'the many' who participate in governance seek the good of all, not only their own private good. For this we probably would have to look among cooperatives, where workers own stakes in the corporation and correspondingly share in its profits. The other condition is, of course, that these 'owner-workers' actively participate in management or governance: that they be 'owner-manager-workers', in effect. The most difficult thing, however, would be to find a corporate equivalent for what in states is called a 'democracy'. This is so, in the first place, because 'the many' will always be relatively poor, and may therefore not have enough capital, to start with, to set up a business. In second place, as is typical in a democracy, people are wont to pursue their own private good instead of the common interest, and this, more often than not, is a surefire recipe for an organizational disaster. In any case, neither should we confuse a 'corporate democracy' with just any manifestation of 'shareholder activism', for example. The latter simply refers to a situation wherein small shareholders come together and unite to exercise their rights, even to the point of challenging top managers and majority shareholders. Democratic corporate governance necessarily goes beyond these incidental activist challenges, and is both broader and deeper, not only in scale but also in scope.

I THE AGNELLIS, ITALY'S UNCROWNED ROYALTY, AND FIAT

In the palace belonging to the family of the count of Brischerasio in Turin hangs a painting by the famous artist, Lorenzo Delleani, depicting the founding of the 'Fabbrica Italiana Automobili Torino' – better known by its acronym, 'Fiat' – in that same place on 1 July, 1899 (Biscaretti di Ruffia, 1952: 40). In the centre of the picture is Count Emanuele Cacherano di Brischerasio, the one who conceived and initiated the business convoking its eight other founders – Count Roberto Biscaretti di Ruffia, Marquis

Alfonso Ferrero di Ventimiglia, Michele Ceriana, Luigi Damevino, Cesare Goria Gatti, Carlo Racca, Ludovico Scarfiotti and Giovanni Agnelli – all of them surrounding him by his desk. A sense of modesty kept Count Emanuele Cacherano di Brischerasio from wanting to be chairman, leaving that position instead for Ludovico Scarfiotti. Count Emanuele Cacherano di Brischerasio only acceded to the position of vice chairman of the newly established company, with Giovanni Agnelli chosen as secretary to the board. From its earliest days, however, the fortunes of Fiat have always been tightly linked, almost identified, one could say, not with those of Brischerasio but with those of the 'cavagliere' (having been named a 'knight of labour' in 1907) Giovanni Agnelli, and later on, with those of his descendants.

In its more than a hundred years of history, Fiat has diversified from its original business of manufacturing cars (Maserati, Ferrari) to producing motorcycles (Piaggio, Vespa), trucks (Iveco), planes (Aeritalia), metallurgical parts (Teksid), electronic components (Magneti Marelli), industrial automation systems (Comau) and agricultural and construction equipment (CNH); it has also engaged in providing construction (Ingest Facility), information technology (ICT), leisure (Sestriere ski resort), media (*La Stampa* newspaper, Itedi, Italiana Edizioni, Publikompass) and financial services (Mediobanca) (Wikipedia, 2006a). With revenues of €46 544 million and a net income of €1333 million in 2005, Fiat is by far Italy's largest industrial concern, employing over 223 000 people (about half of them in its home market) in 61 countries (Wikipedia, 2006a). The Fiat Group is listed in both New York and Milan stockmarkets.

We have chosen to study the Fiat case of corporate governance for two reasons, first of all, because there is a clear concentration of power in its chairman of the board, who at times also carries out the functions of the CEO of the company; secondly, because the prime concern of the one person who governs appears to be a private good rather than the common good of the Fiat stakeholders or the members of its 'corporate polity'. In particular, this private good refers to keeping the reins of power in the corporation within the hands of members of the Agnelli family. This concern seems to trump all others, such as the maximization of shareholder wealth, the welfare of workers, the resistance to fascism or the integrity of institutions of the Italian state, among others.

As we shall soon see, power in Fiat has always been passed on, beginning with Giovanni Agnelli senior to his descendants, albeit with interludes of regency by professional managers who, at a given moment, enjoy the family's trust and confidence. This pattern or cycle started with Giovanni Agnelli senior, who was succeeded by Vittorio Valletta, only to be succeeded in turn by his grandson Giovanni (Gianni) Agnelli junior. It continued when Gianni Agnelli passed on the mantle of company leadership to Cesare Romiti, then to Paolo Fresco, only to be recovered by Umberto Agnelli, Gianni's younger brother. Upon Umberto Agnelli's death in 2004, Luca Cordero di Montezemolo became chairman, but John Philip Elkann, Gianni Agnelli's 28-year-old grandson, was immediately named vice-chairman. As expected, John Elkann is currently being groomed to occupy or 'inherit' the company's top post, something that will occur in due course.

Therefore, although Italy may, for some time now, be a republic, it nevertheless still maintains certain trappings of royalty, at least through the Agnelli dynasty, if not also through other families of the business élite. The Agnellis thus continue to exercise a disproportionate influence over the country's fortunes by means of the company which they rule and control, largely by Fiat.

The following examines how Fiat's history bears out the two distinctive traits which qualify it for what one could call (to borrow a phrase from Aristotelian politics) a 'corporate tyranny': the concentration of power in the hands of a single person in pursuit of a private good.

Probably one of the first sparks of Giovanni Agnelli's strategic vision consisted in his decision to buy Ceirano & Co., producer of the Welleyes model, having been impressed by this car's performance in the Turin–Pinerolo–Avigliana–Turin race in April 1899 (Biscaretti di Ruffia, 1952: 44–6). In that competition the Welleyes had covered a distance of 90 km in three hours and ten minutes, without stopping. Never mind that the winner of the race, a Peugeot model from Gratz, had taken only an hour and 59 minutes for the run. For 30 000 lire, Agnelli instantly got what he wanted: a viable car model, the Faccioli patents, a factory and the workers ready to produce it. That a number of Fiat's incorporators were also part owners of Ceirano & Co. certainly helped in the purchase. This was a way of ensuring that the business was off to a good start, up and running.

Early on, it was likewise Giovanni Agnelli's idea to hire Enrico Marchesi as the manager for administration and sales, and Aristide Faccioli, the inventor of the patents, as the technical manager (Biscaretti di Ruffia, 1952: 46–7). Marchesi's work was crucial in setting up and developing Fiat's first factory in Corso Dante, Turin. Later on, he became the general manager and, when health and age determined that he engage in less taxing tasks, Marchesi was appointed consultant for Fiat's overseas business. Even before joining Ceirano & Co. and, subsequently, Fiat, Faccioli had already registered several engineering patents under his name. He was also credited with having invented the Fiat brand. However, Faccioli's insistence on designing and constructing cars based exclusively on his own models without taking those of others into account led, upon Giovanni Agnelli's initiative, to his dismissal by the board, in April 1901 (Biscaretti di Ruffia, 1952: 62–3).

In 1902, Giovanni Agnelli was formally appointed managing director of Fiat, thereby consolidating the power that he informally already possessed and exercised within the organization. Agnelli was quick to see the importance of races in promoting the brand and he himself participated in the Second Tour of Italy, setting a record for an 8 HP Fiat (Fiat, 2006). In 1908, Fiat set up shop in the United States where its vehicles soon acquired a luxury status, selling at a premium price between $3600 and $8600, compared to the $825 normally charged for the Ford Model Ts (Wikipedia, 2006a). The Fiat plant in New York was operational until World War I, when United States regulations made production there too burdensome. At around that time, the construction of the Lingotto factory, meant to be the largest in Europe, commenced, and Fiat Lubrificanti, the first Italian subsidiary in Russia, opened.

In September 1920, Fiat factories in Italy were taken over by workers and the red flag of communism was hoisted over them (Italiancar, 2006). A couple of months later, however, several thousand employees approached Giovanni Agnelli and asked him to return and run the company once more. He reluctantly agreed and, in November 1920, he became chairman of the board. In the next two years, Fiat downsized its workforce and lowered salaries in an effort to cut costs. Growth did not resume in the company until 1923. On the other side of the equation, by following a policy of mass production in Italy, Fiat contributed to increasing consumer spending and improving overall living standards and social conditions in the country. SAVA, a credit company meant to promote the purchase of cars by instalments, was created by Fiat to take advantage of these new opportunities. Meanwhile, several organizations were founded with the good of the workers primarily in mind, such as the Fiat Employee Health Services, the Central School for Fiat Apprentices and the Fiat Sports Group. In 1928, Professor Vittorio Valletta was named general manager of Fiat.

In the 1930s, with Mussolini's rise to power and autarchy as the official state policy, Fiat had to retrench from the international market and instead concentrate on the domestic one (Italiancar, 2006). Nevertheless, this was a period of significant technological advancements, with the development of the 'Balilla' model – popularly known as the 'Tariffa minima' for its low fuel consumption – and the 'Topolino', then the smallest utilitarian car in the world. These achievements, among others later on, earned for Giovanni Agnelli an appointment as senator from the Duce (Infoplease, 2006). This honour, and the cozy relations it signified with Mussolini, afterwards proved to be a poisoned chalice. It led to the ousting of the Agnelli family from leadership roles in Fiat by decision of the Italian Committee of National Liberation in 1945, soon after the victory of the Allied forces in World War II (Wikipedia, 2006a). That same year Giovanni Agnelli senior died and Valletta began his period of regency as Fiat chairman.

Even before the support for Mussolini and fascism could have influenced succession plans in Fiat, these had already been derailed with the untimely death of Edoardo Agnelli, Giovanni's only son and heir (his daughter Tina had also passed away prematurely, in 1928) in an airplane crash on 14 July 1935 (Quadrone, 1952: 129–31). In addition to being vice chairman of Fiat, Edoardo was already president of La Stampa and RIV. Not only was he his father's prime collaborator, but he was also clearly the new blood meant to continue his father's life-work, had destiny not crossed his path too soon. In this sense he became 'the man whose time had never come'. Edoardo Agnelli was survived by his wife, Virginia Bourbon del Monte, Princess of San Faustino, and seven children, including Giovanni Agnelli junior, better known as Gianni, Umberto and Susanna, who became Italy's foreign minister in the 1990s.

There are no better words to serve as a fitting close to Fiat's initial period of foundation and growth under the 'cavagliere' Giovanni Agnelli than those of Count Carlo Biscaretti di Ruffia, son of Senator Roberto Biscaretti di Ruffia, one of the company's co-founders: 'Among the administrative or technical virtues of the founders and their immediate co-workers, Giovanni Agnelli's steely reserve stood out from the very beginning. Ever since the factory opened its doors, it's as if he lived in the trenches, untiringly fighting against all odds. He always wanted to be right even if he was wrong, and he always won due to his unstinting courage and continued sacrifice. We who have seen him fight like a lion during those difficult and anxiety-filled early hours could very well say so. Fiat has built marvelous cars, but Agnelli has built Fiat and everything great, solid and powerful that that name stands for. And he built it with simple means: a tenacious will, a power of persuasion and of imposing his will which we could almost call hypnotic' (Biscaretti di Ruffia, 1952: 49–50).

At the time of Giovanni Agnelli senior's death on 16 December 1945, his grandson, Giovanni (Gianni) Agnelli junior was only 24 years old and evidently unprepared to take over the patriarch's job. When presented with the issue of assuming the presidency at Fiat, Gianni Agnelli was supposed to have said to Vittorio Valletta, then general manager, 'You go ahead and do it, Professor' (Pagano and Trento, 2002: 2). The relationship between Gianni Agnelli and Valletta at that moment was very similar to the one between an underaged sovereign and an able and trusted regent. 'While Gianni spent his time on fast cars and loose women, Valletta was very much in control of the Fiat Empire, overseeing its reconstruction in the post-war period. Agnelli might have ruled from a distance, but Valletta governed', a biographer remarks (Friedman, 1989: 44).

Referring to the difficulties of running the company during and immediately after World War II, a former Fiat executive had this recollection of Valletta's pragmatic *savoir faire* and survival instincts: 'Valletta always said we would be good Germans, we would be good Fascists, but we had to save Fiat. That was the policy' (Friedman, 1989: 36). And they had to make sure to hand over Fiat in the best possible shape to Gianni and the next-generation Agnellis, the former executive could have very well added. And so they certainly did.

Earnings at Fiat remained flat during World War II, and, in 1946, the company even reported a loss (Italiancar, 2006). However, with the help of American subsidies through the Marshall plan, factories were reconstructed and manufacturing output soon recovered. By 1948, Fiat was solidly back on the road to profitability. In 1951, the company produced Italy's first jet aircraft, the G80 and, five years later, its G91 model was chosen to be one of NATO's tactical fighters. Throughout the decade of the 1950s, Fiat's workforce increased, from 70 000 to 80 000 employees, and car production rose five-fold to almost 340 000 units. The year 1958 saw the beginning of Italy's economic boom, registering a 6.3 per cent yearly growth rate in GDP until 1963, and the automotive sector was generally perceived to be its driving force. By the second half of the 1960s, Fiat factories, staffed by nearly 160 000 workers, were busy churning out more than 1 750 000 vehicles a year, helping to raise the car density in the country to one for every 28 inhabitants. Whereas, at the time of Giovanni Agnelli's death in 1945, Fiat was producing 3260 automobiles a year, by 1966, when his grandson Gianni took over, it was turning out that same number of cars every working day. These are but some of the many achievements of Valletta's regency period, lasting over 20 years.

After Giovanni Agnelli and Vittorio Valletta, the third person to take the helm at Fiat was Gianni Agnelli, popularly known as 'l'avvocato', in reference to his legal training at the University of Turin, although he never really practised the profession (Wikipedia, 2006b). Most significantly, it signalled the return of a scion of the Agnellis to power in the corporation after a two-decade absence. Because of Giovanni Agnelli's collaboration with Mussolini's fascist regime, members of his family as a rule were blackballed from Fiat leadership, but, even then, his grandson Gianni, because of his charm, already stood out as a case apart. Thanks to his fluent English (his mother was half-American and the family had an English nanny) Gianni was able to overcome the threat of expropriation and persuade the Americans to keep Fiat in private hands (*The Economist*, 2003b). His reasoning was that Fiat, as a family-owned company, was vital to staving off the danger of communism and in providing some measure of stability to Italy's post-war economy. It also helped that, having fought on the Russian front as a cavalry officer of the Italian expeditionary force and having participated in the Tunisia campaign with the Italian liberation corps for which he was awarded the War Cross for Military Valor, upon Italy's surrender, he volunteered to serve as a liaison officer with the American troops (Wikipedia, 2006b). As a result, way back in 1953, Gianni Agnelli was already able to hold the post of vice-president and, in 1963, that of managing director of Fiat (Infoplease, 2006). Even before those appointments, however, he became president of the Juventus soccer club in 1947, transforming it into a powerhouse not only of Italian but also of European and world football.

It has become quite customary to speak of a first and a second life of Gianni Agnelli (*The Economist*, 2006). The first one stretches from his youth until 1966, when he assumed chairmanship at Fiat, at the age of 45. It was a time Gianni Agnelli spent in an almost relentless pursuit of beautiful women, racing cars and every sybaritic pleasure imaginable. He was often found in the company of Hollywood stars such as Rita Hayworth and Anita Ekberg, or socialites such as Pamela Harriman (Wikipedia, 2006b). Not even his marriage to Princess Marella Caracciolo di Castagneto, who herself was half-American and half-Neapolitan, and very much a worthy member of the global glamour set in 1953, changed all this. As Gianni Agnelli himself confessed, 'I really loved everything beautiful in life. And a beautiful woman is the most beautiful thing of all' (Achtner, 2003).

Gianni Agnelli's other great passion was, of course, racing cars. In 1952, after a wild night out carousing on the French Riviera, he was in a serious car crash, wrapping his Ferrari round a tree, and although the accident could very well have proved fatal, he managed to wreck only his legs (Achtner, 2003). Gianni Agnelli showed such little interest in business that the communist newspaper *L'Unita* went so far as accusing him of 'absolute indifference' to the problems of the motor industry (*The Economist*, 2006). He more willingly would occupy himself with the arts, coming to own a significant collection of Matisse paintings, for instance. This period of *dolce vita* somehow ended, or at least was greatly tempered, the moment Gianni Agnelli occupied the driver's seat at Fiat.

As head of Fiat in the mid-1960s, Gianni Agnelli oversaw the equivalent of no less than 4.4 per cent of Italy's GNP, 3.1 per cent of its industrial workforce and 16.5 per cent of its industrial research funds. Management then was highly centralized and hardly had any provision for the delegation of decision-making power (Wikipedia, 2006b). Although the system had been effective in the past, its lack of responsiveness and flexibility no longer seemed adequate for Fiat's local expansion and growth abroad. Among the first measures Gianni took was that of liberating managers from Valletta's iron grip, encouraging them to experiment with automotive design, for example (Arnold, 2003). This later paid off in added glitter to Fiat's vehicles in the international markets.

A farther-reaching change Gianni Agnelli spearheaded consisted in reorganizing the company into two main product groups – one for passenger cars and another for tractors and trucks – plus a handful of semi-independent divisions and subsidiaries, all of which were encouraged to be profit-oriented (Wikipedia, 2006b). This liberated top management from minding day-to-day operations and allowed them to focus on more strategic goals instead. In 1967, Fiat acquired Autobianchi and, with revenues of $1.7 billion, it outstripped its main European competitor, Volkswagen. In the following year, with sales reaching $2.1 billion, Fiat came to be called 'the most dynamic automaker in Europe . . . [and that which] may come the closest to changing the worldwide supremacy of Detroit' (Wikipedia, 2006b). It had enough money then to purchase Citroën, a major French car manufacturer, and Ferrari and Lancia shortly afterwards, becoming the third-largest player in the industry world-wide. Fiat also embarked on the construction of a plant in Togliattigrad on the Volga, thanks to an agreement between Valletta and the Russians a few years back.

It was not all smooth sailing in the early years of Gianni Agnelli's reign over Fiat, however. Social and industrial tensions mounted in Italy, as in the rest of Europe, and Gianni Agnelli often had to endure shouts of 'Agnelli, Pirelli, ladri gemelli' (twin thieves) from demonstrators on the streets (*The Economist*, 2003b). Throughout 1969, the company lost a total of 15 million work-hours due to strikes and a proportionate negative impact on profitability (Italiancar, 2006). Gianni Agnelli was forced to cut the dividend for the first time since World War II in 1973.

Having been elected chairman of Confindustria, the Italian employers' association, Gianni Agnelli signed a pact with the communist trade union leader, Luciano Lama, linking wage increases to inflation in January 1975 (*The Economist*, 2003b). With hindsight, Italian economists and businessmen are unanimous in the view that this was a big mistake, for soaring wages only sent inflation into an upward spiral. Gianni Agnelli, however, never accepted this criticism, and he believed to the very end that, with this decision, he saved not only Italian industry, but perhaps the whole country as well. In the mid-1970s, however, four Fiat managers were killed and 27 wounded in terrorist attacks from the far left; factories were burned and equipment routinely sabotaged. Unsurprisingly, absenteeism was running at 20 per cent in Fiat factories. The firing of 61 employees suspected of terrorist connections, in September 1979, marked the end of a decade characterized by hyperinflation, political extremism and violence and overall social unrest.

Meanwhile, still in 1979, Fiat adopted the holding company model, spinning off its operations into independent groups such as Fiat Auto, Fiat Ferroviaria, Fiat Avio, Fiat Trattori and Fiat Engineering, among others (Wikipedia, 2006a).

At the cost of having to oust his younger brother, Umberto, from top management, Gianni Agnelli and his board appointed Cesare Romiti as CEO of the Fiat group in 1980 (Italiancar, 2006). Romiti joined Fiat as Chief Financial Officer in 1974, having worked previously in Alitalia. He proved to be a tough manager, at one point firing – with Gianni Agnelli's approval, no doubt – 23 000 employees involved in a nasty strike. On the other hand, as manager of the car business, Vittorio Ghidella was largely credited with reviving Fiat's fortunes with the introduction of the tremendously popular Uno model in 1983. Thanks to the work of these two professional managers, both of whom turned out to be star performers, Fiat was able to cancel its once crushing debts by the mid-1980s. In 1984, Fiat Auto took over Alfa Romeo, and a couple of years later, in 1987, the Fiat group announced profits of $1.8 billion (*The Economist*, 2003b). This allowed Fiat to undertake a wave of diversification, leading to control of a quarter of Italy's newspaper circulation and 13 per cent of its advertising business.

The 1990s meant another steep decline in Fiat's business, and not exactly for external reasons. One was gross underinvestment in car research and development, spending only $4.5 billion between 1995 and 2001, while rivals such as Renault and Mercedes spent more than double that, and Volkswagen, beyond the $20 billion mark during the same period (*The Economist*, 2003b). Because of this there were several gaping holes among Fiat's product lines and it took an incredibly long time to unveil new models. In the past, the spectacular success of a single car, 'one-trick ponies', managed to cover up these deficiencies, as was the case with the Fiat Uno in the 1980s and the Fiat Punto in the early 1990s, but, as the decade wore on, this no longer proved to be enough. The company was never able to outgrow its reputation abroad as a producer of small cars that were cute and cheap, albeit of dubious quality: Fiat even came to stand for 'Fix It Again, Tony.'

Another problem was that Fiat had become too small to compete effectively in the global car market (*The Economist*, 2003b). During its heyday in the 1980s, the company became so attractive that Ford had wanted to merge it with its European operations. Later on, already in the 1990s, Fiat had also received proposals from BMW, Volkswagen and Daimler-Benz. All of these advances were rebuffed because, as Gianni

Agnelli himself admitted, he just could not bear to lose control. Fiat was hoping to rely on foreign markets for growth and profits, but Brazil suffered a huge economic crisis in the late 1990s and the ascent of South Korean brands in Poland all but eliminated its once enormous market share there.

However, Fiat's major difficulty in the 1990s had to do with leadership. Earlier we mentioned that Romiti was appointed CEO in 1980, against the ambitions of Gianni Agnelli's younger brother, Umberto. Romiti's appointment was said to have been imposed on Gianni Agnelli and Fiat by Enrico Cuccia, the head of Mediobanca, the powerful and secretive Milanese investment bank, and adviser to the members of the exclusive 'salotto buono', the country's industrial élite (Achtner, 1995). We do not know exactly what Cuccia's reasons were in support of Romiti, whether he really believed in the professionalization of Fiat management or he simply preferred Romiti's managerial and business sense to that of Umberto Agnelli. In any case, Gianni Agnelli acquiesced in this state of affairs despite the souring of relations with his younger sibling.

Understandably, there came to be a simmering personal feud between Romiti and Umberto Agnelli since then, one in which the professional manager always gained leverage (Gumbel, 1996a). In the 1970s, Umberto Agnelli already had to be replaced by Romiti as general manager, owing to his inability to cope with the severe cash problems and the industrial unrest plaguing the company. A newspaper headline even put these humiliating words in Umberto's mouth, 'My name is Agnelli and I can't run Fiat!' Two decades later, in 1993, Fiat once more saw itself bogged down by losses of 1.8 trillion lire, a bloated workforce and an uncompetitive production schedule. Major shareholders then made clear (prodded by Romiti) that they did not trust Umberto Agnelli to navigate the company ship through those rough seas and extracted a promise from Gianni Agnelli to hold on for a couple more years instead of relinquishing control to his brother.

Romiti also suffered strained relations with his fellow professional manager, Vittorio Ghidella, ultimately leading to the latter's sudden resignation on 31 December 1988 (Perini, 1989). Conflicts between the two stretch way back to 1985, when Ghidella supported a merger with Ford Europe, a move which Romiti and Agnelli both opposed. Ghidella would have become managing director of what could have been Europe's biggest car manufacturer, but Fiat would have been left with a minority stake. Ghidella, heralded as the man who saved Fiat and the one chiefly responsible for working out its 'second miracle' in the 1980s, lobbied to put a larger share of operations under his control at Fiat Auto, yet Romiti responded by initiating secret investigations of relations with Fiat suppliers without Ghidella's knowledge. That may have been the straw that broke the donkey's back. With Ghidella's departure, Romiti took on his former position in Fiat Auto, in addition to being group CEO. Romiti insisted that he did not want to reduce the importance of cars in Fiat's portfolio – accounting for 67 per cent of profits and 60 per cent of revenues at that moment – he just wanted to diversify and build up other businesses, something with which Gianni Agnelli seemed to agree.

Ever since 1992, however, Romiti's reputation had been sullied by his purported involvement in a country-wide corruption scandal called 'Tangentopoli' (Bribesville) (Wikipedia, 2006a). In April 1997, a Turin court sentenced him to 18 months and about $4700 in fines for setting up an illegal slush fund to pay off politicians and for committing fiscal fraud (*The Economist*, 1997). Fellow Fiat board member Francesco Paolo Mattioli was similarly punished, although jail terms for both of them were suspended on appeal. Far from provoking an unbearable pressure to resign, this decision meant business as usual for Romiti at Fiat. Gianni Agnelli quickly reaffirmed his confidence in his two lieutenants, who he said had always behaved properly through their many years of fruitful collaboration. Fellow billionaire industrialist and comeback prime minister Silvio Berlusconi, despite agreeing with the facts of the case, strongly contested their interpretation, saying 'I'm sorry about the verdict because I know that for many companies these financial donations are necessary to be able to keep working. We all know this, and especially those of us who have tried to build up a business' (Gumbel, 1997).

The stubbornest proof that, despite publicly admitting bribery (Wikipedia, 2006b), Romiti continued to count on Gianni Agnelli's support was his appointment as Fiat chairman in 1996 (Gumbel, 1996b). Gianni Agnelli nonetheless continued as honorary chairman, thereby guaranteeing influence, while Romiti himself, then aged 72, could look forward at most to only three more years in the top post. By then, and coinciding with Fiat's centennial, Giovanni Alberto (Giovannino) Agnelli, Umberto's son and Gianni's nephew, should be ready to assume company leadership.

What about Gianni's own son, Edoardo? Known to his friends as 'crazy Eddy', he seemed to have suffered from a severely dysfunctional personality, taking refuge in mysticism (he studied Religion at Princeton) and in drugs; definitely not one apt to take over the reins of governance at Fiat, as his father Gianni was eventually forced to admit (Gumbel, 1996a). Edoardo was a constant source of embarrassment to his family and to the company, as when he announced at a press conference in the 1986 World Peace Day celebration in Assisi that he was ready to take on the responsibilities of managing Fiat personally, or when he was arrested in 1990 in Kenya for heroin possession. Like his grandfather and namesake, the first Agnelli heir, Edoardo met a tragic end, jumping off a bridge on the Turin–Savona motorway on 15 November 2000 (Achtner, 2003).

On the other hand, since 1993, Giovannino Agnelli was already working as president of Piaggio, Fiat's motorbike subsidiary, and was subequently appointed to the holding company's board of directors (BBC News, 1997). His uncle Gianni proudly announced in 1995 that Giovannino was the most qualified family member to succeed him as head of Fiat. That could have been his father Umberto's sweet revenge. However, fate once more took a cruel turn and Giovannino succumbed to a rare form of intestinal cancer on 14 December 1997, at the age of 33. What was staged to be Romiti's transitional leadership at Fiat had to take a different course.

It is relatively straightforward to draw the parallels between Romiti and Valletta and their respective periods of regency at Fiat. What is more difficult is to spot the differences. Above all, perceived as a self-made man and a ruthless manager, Romiti may represent the antithesis of what the Agnellis had come to stand for (Gumbel, 1996a). Romiti once confessed in an interview, 'The difference between Agnelli [Gianni] and myself is that I'm meaner, really much meaner than he is' (Achtner, 1995). One only has to recall his massive sacking of workers who participated in a 35-day strike that paralysed Fiat in 1979 to be convinced. This toughness plays out in his business philosophy: 'My model of a company is one that tries to reach its primary objective: to produce wealth and thus increase profits. I'm disappointed by politicians who have hesitations about this indisputable concept', as well as in his managerial style: 'Here at Fiat, we have one boss at a time', alluding to his disbelief in power-sharing (Gumbel, 1995). Such was the shadow that Romiti cast over Fiat that even his erstwhile rival, Umberto Agnelli, was prompted to affirm, 'I believe that the age of the family firm is over' (Gumbel, 1995).

Inasmuch as, in 1996, Gianni Agnelli had already officially given up his executive post at Fiat, settling for an honorary chairmanship, his 30-year reign in the company by then could be considered formally over. Although we know for a fact that this was not completely true, and that he continued to pull strings at Fiat practically until his dying day, on 24 January 2003, it would not be totally premature to pass judgment on his tenure until his retirement.

In all his activities, Gianni Agnelli seems to have followed in first place his family's interest, even if this could eventually cause damage to the country as a whole (Wikipedia, 2006b). Certainly he did this most of the time with the connivance of the Italian government and large swathes of the population that benefited from his patronage. Italian politicians, and, through them, the Italian state, had always regarded Fiat as an 'obligation-free' company, for which special concessions in labour and tax laws should always be accommodated. For 50 years, Fiat enjoyed a near-monopoly of the Italian car market, boosted by politicians who built highways, passed tax incentives for buyers and, when all else failed, approved subsidies (Achtner, 2003). But, in the end, only Agnelli and his cronies were getting richer, while ordinary Italians by and large were getting poorer, not least because of the culture of corruption spawned by the businessmen, elected leaders and public servants in their midst. That the common good was not served during Gianni Agnelli's watch at Fiat was not entirely his own fault; many others even swore to do so, but did not also share the blame. As a result, despite having once been the world's fifth-largest economy, on many counts Italy still fails to be a properly functioning modern country.

In June 1998, having reached the mandatory age for retirement of 75 years, Romiti was replaced by Paolo Fresco, former vice-chairman at General Electric, and considered its chief international strategist (Achtner, 2003). Fresco was expected to work hand-in-hand with another professional manager and Fiat veteran, Paolo Cantarella, as CEO. Despite ebbing fortunes, the Fiat group still represented almost 5 per cent of Italy's GDP and, together with the other Agnelli holdings, almost 25 per cent of the Milan stockmarket during that change of guard (Donlon, 1998). The main challenges the pair then faced could be grouped into three (*The Economist*, 1998). First was the overly conservative influence of the Agnelli family, which owned about a third of Fiat through Istituto Finanziario Industriale (IFI) and Istituto Finanziaria di Partecipazioni (IFIL), and which effectively exercised control through 'syndicated pacts' with other Italian financial entities. The Agnellis were wont to block any big strategic moves that would make them lose control.

Second, Fiat Auto, which accounted for more than half of the total revenues, was overly dependent on the Italian market and on small cars, hardly the most profitable business in those days. Machine manufacturing had become a low-margin activity as a result of global competition and Fiat's markets in the developing world, saddled with problems of their own, had not been able to absorb its factories' excess capacity (*The Economist*, 2000). Thirdly, the conglomerate had become so unfashionably diversified, growing into a sprawling collection of unrelated businesses (from robots to leisure parks) too complex to manage from a single control centre.

Early in 2000, Fiat got a new lease on life by entering into a share swap with General Motors (GM) (Popham, 2003). According to the terms of the agreement, the American company acquired 20 per cent of Fiat Auto in exchange for 6 per cent of its own shares, and Fiat, the right to sell the remaining 80 per cent to GM between January 2004 and July 2009, in what is known as a 'put option'. GM signed on to this deal heavily favourable to Fiat as a defence measure for its own European operations, fearful that Fiat would tie the knot with the likes of Daimler-Benz or BMW (*The Economist*, 2002d). Although this put option engineered by Fresco and

Cantarella ended up, in a sense, being Fiat's lifesaver, it did not halt the company's downhill slide.

By June 2002, Fiat's financial situation had become unsustainable, with liabilities amounting to a massive €35.6 billion, €13.4 billion of which was short-term debt (*The Economist*, 2002a). Its market share in Italy was down to less than 30 per cent, and in Europe, just over 7 per cent, cut to half from the 1990s. Having come to symbolize Fiat's misfortunes, Cantarella, its CEO of six years, was finally shown the door, and Fresco temporarily took over his job aside from chairmanship (*The Economist*, 2002b). Whereas barely five years ago, in 1997, Fiat produced 2.6 million cars and made €758 million in profits, by October 2002, when the new CEO, Gabriele Galateri, arrived, production was down to 1.9 million and losses seemingly bottomless (*The Economist*, 2002c). Soon Fiat announced its restructuring plan, which included 8100 layoffs, and it was promptly met by a call from the labour unions for a general strike and a not too subtle hint from Prime Minister Silvio Berlusconi to let the state take over and transform Fiat Auto into 'ItalAuto' (*The Economist*, 2002d). It immediately became clear, however, that the European Union would not look kindly on such an arrangement and an alternative had to be worked out.

In the following months, Fresco and Galateri strove to persuade banks to support their restructuring plan and thus help persuade GM to honour its commitment of buying the remainder of the firm (*The Economist*, 2002e). Yet GM, itself still reeling from an $804 million third-quarter loss, proved increasingly hesitant to make good its part of the deal, and even reduced the value of its stake in Fiat from $2.4 billion to a mere $220 million. Prime Minister Berlusconi, for his part, called on the Milanese investment house Mediobanca to come to Fiat's rescue once more and prevent it from falling into American hands. For their efforts, Berlusconi would expect to acquire Fiat's newspaper interests in *La Stampa* and *Corriere della Serra*, and Mediobanca, Fiat's Toro insurance company. Fresco thought that Berlusconi had 'gone crazy'. However, Umberto Agnelli, who had effectively taken charge of the family's interests because of his older brother Gianni's illness, was said to have warmed to Berlusconi's proposal. The main casualty at this impasse was Galateri, who was forced to tender his resignation after only five months as CEO.

A new twist to the Fiat drama was introduced at the start of 2003, when Roberto Colaninno, formerly with Olivetti and, later on, Telecom Italia, stepped in (*The Economist*, 2003a). Some Fiat banks were unhappy with Berlusconi and Mediobanca's involvement and instead supported Fresco and Galateri, even if that meant pitting them against Umberto Agnelli. Colaninno was willing to invest up to €2 billion in return for managerial control, a move which found Susanna Agnelli, Gianni and Umberto's sibling, apart from Fresco himself, quite receptive. Such was the state of affairs when Gianni Agnelli finally passed away on 23 January 2003. Upon hearing the news, Fiat's share price shot up by a full 6 per cent (Israely, 2003).

Gianni Agnelli's death precipitated Fresco's departure from the top slot in Fiat's board in favour of Umberto Agnelli (BBC News, 2003). When Fresco came in in 1998, it was hoped that his GE experience would boost shareholder value in Fiat, but it did not. His harsh, Jack Welch-like management style, however, was strongly felt, not the least because of the legions of firings which made labour unions recoil. Performance incentives and stock options were introduced for top and middle management. His preference for informality, calling managers by their first names, for example, occasioned conflicts with a tradition set by the founder, Giovanni Agnelli himself, who insisted on addressing each other with his title, such as 'Chairman Fresco' (Wikipedia, 2006a). Fresco's American corporate culture as a whole alienated him from the Agnellis, who had always relied on government support. Given his recent misunderstandings with Umberto Agnelli, Fresco opted to leave several months early, to smoothen succession within Fiat. That same month Giuseppe Morchio became Fiat's fourth CEO in less than a year (Popham, 2003).

The return of an Agnelli as Fiat helmsman was regarded as a conservative choice, since he would certainly put family interests above those of the banks and other shareholders. Likewise, he would most probably be unwilling to take any of the tough measures needed to turn the company performance around. The best Umberto Agnelli could do upon being appointed chairman was to agree to a €250 million capital increase from the family holding, in effect giving Fiat more money to burn (CNN, 2003). Once in the driver's seat, he seemed to have a change of heart. He now pledged allegiance to Fiat Auto, abandoning attempts to sell it in favour of more profitable investments in the service sector (Montani, 2004). As for the difficult negotiations with GM over the put option, he managed to have them delayed until January 2005. In all fairness, however, Umberto Agnelli's tenure as Fiat chair turned out to be a very short, indeed a transitional one, since he passed away on 28 May 2004 (BBC News, 2004b). He did not have much to show in terms of achievements apart from recapitalizing Fiat with family funds and obtaining a stay in the execution of GM's put option.

By the end of May 2004, Luca Cordero di Montezemolo was appointed to succeed Umberto Agnelli as Fiat's fifth chairman of the board (BBC News, 2004a). Since he started working for Ferrari in the 1970s, Montezemolo became one of Gianni Agnelli's favourite managers and, eventually, he was named CEO of the sports car brand. Known to be a man of charm and an excellent team-player, he led Ferrari to record successes both in Formula One races as well as in sales. The not so secret wish was that he could work the same magic with the rest of the companies in the Fiat group. Montezemolo likewise enjoyed a conspicuous public profile, being the head of Confindustria (the employers' association) and the Italian Federation of Newspaper Publishers. Shortly after taking up office, and in the wake of the Parmalat scandal, he issued a call for family firms, the bedrock of the Italian economy, to improve their governance practices through greater transparency, more credible accounting and a clearer separation between ownership and control (*The Economist*, 2004a).

Named vice chairman by the same stroke was John Philip Elkann, the 28-year-old son of Margherita Agnelli, Gianni's daughter (BBC News, 2004a). Apparently, Gianni Agnelli, on his deathbed, extracted a promise from Gianluigi Gabetti, then head of the family holding company, that he would protect the interests of the young dauphin (*The Economist*, 2006). Also appointed to the board was Andrea Agnelli, Umberto's son. The market did not receive this news with much enthusiasm and Fiat shares slid by 3.3 per cent.

Similar to the way that Fresco anticipatedly left office upon Gianni Agnelli's death, thereby allowing Umberto Agnelli to take over, then CEO Morchio also made a dash for the door upon Montezemolo's appointment. As the chief architect of Fiat's restructuring plans, Morchio harboured hopes of being named in the top slot, especially at a time when the Group was showing 'its first positive results after fifteen months of total dedication and intense work at the side of Umberto Agnelli' (BBC News, 2004a).

It was upon the vice chairman John Elkann's suggestion that Sergio Marchionne joined the Fiat Group as its fifth CEO in a span of two years (Institutional Investor, 2006). Although born in Italy, Marchionne's family immigrated to Canada when he was just 14, so he completed his education there. Previous to working for Fiat, Marchionne was CEO of the SGS Group, the Geneva-based testing services company, where he successfully implemented a rigid restructuring plan. During Marchionne's stint between 2002 and 2004, he managed a threefold increase in the SGS share price, much to the delight of the Agnellis, who owned a large stake in the company. Then came John Elkann's invitation, on behalf of the other members of the Agnelli family, and Marchionne willingly obliged.

Montezemolo, Marchionne and Elkann faced a daunting challenge when they took control of Fiat, then considered to be in terminal decline. Losses were mounting: €400 million in 2001, €3.9 billion in 2002, €1.9 billion in 2003 and an estimated €3 billion in 2004; and, according to industry observers, Fiat had an overcapacity of approximately 30 per cent (*The Economist*, 2004b). Furthermore, time had run out on GM's put option to take effect or, in its stead, a difficult agreement had to be brokered. Basically, Fiat's message was that, if GM wanted to be released from its obligation to buy the rest of the company, it had to stump up an enormous amount of money and, furthermore, be willing to renegotiate their partnership in terms favourable to the Italians. GM, on the other hand, had a dire message of its own: if forced to buy Fiat Auto, it would embark on a harsh restructuring plan with thousands of job losses in order to make the company profitable. Besides, GM thought that the put option itself was already rendered invalid by Fiat's decision to sell its finance arm, Fidis, in 2002.

The Fiat–GM relationship unceremoniously ended in what was dubbed a 'Valentine's Day Divorce' in February, 2005 (*The Economist*, 2005a). GM agreed to pay Fiat €1.55 billion, give up its remaining 10 per cent stake and abandon a joint-venture in the manufacture of engines and gearboxes. Despite its heft, the divorce price tag only amounted to about 18 months' cash outflow at Fiat Auto, once again securely in Italian hands. Moreover, Fiat's top managers still had a €3 billion bank loan, convertible to almost 30 per cent of the company's shares, due in September to worry about.

This loan obligation was finally settled in signature Agnelli – and Italian – fashion (*The Economist*, 2005b). First Fiat announced that it would not repay the €3 billion convertible loan in cash. It then appeared that bankers, by converting their loan into shares, would wrestle control over Fiat from IFIL, the Agnelli holding company. To avoid this, IFIL would have to buy more shares, and most probably pay a premium. But, if IFIL raised its holding in Fiat to above 30 per cent, according to Italy's takeover rules, it would then be obliged to bid for the entire firm in cash, something too costly even for the Agnellis. What happened in the end was that, on the due date, while banks converted their loans, IFIL was busy buying just enough shares to retain control of Fiat at €6.50 per share, well below the market price then of €7.30 per share. The seller was IFIL's sister firm, the Exor Group, a private company 70 per cent owned by the Agnellis. Exor, in turn, was purchasing the shares on the same day at €5.60 apiece from Merril Lynch, the investment bank with which it had signed an equity swap. The swap was entered into by both companies in April 2005, when Fiat announced the conversion of the loans and its share price fell to its lowest for years, at €4.50 each.

The €74 million profit that Exor opportunistically made at IFIL's expense indeed seems remarkable. All the more so was the way in which the Agnellis apparently managed to stabilize their control over Fiat. They certainly did this on the cheap, pocketing millions from Exor's sudden windfall on the side, to the detriment of Fiat's minority shareholders (*The*

Economist, 2005b). Because of this series of happy coincidences, Fiat was expected to end 2005 with a pre-tax profit of €1 billion, after suffering losses in excess of €8 billion since 2001.

With Fiat relatively stabilized, Marchionne was now able to proceed with the radical surgery that the firm, nevertheless, still needed (Kahn, 2005). In his own words, the company's major problem was that it 'was overmanaged and underled'. Instead of getting rid of underperforming managers, they were simply transferred to another job within the organization, playing the corporate equivalent of 'musical chairs'. However, Marchionne no doubt had better luck in flattening Fiat's bloated managerial structure than in laying off factory workers, because here he faced staunch opposition from labour unions and politicians. Marchionne also appeared to have pulled off what Cantarella before him attempted but had not: that is, to introduce a more Anglo-American focus on markets and equity in Fiat's stodgy Italian and paternalistic corporate culture (*The Economist*, 2005c). Thus, while chairman Montezemolo dealt with politicians and union leaders with his proverbial charm, Marchionne went on trying to rebuild Fiat's car business step by step.

Having severed links with GM, Marchionne could now enter into a wide range of promising business ventures with other automakers (*Automotive News Europe*, 2005). Throughout 2005, Fiat entered into three cooperation contracts with PSA/Peugeot-Citroën for a light commercial vehicle, a joint production agreement with Ford for a small car in Poland, and a licensing deal with Suzuki to manufacture diesel engines in Asia. Also in the pipeline were alliances with Tata of India and with the Shanghai Automotive Industrial Corporation (SAIC) of China. Furthermore, Marchionne committed over €10 billion in investments in a period of four years to keep Fiat factories busy in the production of 20 new models (*The Economist*, 2005c). Thanks to a strategy of paying off debts, finding investment partners in new products, cutting costs, selling non-core assets and, above all, injecting a sense of urgency into the company's managerial culture, Marchionne seemed to have primed Fiat and made it ready to 'move into higher gear' (Mackintosh, 2006).

How crucial Marchionne's continued involvement in Fiat had become was reflected in the stockmarket's nervousness over rumours of his departure in November 2006 (*El Mundo*, 2006). He quickly had to clarify that he meant to continue as Group CEO at least until 2010 and that he simply wanted to leave his post at Fiat Auto in the hands of someone with a more specialized knowledge of the industry. In three more years he hoped to see the culmination of his business plan, with projected sales of €67 billion and profits of €8.6 billion, about twice Fiat's figures at that moment; production should also rise to around 2.4 million vehicles. The company was expected to end 2006 with an 18 per cent growth in sales, thanks largely to the model Grande Punto.

For the first time in ages, it finally seemed as if the Fiat triumvirate – Montezemolo, Elkann and Marchionne – had reasons to begin the new year, 2007, with relative calm and optimism. But Elkann was the one with grounds for being the most optimistic of all. By the time of Marchionne's announced departure in 2010, Montezemolo would be close to retirement age and Elkann would be in his mid-thirties, old enough to claim his birthright: Fiat's leadership.

Fiat represents an outstanding example of the uniqueness of Italian family capitalism (Pagano and Trento, 2002). Everywhere else, firms are usually begun by entrepreneurs and their families, but among industrialized countries only in Italy are the largest companies normally run by family dynasties. A peculiar trait of Italian corporate governance is that control in large firms is passed generally along hereditary family lines instead of through a mechanism of managerial meritocracy. Although practically all countries have gone through a phase of family capitalism, this has never been overcome in Italy and no version of managerial capitalism has evolved. Going through Fiat's history, we see some sort of cohabitation between family capitalism and State-owned enterprises in the period between the two world wars, and a reinforcement and regulation to a certain degree, but never replacement of family-owned enterprises by institutions such as Mediobanca thereafter. Not even the wave of privatizations in the 1990s or the alliances and equity swap between Fiat and GM at the turn of the 21st century has introduced any major change in the corporate governance style of Italian family capitalism; the model remains intact and, as such, is expected to continue.

II   EMPEROR LI KA SHING OF CHEUNG KONG HOLDINGS AND HUTCHISON WHAMPOA LIMITED

The life of China's last emperor, Pu Yi, is the stuff of legends, not to mention of Hollywood movies. Bernardo Bertolucci's film version of 1987 won in just about every category in which it was nominated, for a total of nine Academy Awards or Oscars, including Best Screenplay, Best Director and Best Picture. Its theme was the life of a man who, despite his title and privileges, had become the objectified plaything of other, sinister forces, ultimately more powerful than he.

Pu Yi had not yet turned three when he ascended to the 'heavenly throne' in 1908 (Spence, 1982; Fairbank, 1987). Until then the country had been ruled by the Dowager Empress Tzu Hsi. It was she who had the nominal emperor and Pu Yi's uncle, Kuang Hsu, imprisoned for conspiring against her; later on, she also had him poisoned, just to make sure he did not interfere with her succession plans. Prince Chun, Pu Yi's father, then served as his own son's regent. As a result of the Xinhai revolution which led to the establishment of the Republic of China, Pu Yi was forced to renounce his throne in 1912. However, a treaty allowed him to retain his imperial title and to remain in the Forbidden City, enjoying all the honours and privileges befitting a 'guest foreign monarch'. He would not leave the Forbidden City – a sumptuous 250 acre compound built by the Ming emperors between 1406 and 1420, composed of 24 palaces, 9000 rooms and countless terraces, gardens and shrines, all surrounded by 35 foot walls and a moat – until he was finally expelled by the warlord Feng Yuxiang in 1924.

In 1931, the Japanese army invaded Manchuria, and some time later they installed Pu Yi, first, as 'chief executive', and afterwards, as 'emperor of Manchukuo', a post that he occupied until 1945. It was intended that Pu Yi play a vital role in the 'japanization' of Manchuria. The imperial family was pressured to marry Japanese women and even to convert to the state religion, Shintoism. After World War II, when the Soviet army took over Manchuria from the Japanese, they brought Pu Yi back with them to Russia, where he stayed for a couple of years. Nonetheless, in 1946, he was transported by the Russians to Tokyo, to testify before the international war crimes tribunal. His account of the treatment received from the Japanese was scathing. In 1950, when Stalin wished to warm his relations with Mao, he repatriated the former emperor to China. Pu Yi was then required to undergo a decade-long process of re-education in Fushun, Liaoning province (Pu Yi, 2000).

By the early 1960s, Pu Yi, already reformed, began to voice support for the Communists and, in consequence, was given work at the Beijing Botanical Gardens. He was made a member of the Chinese People's Political Consultative Conference, a body in which he served between 1964 and 1967, the year in which he died from cancer. At that time, the Cultural Revolution was at its height.

As a man who, very early in life, took the reins of destiny into his own hands, there probably is not anyone more different from Pu Yi in temperament and character than Li Ka Shing, perhaps today's most serious contender to the title of 'emperor of China', albeit coming from a corporate setting. Li Ka Shing was born in Chouzhou, province of Guangdong, southern China, in 1928 (Nohria and Gurtler, 2005), the same year in which revolutionaries desecrated and looted the imperial Manchu tombs. His father, Li Yunjing, was the head of a primary school, although not the same one that Li Ka Shing attended, and belonged to a scholarly family: 'During the late Ching Dynasty, my father's two elder brothers studied PhDs at Tokyo University (known as Imperial University then). Every generation of my family took education very seriously' (Li Ka Shing, 2006). He was the oldest of five siblings, with two brothers and two sisters. In 1940, at the height of the Sino-Japanese war, while Pu Yi was basking in the Japanese-sponsored luxury of Manchuria, the Li family fled as refugees to the relative safety then offered by the British colony of Hong Kong.

By the end of 2006, as a 78-year-old widower with two sons, Li Ka Shing became the richest person of Chinese descent, the second-richest person in Asia (after the Indian steel magnate, Lakshmi Mittal) and the ninth-richest person in the world (with the demise of Kenneth Thomson), attributed an estimated net worth of $18.8 billion (Forbes, 2006). He is chairman of Hutchison Whampoa Limited and Cheung Kong Holdings, two Hong Kong-based conglomerates. Apart from being the world's largest operator of container terminals, his companies are also involved in real estate development, retail, telecommunications and power generation. For all of these reasons, he was named 'Asia's Most Powerful Man' by *Asiaweek* in 2000, and honoured with the first ever 'Malcolm S. Forbes Lifetime Achievement Award' by *Forbes Magazine* in September 2006 (Wikipedia, 2006c).

Our reasons for studying Li Ka Shing's case, however, are not premised exactly on any single one of these accomplishments, but on the manner in which his corporate governance style mirrors what we could call, together with Aristotle, a 'corporate monarchy'. Let us recall the two distinctive features of such a regime, namely, the concentration of power in the hands of just one individual, Li Ka Shing himself, and the precedence of the common good before any other private good, in that individual's course of action (this latter characteristic is precisely what differentiates a 'corporate monarchy' from a 'corporate tyranny').

Like most entrepreneurs, Asian or otherwise, Li Ka Shing was largely dependent on his family for his initial exploits. Yet, unlike their western counterparts, even after the businesses they put up had already gained enough volume and structure, Asian businessmen still kept the top decision-making post to themselves. In this, as chairman and owner of his companies, Li Ka Shing is no exception. As Richard Siemens, an associate in the telecommunications sector comments, 'One of the reasons American firms have difficulty in Asia is that they only have short-term chairmen, with two or three years' tenures. In Asia, the chairmen probably started the company like K.S. [Ka Shing] did, and will be there until he dies. And when this chairman speaks, everybody else holds his breath because what he says goes' (Nohria and Gurtler, 2005: 6).

Certainly, Li Ka Shing may have handed day-to-day management in both Cheung Kong and Hutchison Whampoa over to his older son, Victor

Li Tzar Kuoi, supported by an army of professionals, but it is clear that he continues to control the levers of power at the board level. In a 1999 interview he confessed, 'I have already retired as Managing Director of Cheung Kong, just keeping my capacity as Chairman. The duties are now shared by my son Victor and a team of young Executive Directors; on major decisions, they will consult me. Both Victor and I get along very well with our senior executives, and I believe there won't be a problem with succession' (Li Ka Shing, 1999). Victor himself seems quite comfortable with the arrangement, having this much to say of his father: 'We're good partners working together. When we reach decisions, we almost always arrive at similar conclusions' (Schuman, 2004).

Not content with simply being the founding chairman – at least of Cheung Kong, since he took over Hutchison Whampoa only in 1979 – Li Ka Shing also seems bent on becoming chairman for life. He has always had his own peculiar understanding of retirement: 'I have my own definition for the term "retirement"'. Life was extremely hard when I was young; today working without the burden of pressure to me is the same as the luxury of retirement' (Li Ka Shing, 2002). And finally, as if to put all doubts to rest, when asked in December 2006 whether or not he had any retirement plans, Li Ka Shing came up with this crystal-clear response, 'No, no plan' (Li Ka Shing, 2006).

Li Ka Shing's tight control of his empire is reflected in the cascading, pyramid-like ownership structures of Cheung Kong Holdings Limited and Hutchison Whampoa Limited, as well as in the cross-shareholding arrangements with dual class equities between the two. Because of this, he is able to retain a disproportionate control of the companies without incurring the cost of owning an equivalent economic interest. Thus Cheung Kong Holdings owns, among the companies listed in Hong Kong, 49.97 per cent of Hutchison Whampoa Limited, through which it controls through combined holdings Hutchison Telecommunications International Limited (50.83 per cent), Cheung Kong Infrastructure Holdings Limited (84.58 per cent), Hutchison Harbour Ring Limited (61.97 per cent) and Tom Online, Inc. (66.06 per cent), apart from significant stakes in Cheung Kong Sciences Holding International, Inc. (44.30 per cent), Hong Kong Electric Holdings Limited (38.87 per cent) and Tom Group Limited (36.70 per cent), for a total group market capitalization of HK$ 793 billion as of December 2006 (Cheung Kong Holdings Limited, 2006). Similarly, Hutchison Whampoa Limited, apart from its five core businesses consisting of ports and related services, property and hotels, retail, telecommunications and infrastructure, also owns 71.60 per cent of Hutchison China MediTech Limited and 34.61 per cent of Husky Energy Inc. (Hutchison Whampoa Limited, 2006).

Although current research suggests that entrusting extensive corporate control to a single family is generally undesirable, it also acknowledges that family control pyramids may be a sensible adaptation to certain markets and institutions, especially in developing countries (Morck and Yeung, 2004).

How did Li Ka Shing build his business empire? In his acceptance speech delivered on 6 June 2000 for the International Distinguished Entrepreneur Award received from the University of Manitoba (Canada), Li Ka Shing made the following reflections: 'A month ago, on the first of May, I quietly celebrated the 50th anniversary of the company I first built. On that day, I reflected on those past years, the sadness of lost childhood in the turmoil of war, the helplessness of watching my father's suffering, the loneliness of poverty, the desperation of seeking employment as a 12-year-old, the joy of receiving my first paycheck, the enthusiasm in getting the first deal, the setting up of my own company, the comfort of my first home, and ever eventful participation in global changes and development, the sheer magnificent feeling of accomplishments and recognition. It has not been an easy journey. My life has been filled with challenges and competition. The constant demand for one to be wise, to be far-seeing and to be creative is certainly tiring, yet all in all I am glad that I can say I am a happy man, for I have tried to serve society to the best of my ability as a human being, as a citizen and as a businessman' (Li Ka Shing, 2000).

In its early stages, life has definitely been a steep and steady uphill climb for Li Ka Shing. Despite displaying precocious intelligence, he was forced to leave school at the age of 10 because family finances had deteriorated sharply and even his paternal uncles who had gone to Tokyo for advanced studies could not offer any help. Two years later, the family arrived in Hong Kong: 'I was facing life for the first time. I was 12 years old, but I felt like a 20-year-old. I knew then what life was' (Li Ka Shing, 2006). Li Ka Shing soon enrolled in a colonial middle school and quickly caught up with his classmates. Classes were interrupted abruptly, however, by the Japanese invasion, and when they resumed, students were then required to learn the Japanese language. Changes of this sort did not sit well with Li Ka Shing's father, who was very patriotic and had even joined an underground resistance movement. When conditions in Hong Kong had become unbearable, the Li patriarch decided to send his wife, two daughters and two sons back to China, choosing only his eldest, Li Ka Shing, to remain with him. It did not take very long for Li Ka Shing's father, Li Yuan Jing, to succumb to tuberculosis, which eventually caused his death in 1943: 'TB was a difficult disease to treat at the time, [it] was as devastating as cancer is today. If you were rich and could afford proper care, you might have a better chance. We had no choice. I needed to be strong, and needed to find some way to secure a future' (Li Ka Shing, 2006).

On his deathbed, aside from lamenting his failure to provide for his son's education, Li Yuan Jing was said to have confided to his first born, 'A man must have ambitions. You must have the strength of character. Then you can rise as tall the sky. And remember, at any time, if things don't go well, never be discouraged', to which Li Ka Shing replied, 'Father, don't worry. I will learn to do business and make lots of money' (Nohria and Gurtler, 2005: 2). At the age of 15, because he was the eldest son, Li Ka Shing assumed the responsibility of caring for his family in China. He began working as a clerk in a maternal uncle's small watch and clock shop. 'During the Japanese occupation of Hong Kong, [. . .] I sent 90 per cent of my salary to my mother. I spent nothing. I had a haircut every three months. I shaved my head like a monk. Nor did I go to see a movie during this period. Seeing a movie was very cheap at the time, but I needed to save every penny' (Li Ka Shing, 2006). Nonetheless, because of what he perceived to be his uncle's arrogance, or perhaps because of his own driving ambition, he did not stay at his uncle's store for long.

Li Ka Shing's next job was at a plastics trading firm selling belts and wrist straps. Although he clocked 16-hour workdays, he still managed to study with a private tutor twice a week. This extra knowledge ended up giving him a lucky edge: 'My boss needed a letter written. He had a secretary who wrote his letters for him, but he was on sick leave. When he asked around the office to see who could take his place temporarily, my colleagues recommended me. My boss said that my letters were quick and nice, and I got his meaning. He was happy with my work and I was promoted to head a small department. I always believe that knowledge can change life [knowledge reshapes destiny]. It was a case of knowledge changing my life' (Li Ka Shing, 2006).

Soon afterwards, teen-aged Li Ka Shing was reassigned as a wholesale salesman for the plastics company. His boss then announced that bonuses would be based on sales. 'At the end of the year, my sales figure was seven times higher than the second best. If they paid my bonus based on my sales, my bonus would have been higher than the General Manager's. The other salesmen were already jealous. So I said to my boss, "Just pay me the same as the second best salesman, it would make everyone happy." As a result, I became manager when I was 17 going on 18. I was second in command only to the boss. At 19, I became the general manager of the factory' (Li Ka Shing, 2006). Having reached the top rung of the ladder, Li Ka Shing decided it was time to start a business of his own.

Li Ka Shing founded the Cheung Kong Plastics Company in 1950 with a capital investment of HK$50 000 sourced from his personal savings and loans from relatives and friends. The company was named after the Cheung Kong River, also known as the Yangtze, the longest river in China, as a constant reminder of the need for alliances in business. In the words of its founding chairman, 'If you want to be successful, whatever your business or position, you need to accept different opinions and different people. Why did the Yangtze become a long river? It's because it can accept smaller rivers and become big. Outside, I was polite to everybody, but inside I knew I was too powerful. So I told myself: when you start your own business, you need to be more polite, more acceptable to people. If you're too powerful and reject the smaller waters, you cannot become a long river' (Nohria and Gurtler, 2005: 2).

Cheung Kong produced combs, soapboxes and simple toys sold primarily in Hong Kong and China, although it also made small forays into the international market. The company was robust enough to have survived the United Nations-imposed trade embargo on China for its role in the Korean War of the 1950s. Meanwhile, Li Ka Shing never stopped learning and innovating in his trade, even going to Italy for this purpose, until he carved a niche for himself as the 'King of Plastic Flowers'. As a result he landed very lucrative foreign deals, as with the American Natural Fern Company of New York, for example.

In 1958, Li Ka Shing brought his empire building to the next higher stage with his entry into real estate. Unable to renew the lease for his factory, he was forced to buy and develop land himself. He did this against all odds, given that three other factories then located at Smithfield Road were already on the verge of closing down: the place was just plain unlucky for business. Nonetheless, since he already had orders and bought new machines, Li Ka Shing went ahead in order not to let his clients down. In the end, business turned out to be so good that he had earned a full year's operating expenses by the first month. He even had to rent the premises vacated by the other two factories next door to keep up with production. 'You can believe in Feng Shui [chinese geomancy] if you want, but ultimately people control their own fate. The most important thing is to improve yourself and give it your best. The many things previously thought to be impossible will become possible. Broaden your vision, and maintain stability while advancing forward' is the lesson he drew from this experience (Li Ka Shing, 1999).

Because of the turmoil caused by the Red Guards and the Cultural Revolution in China in 1967 – the same year that the last emperor Pu Yi died – people in Hong Kong panicked, selling their land and property at rock-bottom prices as they fled. 'A completed new building could be bought cheaper than the cost of the land. For example, I paid 60 per cent of the replacement cost for a building in Kwun Tong. The seller wanted me to pay in US dollars. I made the decision in five minutes. The seller, an American company, lost confidence in Hong Kong. The building had a floor area of about 330 000 sq. ft. I made my money back in fifteen months. In other cases, the site had only half of the pilings done, and the seller would offer to sell the site on the cheap because they could not complete the construction', recounts Li Ka Shing (Li Ka Shing, 2006).

Believing the crisis to be only temporary, he quickly bought whatever was for sale. He reasoned, 'If China took back Hong Kong, it would become a burden for them. They would get five to six million more people, but they already had enough people. What benefit would they have had? Hong Kong doesn't have natural resources. Its greatest asset is its hardworking people. Of course I was quite clear at the time when I bought the property. But I did not borrow money; I used my cash reserves to invest' (Li Ka Shing, 2006). In effect, Li Ka Shing had always personally avoided going into debt. He would use his own cash, and if that was not sufficient, he would form joint ventures with landowners and presell apartments to raise capital. When Cheung Kong went public in 1972, it had almost no debt. 'By 1958 or 59, I owned my factory site as well as other real estate. By 1960, we were the biggest manufacturer in Hong Kong in terms of dollar value export. I started working in 1940, I started business in 1950, and by 1960 I was the biggest manufacturer' and by 1979, Hong Kong's largest private landlord, Li Ka Shing could very well add (Li Ka Shing, 2006).

This also marks the year (1979) in which Li Ka Shing acquired Hutchison Whampoa Limited, one of the oldest British 'hongs' or 'trading companies' which dominate the Hong Kong economy, thereby foreshadowing the handover of power back to the Chinese by almost 20 years. The 'hongs' originally refer to the guild of Chinese merchant houses authorized by the Beijing central government to trade with Westerners in the port of Guangdong prior to the first Opium War (1839–42). Each foreign vessel had to be supervised by a hong merchant who, in turn, would guarantee the Chinese government the payment of duties and the proper behaviour of the foreigners. Hutchison Whampoa Limited finds its roots in the A.S. Watson dispensary founded in Guangzhou in 1828 and which transferred to Hong Kong in 1841 (Hutchison Whampoa Limited, 2006). The Whampoa name comes from the Hong Kong and Whampoa Dock Company established in 1863, with operations in Aberdeen, Hong Kong Island and Whampoa, on the banks of the Pearl River in China. The Hutchison part refers to the John D. Hutchison Company which began in 1877. In the 1960s, Sir Douglas Clague embarked on the acquisition and control of A.S. Watson, Davie, Boag and Co. Ltd, Hong Kong and Whampoa Dock Co. Ltd., and China Provident Co. Ltd. under the Hutchison International Limited flagship. A decade later, however, the conglomerate reported losses of HK$130 million and became unable to service its growing debt. The Hong Kong Shanghai Banking Corporation (HSBC) then acquired 150 million shares of Hutchison International at a discounted price, gaining control of 33 per cent of the company (Nohria and Gurtler, 2005).

At around the same time, Li Ka Shing had agreed to sell 28 per cent of Kowloon Godown to Pao Yuekong, owner of World Wide Shipping and member of the HSBC board. In exchange, Pao used his influence over the new HSBC CEO, Michael Sandberg, to consider selling the bank's stakes in Hutchison International to Li Ka Shing. Sandberg agreed and Li Ka Shing went away with the bank's entire stake (he was the only bidder allowed access) for HK$639 million, becoming Hutchison Whampoa's largest shareholder (Nohria and Gurtler, 2005). From then on, Li Ka Shing gradually increased his equity in Hutchison Whampoa.

The following are his comments on this milestone event: 'Our acquisition of Hutchison Whampoa was indeed very significant. But if I had not taken control of Hutchison at that time, I would have purchased another foreign-owned conglomerate. Back in the late 1970s, we had already established a solid foundation with Cheung Kong, and I began to take notice of foreign-owned companies, whose shareholders were able to control sizeable assets with only a relatively minor stake. I had a clear intention of taking over one of these companies with underperforming assets and developing it into a multinational corporation. At the time, Hutchison had negligible operations outside of Hong Kong. Now it has investments and operations in 41 countries and employs 150 000 worldwide. When the transaction was announced, the press neglected one important factor in Hong Kong Bank's decision to sell the Hutchison shares to me: Hong Kong Bank's management was confident that I am better suited to lead this company. I believe I have not disappointed them. Hutchison Whampoa is now a world renowned multinational conglomerate. When I first took control of Hutchison, there were many internal problems that others were not aware of. I eradicated those problems, improved the company's operations and grew the company. Some people seem to think that the acquisition of Hutchison was a sweet deal for me, but only because they did not know the full picture' (Li Ka Shing, 2002). In 2006, Hutchison Whampoa had expanded operations to 56 countries, staffed by 220 000 employees. The group's achievements include being the world's biggest port operator, the largest retailer of health and beauty products, a mobile multimedia communications pioneer (3G phones) and a leading international telecommunications service provider.

Indeed, Li Ka Shing's acquisition of Hutchison Whampoa signals the momentous growth of his empire beyond China through a unique business and management philosophy that combines western structures with traditional Chinese thinking. He explains, 'To me, when CKH [Cheung Kong Holdings] took over Hutchison in 1979, I focused on establishing a management structure and corporate culture that could align the interests of management and shareholders and within which our executives have maximum flexibility to realize the full scope of their professional expertise and enterprising spirit. Truly great talents with capabilities and strategy are extremely rare and the extra margin on inventiveness, courage and prudence is even rarer and must be rewarded. I started with identifying within the fluidity of Chinese philosophical thinking and the science of western management, the coordinates upon which we could format a seamless management structure. Building on this foundation, the company structure becomes a life-force that supports the development of each division of business. Even should I myself retire or any senior management retire from office, it would not have any real effect [. . .] As the chairman and a shareholder, I have a duty and responsibillity to create long-term value and achieve short-term returns for all shareholders' (Li Ka Shing, 2002).

Apart from their equity structures, Li Ka Shing also exerts control over companies through their boards. In 2006, six directors sat on the boards of both Cheung Kong and Hutchison Whampoa (Cheung Kong Holdings Limited, 2006; Hutchison Whampoa Limited, 2006). Included among these, aside from Li Ka Shing himself, are his eldest son, Victor Li Tzar Kuoi, as deputy chairman of both conglomerates, and his brother-in-law and Victor's uncle, Kam Hing Lam. Executive directors are a minority in Cheung Kong as well as in Hutchison Whampoa. However, a number of the non-executive directors, such as George Colin Magnus, the former deputy chairman of Cheung Kong, had previously worked for Li Ka Shing until his retirement. There is also quite a shuffle between non-executive and independent non-executive directors on both boards, many of whom had held their posts through criss-crossing directorships since the early 1980s. The members of the Cheung Kong and Hutchison Whampoa boards, therefore, are a tighly-knit group of Li Ka Shing friends.

An indisputable advantage of such concentration of power is that decision making is quick and, to that extent, effective. Little time is lost in consultations when business opportunities knock on the door. In 1999, Li Ka Shing sold Orange, the leading mobile phone carrier based in the United Kingdom, to Mannesman in exchange for 10 per cent of the German firm and cash; a few months later, in February 2000, Mannesman was bought by Vodaphone in what was then the world's biggest corporate takeover and Li Ka Shing ended up with a profit estimated between $14.6 and $15 billion; shortly afterwards, the tech bubble bursted (*Time Asia*, 2000). No wonder he is called 'Chiu Yan' (Superman) by fellow Hong Kongers. Here is his account in a 2001 interview: 'Orange was a miracle. About eleven years ago, we were going in two directions – we were operating a one-way mobile system, and at the same time we registered Orange, which was a PCS system. I tried it for myself, and the reception was very clear. The operation was very successful. However, very few people know why we finally sold the business. The value of the business was extremely high. Someone came to Hong Kong and offered us US$30 billion, but they were not the only interested buyers. Someone else had offered about the same amount. I felt we should sell right away. [. . .] So the transaction took place less than two hourse after we met, and it became one of the largest transactions and the most profitable deal in history' (Li Ka Shing, 2001). Elsewhere he adds, 'the sale of Orange to Mannesman in 1999 was the most memorable in recent years. It was the most profitable transaction in history, and represented a win-win-win situation for shareholders of Hutchison, Mannesman and Orange' (Li Ka Shing, 2002). Do we need greater proof of the way Li Ka Shing single-handedly runs his empire?

The next issue we would have to defend is that, unlike the Agnellis with Fiat, Li Ka Shing is concerned above all with the common good in the running of his vast business empire. That distinguishes a 'corporate monarchy' from a 'corporate tyranny' as we have already said. Li Ka Shing may be the closest we now have to a Chinese Emperor, but he is certainly no saint. Nonetheless, despite all his faults, a case could still be built on the premise that, in his business dealings, he strives to seek the good of all rather than just his private good or interest. This is no guarantee that he always hits the mark, and in certain instances, we rather have evidence to the contrary, yet the hypothesis is definitely still worth exploring. We shall base our arguments on the following reasons: the continued growth and profitability of his companies to the benefit of shareholders, the professionalism and low turnover levels among his executives, his philanthropic activities and his patriotism or love for his country, China, which has caused a lot of misunderstanding. All of these characteristics coalesce into what is perhaps his most important business asset, a good reputation.

The Hutchison Whampoa Limited webpage offers, apart from annual reports, a 10-year summary of the group's financial performance from 1996 to 2005 (Hutchison Whampoa Limited, 2006). As we have already explained, owing to the results of the Orange–Mannesman transaction, the figures corresponding to 1999 – a profit attributable to shareholders of HK$117 882 million, with an earnings per share of HK$27.65 and a return on average of shareholders' funds of 72.4 per cent – may be deemed statistically insignificant. Just the same, with the exception of 1999, the average profit attributable to shareholders has been HK$13 742 million for the past decade; the average earnings per share HK$3.248; and the average dividends per share, HK$1.593.

The Cheung Kong Holdings Limited group financial summary paints a similar picture (Cheung Kong Holdings Limited, 2006). Always with the exception of the banner year 1999, the average profit attributable to shareholders between 1996 and 2005 has been HK$11 170 million; the average earnings per share, HK$4.843 and the average dividends per share, HK$1.604. Because of all this, it should come as no surprise that, when Tom.com (later renamed Tom Group) had its IPO in 2000, it was oversubscribed by 669 times (*Time Asia*, 2000). Some 50 000 people lined up in the streets, a hundred policemen were dispatched to keep order and traffic even had to be rerouted on Nathan Road, Hong Kong's prime tourist boulevard.

Li Ka Shing establishes his boundaries, however, and there are certain businesses he will not get into, no matter how lucrative. Having built container terminals, an airport, hotels and a golf course, he became the largest investor in the Bahamas. The Bahamas government then offered him a much sought-after casino licence as a gesture of thanks. But not even the Prime Minister was able to convince him to accept the deal. Li Ka Shing then thought of the following compromise: he would construct a new building outside of the hotels for a casino to be operated by a third party. The Bahamas government could then grant the licence to whomsoever it wished, but Hutchison Whampoa would only receive rent from the casino. Li Ka Shing argued, 'I don't care where our hotel guests go, but the casino will not be built inside my hotels. This is my principle, and I will stick to it' (Li Ka Shing, 1999). At some other instance, commenting on this same event, he added, 'My managers always say that I don't like to make easy money, that I only like to earn money the hard way. So this is my business philosophy: you should make money only in a legitimate fashion. In the US, they teach MBA students how to squeeze the last penny out of a deal. But we Chinese think differently. Making money is good, but not if it causes harm' (Li Ka Shing, 2001).

A second reason for claiming an overriding concern for the common good in Li Ka Shing's style of governance is his ability to keep and nurture talent among his ranks. 'I feel very fortunate that I have a very good relationship with my colleagues. I was once an employee myself, so I know what employees want. The turnover rate for senior executives at my company is the lowest of any major company in Hong Kong, probably under 1 per cent over the last ten years. To attract and retain good staff, you have to offer them good remuneration and good prospects, and to make them feel important. Of course you also need a good system of checks and balances, which is vital to the health of a company. Even the best people can turn bad if you leave them isolated' (Li Ka Shing, 2001).

Although Li Ka Shing has never fired any senior executive, he did intervene in the dismissal of one from the lower ranks: 'He was a well-educated middle manager, but he took advantage of his position for personal gains on many occasions. His behaviour was not in line with his remuneration, so I decided to fire him. If a staff is sloppy in his work, I will get very angry and criticize him. But if he makes a mistake, you should give him a chance.

Once a staff member broke a very precious Tang dynasty tri-coloured pottery horse in my office. I just told him to be more careful next time. The horse is shattered; he is blaming himself; why do you need to say more? This is not a question of money; it's a personal philosophy. I believe our turnover rate at the senior level is the lowest among similar companies. They are always sad to leave when they retire' (Li Ka Shing, 1999). The organization also seems to share that feeling.

There is something about the Chinese character that makes it more indulgent with other people's honest shortcomings than westerners. As Li Ka Shing expounds, 'In foreign companies, there are many Quarter CEOs who are forced to resign if their company fails to perform. But we are not like that. We are a compassionate organization. For instance, if our peers in the same industry have reported a 580 profit loss, and we record a loss of 60 per cent, then I would reward the CEO. Conversely, if other companies are making $100, and we are only making $80, then I have to ask why we are not performing as well as other companies. Foreign companies tend to focus on efficiency; Chinese companies lean toward compassion' (Li Ka Shing, 2001).

Compassion does not mean, however, squandering trust in the organization, much less when one is dealing with family members, no matter how un-Chinese that may sound. 'You can't trust someone just because he is a relative. You have to spend time with that person, understand his way of thinking, and if it is positive like your own, then you can trust him. If you employ someone solely because he is your relative, then the company will certainly suffer. On the other hand, if you have worked with someone for a length of time, and you feel that he is heading in the right direction in life, and he takes care of every important assignment that you give him, then you can trust him as if he were your own family' (Li Ka Shing, 2001).

Thirdly, let us consider Li Ka Shing's philanthropic activities. In 1980, he set up the Li Ka Shing Foundation – to which he refers as his 'third son' – focusing on educational and health-care projects. He tells the story of the birth of his 'third son' as follows: 'I was tossing and turning one night. The next day, when I was having dinner with my family, I told them that I have a third child. They fell silent. They were shocked and thought that I had finally lost it. Actually it was an epiphany. If I had a third child, wouldn't I want to build a solid foundation for his future? By treating my private foundation as my third son, I could allocate more assets to it and enable it to benefit more people. I hope our 1.3 billion compatriots can understand this reasoning because our Chinese tradition is to pass on our wealth from one generation to the next. But if we can use our wealth to benefit society, then everyone will be happier' (Li Ka Shing, 2005). In a very Chinese fashion, Li Ka Shing has assured his two sons that their 'brother' will not cause them any trouble, so neither should they cause any trouble for their 'brother'. In fact, he has established that no family member or director of his companies will benefit from the foundation; it is 100 per cent for charity.

Li Ka Shing's desire is to donate one-third of his wealth to the foundation (Li Ka Shing, 2006). Unlike many wealthy individuals who use private foundations basically as tax shelters, he does not finance the Li Ka Shing Foundation with shares from his listed companies; instead he makes outright donations from non-core assets. In January 2005, for example, the sale of 17 million shares in the Canadian Imperial Bank of Commerce netted him US$1 billion, a considerable sum which he, in turn, injected into the Foundation (Li Ka Shing, 2005). That represented the largest charitable donation in history by a Chinese person.

The Li Ka Shing foundation is engaged primarily in the two areas in which its founding patron experienced greatest hardships and deprivations: in medicine and in education. 'My father died of tuberculosis when we could not afford medical care. I know the feeling of helplessness and loneliness. This is why I am very dedicated to developing better medical care services' (Li Ka Shing, 2002). Furthermore, knowing only too well the difficulties of a lack of formal education, and firmly entrenched in the belief that knowledge can change one's fate, the foundation supports a myriad of educational institutions and projects, notably the Shantou University in Li Ka Shing's native Guangdong, founded in 1981, and specific initiatives from the University of Hong Kong and the Singapore Management University, among others. This patronage is over and above that carried out by his companies, through the Cheung Kong scholars, for example.

For Li Ka Shing, compassion did not come as an afterthought, once he had already made a huge pile of money, as a way to assuage guilty feelings. In the early 1960s, his factory was located in Western District, Hong Kong, while his office was on Ice House Street, Central. He noticed a woman who often stood on the street corner, accepting money from whoever offered, although she herself did not beg. Believing her to be an honest person, Li Ka Shing approached her and told her one day after work, 'Do you have any relatives in Hong Kong? If you can arrange for someone to transfer to you a licence to sell newspapers in front of the restaurant, I can offer you the financial support. This way you won't have to stand on a street corner to beg' (Li Ka Shing, 2005). But on the day Li Ka Shing promised to give the woman money, a customer requested a visit to his factory in Western. To keep his word to the woman, he left in the midst of a meeting, telling the staff, 'I have to go out for a while. If the client asks, tell him I went to the bathroom'. Li Ka Shing then sped to Central – 'the fastest I had ever driven' – stopped next to the curb, and found the woman. When she showed proof of obtaining the licence, he gave her the money and returned to the factory. No one knew that he disappeared to do a good deed, much less the client visiting the factory.

As for the motives of such charitable giving, Li Ka Shing confesses, 'I have no need for more wealth. But if I can do more for mankind, for our people, and for our country, I would be more than happy to do so' (Li Ka Shing, 1999). A couple of years later, he spells out the connection between philanthropy, his work, and his philosophy of life: 'To be able to contribute to society and to help those in need to build a better life, that is the ultimate meaning in life. I would gladly consider this to be my life's work' (Li Ka Shing, 2005). He does not consider himself to have special religious beliefs, although he has read many books on Christianity, Buddhism, Confucianism and Taoism, and admires the wisdom contained therein. He believes, however, that moral education is the most important task of schooling, rather than vocational training or merely honing one's intelligence: 'What good is a talented person if you need three people to watch over him day in and day out?' (Li Ka Shing, 2001).

A facet of Li Ka Shing's life that has been most prone to misunderstanding refers to his relationship with China, in particular, to his government and army connections. Part of the western press has all but accused him of being a spy or a straw man for the powers that be in Beijing and an associate of the Chinese Triad ganglords (Smith, 2000). These claims are based on documents from the US Commerce Department, according to which Li Ka Shing obtained permission to build his \$2 billion Oriental Plaza in Beijing's prime Wangfujing area because of those special connections; these relations were also said to have played a part in the swift arrest and execution in China of the man responsible for the 1996 kidnapping of Li Ka Shing's son, Victor. Furthermore, Hutchison Whampoa's operation of port facilities in Panama and the Bahamas was reported to favour the illegal traffic of drugs, arms and secret military equipment between the United States and China. The China International Trust and Investment Company (CITIC), a Beijing-based firm formed by Li Ka Shing in partnership with purported Triad members, Robert Kwok and Henry Fok, was also singled out by a Rand Corporation report as a front for Poly Technologies Inc, a weapons manufacturer owned directly by the Chinese People's Liberation Army (PLA).

That is why, between 2002 and 2003, when Li Ka Shing attempted to purchase Global Crossing, the largest US telecom company then in bankruptcy protection, his offer was rebuffed, partly owing to opposition from Congress. A national security adviser even remarked, 'The purchase of Global Crossing by Li Ka Shing is another step in his role of a stalker for the People's Republic of China' (Smith, 2002a, 2002b, 2003a, 2003b). The insistence of Hutchison spokeswoman Laura Cheung that 'the Chinese government doesn't have any official on our board, and therefore has no influence at all over our business' was to no avail, and simply received this reply: 'Since when does one have to sit on a board of a company to exert influence?' (Smith, 2003b). David Chu, a human rights advocate who supports the boycott of Chinese goods rejoins, 'All that the dictators in Beijing need to do is to threaten Li Ka Shing in no uncertain terms. Do people honestly believe that he wouldn't accommodate their requests, as if he hasn't already? Li Ka Shing operates from Hong Kong that is now part of the Motherland, Communist China' (Smith, 2003b).

Li Ka Shing's ties to Beijing are well known in public. He advised Deng Xiaoping during the Sino-British talks leading to the 1984 Joint Declaration on Hong Kong's future, and afterwards, between 1985 and 1990, he was a member of the Drafting Committee for the Basic Law of the Hong Kong Special Administrative Region. Deng Xiaoping himself was said to have invited Li Ka Shing to the board of directors of CITIC, the firm that spearheaded the country's economic reform initiatives. He accepted, albeit only for a year. CITIC is China's largest conglomerate and the government's chief investment arm. While 42 per cent of CITIC is owned by the government, its leader holds ministry status on the Chinese State Council (Wikipedia, 2006c). The subsequent changes of guard in Beijing have not affected Li Ka Shing's privileged relationship, as he was known to talk directly with President Jiang Zemin and Premier Zhu Rongji. At present, there are no reasons to think of ties with President Hu Jintao and Prime Minister Wen Jiabao having loosened either. But in any case, it does not seem reasonable to conclude that Li Ka Shing was able to build his extensive business empire purely on the basis of enjoying Beijing's favour or by following directives from the Chinese communist party. After all, more than 80 per cent of the Group's total profit comes from overseas, not China (Li Ka Shing, 2005).

Li Ka Shing has always been loyal to Hong Kong and this has served him well, even financially. Despite the Red Guard-induced jitters in 1967, for example, his companies reported 50 per cent more profits than usual that year (Li Ka Shing, 2006). That experience encouraged him to continue to invest in properties in spite of the bank runs in the 1960s, the Thatcher visit to China in 1982, and other tumultuous events. The political turmoil in 1989 corresponding to the Tiananmen massacre, however, prompted him to withdraw from a HK$10 billion investment and made people think that he would leave Hong Kong altogether. 'Many of our local and overseas partners, even our own directors, urged me to take our company registration overseas. But I refused. [. . .] I told everyone during a meeting that if they want to move, they first have to remove me as chairman. Of course, no one mentioned this topic again. [. . .] I said we would withdraw from this one single project, but I also said that Hong Kong would remain the base for our Group and that we would continue to make other investments' (Li Ka Shing, 1999).

Regarding China, there is of course the possibility that what critics perceive to be kowtowing to government's demands may simply be an offshoot of Li Ka Shing's patriotism and desire to help in the development of his own country. What is more, neither is his love for China necessarily at odds with his commitment to democracy and the rule of law. His strategy of engagement may even be more effective, in fact, than that of confrontation favoured by many. 'I am Chinese and I have a great love for my country. I more cherish democratic and humanistic values; they are dear to my heart. The first time I returned to China was in 1977. My activities on the mainland were primarily charity-related. It wasn't until the early 1990s, when Deng Xiaoping made his famous southern tour and committed the country on the path to further reform and opening-up policies that we commenced venturing into China. [. . .] The Chinese economy has grown significantly over the years. Following its accession to the WTO [World Trade Organization], commercial activities have become better regulated, falling in line with international standards. It is certainly very encouraging, and our Group will continue to explore new opportunities on the mainland' (Li Ka Shing, 2002).

Proof of the internationalization of business standards is the diminishing importance of Guanxi or the kind of preferential relationships used in forming and getting around the so-called 'bamboo network'. As Li Ka Shing observes, at present 'many properties are being auctioned publicly. Cheung Kong and Hutchison have acquired many property projects in China through an auction process. China has made good progress in this area. Did you see any property auctions ten years ago? Now 90 per cent of our land bank is acquired from auctions' (Li Ka Shing, 2006).

By 2006, Li Ka Shing had invested over $15 billion in infrastructure (highways, power stations, bridges, a container terminal) and different kinds of real estate ventures in China. He continues to be confident that greater improvements would materialize, although he asks for a little more patience: 'It takes time. 1.3 billion people. 30 or 40 years ago, there was no contact with the outside world. Now the Government is trying very hard to improve the rule of law, including commercial law' (Li Ka Shing, 2006). And when asked recently about his vision for China, Li Ka Shing related the following story. 'In 1978, when I was in China, I went to see some friends in the guesthouse. They would write notes to me because they were afraid of being eavesdropped. They had been scared by the Cultural Revolution. Today they can openly criticize the Government. I love democracy, but I also understand that different countries and peoples have

different values. However, democracy without law and order is no democracy. We have many investments in democratic countries. A liberal society
has to be founded not only on law and order but [also on] a prosperous
economy' (Li Ka Shing, 2006).

On the twin issues of direct elections for Hong Kong's chief executive in
2007 and for the whole of its legislature in 2008, Li Ka Shing has publicly
advocated a cautious, step-by-step approach. 'We cannot afford to have
instability in Hong Kong. We have to act for the true benefit of Hong
Kong's future. People should not pull any stunt for votes. [. . .] We should
take things gradually, one step at a time. If we rush into things and get emotional, usually it will lead to unexpected mistakes' (Kyodo, 2004). His
remarks would have been gravely suspicious had they not coincided, in substance, with those of Donald Tsang, Hong Kong's Chief Secretary for
Administration: 'If Hong Kong takes a shortcut by putting forward proposals hastily and unilaterally, it will breach its constitutional obligation
that discussion on matters relating to constitutional development must be
held with the central authorities. In political reality, if concrete proposals
put forward in future do not go in line with the principles of the Basic Law,
it will deal a blow to the local community and give rise to more controver-
sies. In the end, it is the people of Hong Kong who suffer' (Kyodo, 2004).

If Li Ka Shing's style of corporate governance truly is an example of
monarchy, that is, one in which a single ruler seeks the common good above
all, what are we to make of his insider trading conviction in 1987 (Nohria
and Gurtler, 2005)? A Hong Kong Tribunal declared that Li Ka Shing and
Wang Guangying, one of his associates belonging to a prominent Chinese
family with close connections to Beijing, engaged in transactions with no
other purpose than to drive up the shares of International City Holdings,
one of the Group's companies. Although the ruling had no jail sentence or
fine attached, Li Ka Shing brought the case on appeal to the Hong Kong
High Court, if only to clear his name. Yet the Court maintained the previous ruling, which found Li Ka Shing guilty, although the judge admittedly
stated that culpability 'need not be equated to a finding of dishonesty or
fraud' (Nohria and Gurtler, 2005).

In 2006, the controversial sale of a major stake in Pacific Century
CyberWorks (PCCW), Hong Kong's dominant telecommunications firm,
cast another cloud on Li Ka Shing's reputation (*South China Morning Post*,
2006). In July of that year, Richard Li Tzar Kai, Li Ka Shing's second son
and chairman of PCCW, announced the sale of a 22.66 per cent stake in
the company to Francis Leung Pak To for $1.17 billion. This amount was
far below offers for as much as $7 billion coming from Australia and the
United States. The rejection was widely interpreted as the result of objections by state-owned China Netcom, PCCW's second-largest shareholder,

over sensitive assets falling into the hands of foreigners. In early November, however, Francis Leung Pak To finally revealed the identity of the main buyers for whom he was fronting. They were none other than Li Ka Shing – injecting $622 million from his charity funds for a 12 per cent stake – and Telefónica of Spain. When asked for a comment, Li Ka Shing simply refused and said, 'The Foundation has invested in a lot of companies with good returns and they are 100 per cent for charity. One of the items is almost five times bigger than the PCCW investment. This matter is over' (Li Ka Shing, 2006). It also emerged that China Netcom had entered into an alliance with Telefónica, raising its equity stakes to 27.97 per cent of the ailing company.

That was not the first time that Richard Li Tzar Kai occasioned his father trouble and embarrassment. In 2000, he used inflated stock from PCCW (then an Internet firm) to buy Hong Kong's dominant phone company for $28 billion. Yet his vision for the world's largest broadband Internet business imploded, together with the hi-tech bubble (Schuman, 2004). In July 2003, Richard Li Tzar Kai turned over the job of CEO to a former manager of Hong Kong's subway system and, by August, the share price had plunged to its lowest level, at 97 per cent from its peak.

So there may have been some amount of fatherly pride trying to buy out a son's reputation that lay in tatters because of the PCCW affair. But that certainly is no excuse for possible violations of market regulations and minority shareholder rights, although the ones affected are mainly the investors of PCCW, not those of Cheung Kong or Hutchison Whampoa.

These blemishes on Li Ka Shing's reputation may be what hurt him most, for, as he himself says, 'The most important thing is to build the best reputation. Anytime I say "yes" to someone, it is a contract' (Li Ka Shing, 2006). He then backs up the lesson with an anecdote. 'In 1956, when I was in the plastics business, my first order was for a three to six month production. I calculated a profit of 20 per cent. My competitors were making 100 per cent profit. A large US competitor of my buyer approached me and offered to pay me an extra 30 per cent profit for the merchandise my buyer had ordered. He said that, with the extra profit, I could expand my factory. I said, "Look, I am also a businessman. I'll make a deal with you. I will start another factory in nine months' time, a much bigger one, and I will take your order. But this time I have already promised this buyer, and I will finish the order for him as I am his only supplier." I did not tell my buyer this story but he learned it from elsewhere. So when the buyer came to Hong Kong, he humoured me and said that he thought I would be bankrupt by now. He said, "Why didn't you take the extra profit from my competitor?" I said, "I already promised you." He said, "but at least you could have told me and requested a price increase." I said, "Next time, I will increase the price."

After that we became even better friends, even after I quit the plastics business. Reputation is the key to success. You have to be loyal to your customers' (Li Ka Shing, 2006).

Li Ka Shing likewise insists on treating people with honesty and sincerity, rather than just banking on charisma, to keep an organization together. 'If you are not honest and sincere, people will leave you sooner or later. A company is built on the efforts of many individuals, and not just on one person. A single individual cannot accomplish much. In the Han Dynasty, Xiang Yu was very brave and won many battles, but in the end he failed. You can't succeed on charisma alone. Treat people with sincerity and build a good organization. Otherwise it doesn't matter how famous or how capable you are. A company needs a good structure, good organization, and good people. If everyone works in concert, then you can succeed' (Li Ka Shing, 2001).

Li Ka Shing also makes a strong case for leading a simple, frugal life. He confesses that his standard of living has not risen for the past 40 years, that he still sports an inexpensive watch (albeit 20 minutes fast) and wears the same practical, durable shoes (Li Ka Shing, 1999, 2002). Such a lifestyle has actually helped him achieve the best results and returns for his shareholders. This illustrates a contrast even with traditional Chinese thinking that regards merchants and traders as being the lowest among social classes, behind mandarins, farmers and labourers, because of their opportunism and profiteering. Citing the historian Sima Quian, he says that merchants serve society by distributing resources, managing risks and using capital efficiently. While it is true that many business people sacrifice their moral integrity for the bottom line, the majority understands 'that social progress requires courage, hard work and perseverance; more importantly, they know that a fair and equitable society is built on trust and integrity' (Li Ka Shing, 2004).

To be sure, in spite of his undeniable errors and false steps, Li Ka Shing continues to be the most admired person in Hong Kong for ten years running (Li Ka Shing, 2005). He once donated some personal effects to an auction conducted by a volunteer youth group in order to raise funds. Leather wallets bearing his signature were sold for $8888 each and ties fetched up to $3888 apiece. Bidders believe that Li Ka Shing's belongings could bring them good fortune. 'Your life is meaningful if you can honestly say that you have done your best to do some good' (Li Ka Shing, 2005).

In evaluating the particular corporate governance style Li Ka Shing has imprinted on his business empire, we have chosen to examine factors such as growth and profitability, employee satisfaction, philanthropic activities and other virtues or values that its chairman manifests, always in relation to the concentration of power and the common good. This does not mean, however, that a more conventional examination based on a compliance checklist of the usual corporate governance issues (information disclosure and transparency, board structure and board committees, code of conduct, and so forth) and corporate social responsibility issues cannot be effected (Shea, 2006). What is striking is that, even through a different route, one could reach the same conclusion. Family firms with dominant shareholders, of which Li Ka Shing's conglomerates are sound examples, could also adopt good corporate governance and social responsibility practices while keeping the family interest alive and the business prosperous (Sycip, 2003). In other words, the 'faults' regularly attributed to family firms, such as the non-separation of ownership and management, the dearth of professional managers and the exploitation of minority shareholders, are not always true, nor are they insurmountable.

III   ONE MAN RULES

A more detailed reading of Aristotle's *Politics* reveals that, apart from the fundamental division between a monarchy and a tyranny – depending on whether the single ruler pursues the common good or a private good – there are further subcategories for each and even crossovers between the two.

Initially, Aristotle considers up to five different kinds of monarchies or kingships (Pltcs, 1285a–b). The first one, which he attributes to the Lacedaemonians, consists in having a hereditary and life-long sovereign power. This power, however, is not absolute: the sovereign does not have power over the life and death of his subjects except in particular cases, as in a military campaign, for example. His rule is more akin to that of a generalship. The second version is similar to the first in that it is also hereditary and found among foreigners, particularly, among those who are 'by nature slaves' and thus tolerate a 'legitimate despot'. There is no danger here of the king being overthrown, and he is guarded, not by mercenaries, but by fellow citizens. The third one is said to be prevalent among the Aesmynetes. It comprises an elective tyranny, either for life or for a set number of years, until certain duties are fulfilled; nonetheless, it is legitimate because the subjects acquiesce in it. The fourth refers to a monarchy as established during Heroic times; one that was hereditary, legal and exercised over willing subjects. In this system, the first kings were originally benefactors of their subjects. In exchange for their good deeds, these benefactors were allowed to take command in war, preside over sacrifices or decide in lawsuits. Subsequently, these kings either relinquished some of these privileges, retaining only a few, or their subjects took these prerogatives back from them. Lastly, there is the absolute monarchy where one man has the entire state at his disposal, just like the father over his household.

On the other hand, when dealing with the different kinds of tyrannies, Aristotle enumerates three, although he admits that the first two correspond to types two ('foreign kingship') and three (Aesmynete) among the monarchies: these are 'royal, in so far as the monarch rules according to law over willing subjects; but they are tyrannical in so far as he is despotic and rules according to his own fancy' (Pltcs, 1295a). Only the third kind of tyranny is without mixture and as such is a worthy counterpart of the perfect monarchy: 'This tyranny is just that arbitrary power of an individual which is responsible to no one, and governs all alike, whether equals or betters, with a view to its own advantage; not to that of its subjects, and therefore against their will. No freeman willingly endures such a government' (Pltcs, 1295a).

We can see from the foregoing how difficult it is to distinguish a monarchy from a tyranny except in their pure forms. This should serve as a reminder whenever we have to classify corporations under these categories according to their manner of corporate governance, for it is nearly impossible that they exemplify either an absolute monarchy or an absolute tyranny. However, the criterion of whether the common good of the corporate citizens or the private good of the lone ruler comes first should hold its rightful place in our discernment, notwithstanding its difficulty. Hence our attempt with Fiat under the Agnellis and with Li Ka Shing's holdings. For this we will have to look not only into the ruler's actions but also into his intentions and motives, and the manner in which he realizes them. Under closer scrutiny, what apparently is a form of monarchy could very well turn out to be a form of tyranny, or the reverse.

There are several factors which could explain the crossovers between monarchies and tyrannies. One depends on the 'nature' of the subjects themselves, on their 'natural drift' towards slavishness, on the one hand, or liberty and freedom, on the other. Hence, a people could actually legitimize a despot or tyrant to rule over them, either by putting up no resistance or by actively desiring it. Such a regime would be legal – in the sense that it would be in accordance with law – although it would not be just, because it would be contrary to the common good and utterly dependent on the tyrant's fancy. A government's being monarchical or tyrannical thus also depends on the understanding of law in a particular case. Analogically, to distinguish between a corporate monarchy and a corporate tyranny, it would not be enough to study the ruler's actions; it would also be necessary to examine the attitudes of the other corporate members and their notion of the law.

Not only could there be confusion between monarchies and tyrannies, but also, regimes could evolve from one form of monarchy into another;

and the same holds true with tyrannies. With regard to corporations, it is fairly frequent that they begin as absolute monarchies, especially if they are family firms, since clearly defined boundaries between family and business at the start hardly makes sense. The founder gains precedence over family and non-family firm members, that is, over the corporate citizens, insofar as he proves beneficial to them, just as in heroic monarchies. Gladly would the people cede decision making and executive powers as well as honours; they may even agree to make the position hereditary, as long as they see the monarch and his offspring work to their advantage.

Yet a wise monarch would guard against his own weakness by institutionalizing limits to his own power through the instrument of law; a foolish one would abuse his privileges, turning the law into his servant, then being well on his way to becoming a tyrant. In the corporate context, a founding chairman could either adopt good corporate governance measures or simply ignore them, enjoining his family heir and corporate successor to do the same. Concurrently, people with a natural drift towards freedom could take legal measures that would prevent their monarch from turning into a tyrant, while those who are by nature slavish would do none of this but simply allow the despot to reign over them. Within firms, members of the corporate community may decide to be actively involved in the running of the enterprise as befits free and rational agents, or they may resign themselves to passively receiving profits, without supervising management or intervening in governance, as is proper of slaves.

A heroic monarchy could then evolve, in the better of cases, into a Lacedaemonian or a foreign one, which are both hereditary yet somewhat limited in their powers, by certain laws or circumstances or by the nature of the subjects themselves. Another possibility is the Aesmynete solution, which is an elective tyranny, not a hereditary one. These regimes are reflected in the governance codes that corporations adopt, specifically in what refers to nomination, succession, compliance, audit and compensation functions. Research has shown, for example, that a founder's decision to leave management to a professional or to an heir depends on the prevailing legal environment: legal regimes with strong minority shareholder protection favour professionalization, those with intermediate protection resort to a professional but with the family staying on to monitor the manager, while those with weak protection normally keep control and ownership within the family (Panunzi, Burkart and Shleifer, 2002). The worst case is, of course, that a heroic monarchy degenerate into a complete and absolute tyranny. This occurs with an emasculated board that exercises no supervision over management whatsoever because of passivity, fear or corruption.

In this discussion on monarchies and tyrannies, the background issue seems to be whether it is better for a man or for the law to govern (Pltcs,

1286a). An individual is able to deliberate and decide on particular cases, while the law only speaks in general terms; yet, while a ruler cannot be entirely free from passion, the law is without passion and listens to reason alone. In theory, the optimum solution is that the best man legislate and pass the best law, but how are we to know who the best man is? Even if we did in a particular instance, could nature guarantee the heritability of this trait? Perhaps that would be too much to ask of human nature (Pltcs, 1286b).

Therefore, neither the best man nor the best law is, by itself, sufficient to govern, and even the best man has need of others to do so effectively. Aristotle advocates the rule of law rather than the rule of the individual and, among laws, he deems customary laws to be more important than written laws. In fact, in the end he even admits that 'a man may be a safer ruler than the written law, but no safer than the customary law' (Pltcs, 1287b). And, as for the excellent man's need for others to assist him in governing, he says: 'the good man has a right to rule because he is better, still two good men are better than one' (Pltcs, 1287b).

Therefore, although a monarchy may be defensible as the best regime in theory, it does not play out as such in practice. And the best way a monarchy is preserved is through the limitation of the ruler's powers, by written laws and by unwritten customs. Ultimately, however, it is from the integrity of character of both rulers and subjects that those laws and customs draw strength.

IV   IN BRIEF

- An analogy could be drawn between states and corporations on the basis of their regimes or constitutions. Aristotle's classification of political regimes depending on whether they aim at the common good ('constitutional') or not ('despotic') as well as on the number of rulers (among constitutional regimes, a monarchy, when there is one, an aristocracy, when there are a few, and a constitutional rule or polity, when there are many; among despotic regimes, a tyranny, when there is one, an oligarchy, when there are a few, and a democracy, when there are many) could also apply to corporations. Hence we could speak of corporate monarchies and tyrannies, corporate aristocracies and oligarchies, corporate polities and democracies.
- The corporate governance of Fiat under the Agnellis could be considered an example of a corporate tyranny. Power is concentrated in the hands of just one man whose overriding concern is to keep the control of the conglomerate within the Agnelli family. This objective has been maintained throughout Fiat's history despite periods of regency by professional managers. Because of this, the good of the

other members of the corporate polity – other shareholders outside of the Agnellis, Fiat workers, alliance partners such as GM, Italian society and even the Italian state, among others – have been relegated to a distant second place. It is not that the interests of these other groups have never been served; it is just that they have always come after the private good of the Agnellis' continuance in power.

• By contrast, the corporate governance of Cheung Kong Holdings and Hutchison Whampoa Limited under Li Ka Shing could be likened to a corporate monarchy. Once again, decision-making power and authority are concentrated in their imperial Chairman (and, in the case of Cheung Kong, founder) Li Ka Shing. Yet, apparently, great care has been taken to harmonize family concerns (eldest son Victor Li Tzar Kuoi is his heir apparent) with the good of the other members of the corporate polity, such as shareholders, who get good returns on their investments, professional managers, whose low turnover rates indicate high job satisfaction, and the Hong Kong community and Chinese society at large, which benefits from Li Ka Shing's philanthropy. Certainly, Li Ka Shing has made his share of errors, as with the insider trading conviction, for instance. However, when put in overall context, this seems to be but a minor blemish on his reputation, for he continues to be the most admired person in Hong Kong.

• In theory, the concentration of power in the hands of a single individual by itself should not discredit a governance regime, be it in a political or in a corporate context. That is why we distinguish between monarchies and tyrannies, and their various subtypes. In practice, however, Aristotle advocates the rule of law, which he equates to the rule of reason, rather than the rule of man, which is subject to the disturbing influence of passion. Within law, he grants greater importance to customary law over written law. Aristotle also favours placing limits to the power of royalty, either through law or through other people who assist the monarch in the task of government. Furthermore, it is not only the nature of the ruler, but also the nature of the ruled, that has to be considered, whether it is slavish or free. In consequence, the determining factor in a good one man rule is the excellence of the moral character of both the ruler and the ruled, which necessarily leaves its mark in law as well as in custom.

REFERENCES

Achtner, Wolfgang (1995), 'The tough cop takes the wheel; profile; Cesare Romiti', *The (London) Independent*, 17 December.

Achtner, Wolfgang (2003), 'Obituary: Gianni Agnelli', *The (London) Independent*, 25 January.

Aristotle (1990), *The Politics*, ed. Stephen Everson, Cambridge: Cambridge University Press.

Arnold, James (2003), 'Gianni Agnelli: a troubled tycoon', BBC News, 24 January, http://bbc.co.uk/1/hi/business/2690547.stm (accessed 27 November 2006).

Automotive News Europe (2005), 'Talk from the top. Marchionne says Fiat is now market-oriented', 14 November.

BBC News (1997), 'World: Europe. Fiat heir dies at 33', BBC News, 14 December, http://bbc.co.uk/2/hi/europe/39500.stm (accessed 27 November 2006).

BBC News (2003), 'Agnelli's brother to head Fiat', BBC News, 25 February, http: // bbc.co.uk/go/pr/fr/-/1/hi/business/2799553.stm (accessed 27 November 2006).

BBC News (2004a), 'Fiat shares slide after shake-up', BBC News, 31 May, http: // bbc.co.uk/go/pr/fr/-/2/hi/business/3763373.stm (accessed 27 November 2006).

BBC News (2004b), 'Fiat boss Umberto Agnelli dies', BBC News, 28 May, http: // news.bbc.co.uk/go/pr/fr/-/1/hi/business/3756043.stm (accessed 27 November).

Biscaretti di Ruffia, Carlo (1952), 'Orígenes, Nacimiento y Primeros Pasos de la Fiat', in *Los Cincuenta Años de la Fiat*, Milan: Arnoldo Mondadori Editore.

Cheung Kong Holdings Limited (2006), 'Group structure', *About Cheung Kong Holdings*, www.ckh.com.hk/eng/about/about_group.htm (accessed 10 January 2007).

CNN (2003), 'Umberto to take wheel at Fiat', *CNN.com*, 26 February, http: //edition.cnn.com/2003/BUSINESS/02/26/fiat/index.html. (accessed 27 November 2006).

Donlon, J.P. (1998), 'Fiat looks for its global gear – interview with Fiat CEO Paolo Cantarella', *The Chief Executive*, April.

The Economist (1997), 'Free the Turin two', 24 April.

The Economist (1998), 'Driven by fiat', 23 April.

The Economist (2000), 'In search of Fiat's soul', 1 June.

The Economist (2002a), 'Running on empty', 30 May.

The Economist (2002b), 'Ciao, Paolo', 13 June.

The Economist (2002c), 'Fiat redux', 10 October.

The Economist (2002d), 'Under siege', 17 October.

The Economist (2002e), 'Imbroglio', 12 December.

The Economist (2003a), 'The boss as Superman', 9 January.

The Economist (2003b), 'The party's over', 30 January.

The Economist (2004a), 'Putting Italy back on the podium', 20 May.

The Economist (2004b), 'Divorce Italian-style', 9 December.

The Economist (2005a), 'Valentine's Day divorce', 17 February.

The Economist (2005b), 'Still in the driving seat', 13 October.

The Economist (2005c), 'Saving Fiat', 1 December.

The Economist (2006), 'Fading family firms', 22 May.

Fairbank, John King (1987), *The Great Chinese Revolution 1800–1985*, New York: Harper & Row.

Fiat (2006), 'History of Fiat', *The Fiat Brand*, www.fiat.com/cgi-bin/pbrand.dll/FIAT_COM/fbrand/fbrand.jsp?BV_SessionID=@@@@1096381272.1166090543 @@@@&BV_EngineID=cccfaddjjdjelglcefecejgdfiidgnj.0&categoryOID=-1073765237&contentOID=1073903999 (accessed 14 December 2006).

Forbes (2006), '#10 Li Ka Shing', The World's Richest People, *Forbes.com*, www.forbes.com/lists/2006/10/SO0W.html (accessed 9 January 2007).

Friedman, Alan (1989), *Agnelli and the Italian Network of Power*, London: Mandarin Paperbacks.

Gumbel, Andrew (1995), 'Agnelli to step down at Fiat', *The (London) Independent*, 12 December.

Gumbel, Andrew (1996a), 'Ciao Gianni, but now what?', *The (London) Independent*, 29 February.

Gumbel, Andrew (1996b), 'Agnelli hands over the reins at Fiat', *The (London) Independent*, 29 February.

Gumbel, Andrew (1997), 'A battle against sticky hands', *The (London) Independent*, 18 May.

Hutchison Whampoa Limited (2006), 'Group structure', *About Hutchison Whampoa Limited*, www.hutchison-whampoa.com/eng/about/structure/structure.htm (accessed 10 January 2007).

Infoplease (2006), *Agnelli*, http://infoplease.com/ce6/people/A0932910.html (accessed 27 November 2006).

Institutional Investor (2006), 'Sergio Marchionne of Fiat Group. Getting back in gear', 17–18 April.

Israely, Jeff (2003), 'The end of the road', *Time Europe*, **161** (5) 3 February.

Italiancar (2006), *Fiat*, www.italiancar.net/site/cars/fiat/index/fiat3.html (accessed 27 November 2006).

Kahn, Gabriel (2005), 'Fiat CEO says major surgery drives revival', *The Wall Street Journal Europe*, 4 November.

Kyodo (2004), 'H.K. businessman Li Ka-shing opposes direct elections in 2007', *Asian Economic News*, 22 March, http://findarticles.com/p/articles/mi_m0WDP/is_2004_March_22/ai_114484605 (accessed 10 January 2007).

Li Ka Shing (1999), 'Create a new legend (Yazhou zhoukan)', *Li Ka Shing Foundation*, www.lksf.org/eng/media/interview/print/19990621.shtml (accessed 9 January 2007).

Li Ka Shing (2000), 'A new fraternity', *Li Ka Shing Foundation*, www.lksf.org/eng/media/speech/print/20000606.shtml (accessed 9 January 2007).

Li Ka Shing (2001), 'On corporate strategy. Shantou University Business School Economic Forum', *Li Ka Shing Foundation*, www.lksf.org/eng/media/interview/print/20010517.shtml (accessed 9 January 2007).

Li Ka Shing (2002), 'Bloomberg Markets interviews Mr. Li Ka Shing', *Li Ka Shing Foundation*, www.lksf.org/eng/media/interview/print/20021222.shtml (accessed 9 January 2007).

Li Ka Shing (2004), 'The Art of Giving', *Li Ka Shing Foundation*, www.lksf.org/eng/media/speech/print/20040628.shtml (accessed 9 January 2007).

Li Ka Shing (2005), 'The third son also rises (Yazhou Zhoukan)', *Li Ka Shing Foundation*, www.lksf.org/eng/media/interview/print/20050206.shtml (accessed 9 January 2007).

Li Ka Shing (2006), 'Forbes interview Mr. Li Ka Shing', *Li Ka Shing Foundation*, www.lksf.org/eng/media/interview/print/20061204.shtml (accessed 9 January 2007).

Mackintosh, James (2006), 'The impetus behind a move into higher gear', *Financial Times*, 22 May.

Montani, Gianni (2004), 'Obituary. Umberto Agnelli, Italy's first family mourns again', Forbes.com, 28 May (accessed 15 December 2006).

Morck, Randall and Bernard Yeung (2004), 'Special issues relating to corporate governance and family control', *World Bank Policy Research Working Paper*, no. 3406, September.

El Mundo (2006), 'Marchionne rectifica y dice que seguirá en Fiat Auto hasta 2010', 22 December.

Nohria, Nitin and Bridget Gurtler (2005), 'Li Ka Shing', *Harvard Business School Case*, 9-405-026, Rev. December 19.

Pagano, Ugo and Sandro Trento (2002), 'Continuity and change in Italian corporate governance: the institutional stability of one variety of capitalism', *Quaderni. Dipartamento di Economia Politica. Università degli Studi di Siena*, no. 366, September.

Panunzi, Fausto, Mike C. Burkart and Andrei Shleifer (2002), 'Family firms', *Fondazione Eni Enrico Mattei FEEM Working Paper*, no. 74.2002/ *Institute of Economic Research Harvard University Paper*, no. 1944/ *Social Science Research Network Electronic Paper Collection*, http://papers.ssrn.com/abstract_id= 298631.

Perini, Giancarlo (1989), 'Fiat's Romiti era begins – Cesare Romiti', *Ward's Auto World*, January.

Popham, Peter (2003), 'Business analysis: Fiat drives ahead with £13M plan', *The (London) Independent*, 27 June.

Pu Yi, Aisin Gioro (2000), *From Emperor to Citizen*, Beijing: Foreign Languages Press.

Quadrone, Ernesto (1952), 'El hombre que no habría tenido tiempo', in *Los Cincuenta Años de la Fiat*, Milan: Arnoldo Mondadori Editore.

Schuman, Michael (2004), 'The families that own Asia. The Lis', *Time Magazine*, 16 February, www.time.com/time/magazine/article/0,9171,591367,00.html (accessed 11 January 2007).

Shea, Hubert (2006), 'Corporate governance and social responsibility of family firms in Hong Kong: a case study of Hutchison Whampoa Limited (HWL)', University of Newcastle, Graduate School of Business and Law, http:// papers.ssrn.com/sol3/papers.cfm?abstract_id=935101 (accessed 10 January 2007).

Smith, Charles (2000), 'Cash register' Li Ka Shing, *WorldNetDaily*, 7 June, www.worldnetdaily.com/news/article.asp?ARTICLE_ID=20569 (accessed 10 January 2007).

Smith, Charles (2002a), 'Chinese billionaire wants global crossing', *NewsMax*, 11 February, www.newsmax.com/archives/articles/2002/2/11/184102.shtml (accessed 10 January 2007).

Smith (2002b), 'Li Ka Shing seeks U.S. contract', *NewsMax*, 6 August, www. newsmax.com/archives/articles/2002/8/5/181935.shtml (accessed 10 January 2007).

Smith (2003a), 'Global double crossing', *NewsMax*, 27 February, www.newsmax. com/archives/articles/2003/2/26/182009.shtml (accessed 10 January 2007).

Smith (2003b), 'Billionaire fails in bid for global crossing', *NewsMax*, 6 March, www.newsmax.com/archives/articles/2003/3/5/162452.shtml (accessed 10 January 2007).

South China Morning Post (2006), 'Hong Kong: PCCW sale raises hackles over corporate governance', 20 November, http://asiamedia.ucla.edu/article.asp? parentid=57999 (accessed 9 January 2007).

Spence, Jonathan D. (1982), *The Gate of Heavenly Peace: The Chinese and Their Revolution*, New York: Penguin Books.

Sycip, Washington (2003), 'Managing corporate governance in Asia', *Finance India*, **17**(4), 1389–97.

Time Asia (2000), 'The rise and rise of the Li dynasty', *Time Asia*, **155**(10), 13 March, http://time.com/time/asia/magazine/2000/0313/cover/timeline.html (accessed 11 January 2007).

Wikipedia (2006a), *Fiat*, http://en.wikipedia.org/wiki/Fiat (accessed 27 November 2006).

Wikipedia (2006b), *Gianni Agnelli*, http://en.wikipedia.org/wiki/Gianni_Agnelli (accessed 27 November 2006).

Wikipedia (2006c), *Li Ka Shing*, http://en.wikipedia.org/wiki/Li_Ka_Shing (accessed 9 January 2007).

6.   A few good men?

Let us now consider aristocratic and oligarchical corporate governance regimes. We may recall from Aristotle's *Politics* that aristocracies and oligarchies are similar because, in both of them, only a few people rule; on the other hand, they differ from each other in that aristocracies are a form of 'true' or 'constitutional' rules wherein the common good presides, while oligarchies are 'defective' or 'perverted' rules in which private interests predominate (Pltcs, 1279a–b). From the viewpoint of the rulers themselves we are also told that the few who rule in aristocracies are the 'best' in terms of merit and qualifications, whereas, in oligarchies, they are simply the wealthier ones. The two may be said to have the same idea of justice, according to which those who are unequal in one respect – say merit or wealth – should be treated unequally in all others, including the distribution of tasks, duties, honours and privileges within the state (Pltcs, 1280a). Perhaps a few good (or wealthy) men would be enough to run not only a state but also a company properly.

In the following we shall see how these two models apply to different corporations. Likewise we shall look into their particular strengths and weaknesses. It would be quite surprising to discover just how many of these advantages and disadvantages, dangers and challenges have already been somewhat foreshadowed in Aristotle's treatise on government, despite the difference in context.

I   WHEN EVEN TWO IS TOO MUCH: THE SIMON SIBLINGS AT AIMC

David Simon was barely in his thirties when he had no choice but to assume the presidency of Abelardo Investment and Manufacturing Corporation (AIMC), the family-owned holding firm, in 1968 (Ty, 1999: 31). He started out working as a warehouse checker and was currently occupying the post of Assistant Treasurer of the Abelardo Flour Mills, helping his mother Bernarda out in the overall running of AIMC, when the new appointment came. The trigger for all of these changes was the serious stroke that his father Abelardo suffered the year before, in 1967. Never again would Abelardo return to manage the business.

At that moment, AIMC's affairs were in frank disarray, with motley investments in automotive assembly and distribution (Abelardo Motor Corporation), insurance (Abelardo Insurance Company), finance (Abelardo Bank and Trust Company, Abelardo Finance Corporation, Kosme Bank of Manila) and wood products (Green Wood Industries Corporation), apart from real estate (AIMC, formerly Abelardo Realty Corporation) and milling (Bernarda Papel Mill and AIMC's flour milling activities, the holding company's flagship) (Ty, 1999: 30–31). Besides, David found that the family had to pay off several bad loans of his father's friends, since Abelardo had guaranteed them. There were also economic obligations to be met arising from the needs of Abelardo's distant relatives, immigrants from China, whom he supported. For all of these reasons Xavier, David's step-brother born of his father's first marriage in China, decided to claim his inheritance and was given Abelardo Bank and Trust.

Abelardo first came to the Philippines from China in 1930, as a young man in his teens wanting to explore the possibilities of earning a decent livelihood (Ty, 1999: 26). A relative who ran a trading business took him in and offered him his first job. Soon afterwards, however, he was recalled to China to get married to Xavier's mother.

Abelardo returned to the Philippines a few years later. This time around, he worked as a salesman for a textile company based in the Divisoria district of Manila. That was how he met his second wife, Bernarda, who tended a store in the Yangco market. Bernarda was the second daughter of a widow with eight children. She started working right after her eldest sister married in order to help the family with its finances. Although, apparently, Bernarda had many suitors, her mother chose Abelardo to be her future son-in-law because she found him 'courteous, hard-working and responsible' (Ty, 1999: 27).

Abelardo and Bernarda wed in 1936, and the entrepreneurial couple decided to resign from their respective jobs and to set up the Abelardo Company instead, engaged in the wholesale and retail of imported textiles. The business prospered, with Abelardo providing the 'vision' and Bernarda, the necessary 'revision'. He had a knack for spotting opportunities while she put in hard work and perseverance, not to mention the needed financing on favourable terms from various banks, thanks to her good credit standing. World War II brought along with it textile stock confiscation, yet nevertheless, the couple was able to pull through. After the liberation from the Japanese forces, Bernarda's good reputation once more came in handy to take advantage of new credit lines, bank loans and merchandise on consignment. By the time an import control law came into effect in the 1950s, Abelardo and Bernarda then had a huge inventory of textiles. This brought the business substantial profits.

Meanwhile, on the more personal front, between 1937 and 1951, Bernarda gave birth to ten children, five boys and five girls: Carmen, David, Ernesto, Fatima, Gloria, Horacio, Imelda, Jasmin, Kosme and Luis (Ty, 1999: 27–8). However, the ten children never became close as a group. That Carmen and David spent their childhood with their maternal grandmother, Soledad, whereas the rest of their siblings stayed under the care of their maternal grand-aunt and Soledad's sister, Victoria, may have had something to do with this. Instead, the children on the whole tended to bond according to age. Carmen, the eldest of the brood, exhibited a strong personality and clearly enjoyed preferential treatment from the family adults that made her sisters jealous. David, the eldest boy, was considered to be the most reliable, trustworthy and responsible among the siblings. Ernesto was generally independent and pleasant to everyone, which made him well-liked. He had a soft spot for Fatima and Gloria, who came immediately after him. Horacio was their mother Bernarda's favourite son, because of his close resemblance to Abelardo, and Imelda was close to Jasmin for the same reasons that Kosme was to Luis. Their step-brother, Xavier, was given such attention and consideration by the family elders that he always ended up having things his own way, much to the chagrin of the younger members. Bernarda was always accommodating and generous with Abelardo's relatives. In fact, one of the reasons AIMC was incorporated was Abelardo's desire to give part-ownership in the business to his first wife and family, as well as to his nephews who had come to the Philippines after World War II.

When the government decided to provide incentives for pioneering industries in order to rebuild the country and the economy, the couple invested profits from the textile trade into a paper mill joint venture. At around the same time, Bernarda was able to secure a loan to purchase a 5200 sq. m. lot beside the Binondo Church, at the heart of Manila's Chinatown. That was when the Abelardo Realty Corporation was established. Thus, starting from textiles and real estate, the couple diversified into manufacturing, with the Abelardo Realty Corporation being renamed Abelardo Investment and Manufacturing Corporation (AIMC) in 1954, and, eventually, wheat flour milling, in 1960 (Ty, 1999: 29–30).

Although flour milling had been present in the Philippines since the 17th century, when it was introduced by Spanish missionaries in order to prepare Eucharistic wafers, it was only established and recognized as a manufacturing industry in 1958, with the founding of the Jacinto Flour Mills (Ty, 1999: 32). Before then, all of the country's requirements were imported from the United States, Canada or Australia, by which time the Philippines had already become the world's second-largest flour importer after Great Britain. Flour purchases, amounting to PHP 56.2 million in 1958, therefore constituted an enormous drain on the country's meagre foreign exchange reserves. Because of this, the government supported the fledgling industry with foreign exchange concessions, tax exemptions and unrestricted wheat importation during its first decade of operations. AIMC took advantage of this favourable environment and became the second flour mill in the country. Aside from Jacinto Flour Mills and AIMC, four other players joined the sector and, together, they were able to reduce flour imports in 1963, almost to a tenth of the all-time high figure of 297 945 metric tons in 1958. AIMC rode high on the wave of the flour milling success, growing in both capacity and production (Ty, 1999: 33). During the 1960s, the board of AIMC consisted mainly of Bernarda's brothers and sisters, who were all native-born Filipino citizens (Ty, 1999: 34).

Immediately upon assuming the presidency of AIMC in 1968, David, with Bernarda's approval, decided to have each of the family's firms audited, to see which among them were the most sustainable (Ty, 1999: 35). A study by a large consultancy firm revealed that only the flour mill and the real estate leasing businesses were worth retaining, and David followed the advice. Two professional managers were also given nominal shares and elected to directorships in the board. Having jettisoned losing affiliates, AIMC quickly returned to profit, yet David thought that AIMC could do even better, so he brought in a couple of consultants to tackle operational problems such as high procurement costs, pilferage and lack of motivation among distributors (Ty, 1999: 36).

During the decade of the 1970s, as Abelardo and Bernarda's children came to age and married, they were little by little introduced onto the board, sub-stituting for their maternal aunts and uncles (Ty, 1999: 34–5). Carmen married Gualberto Gomez of the Gomez Bank Group. However, being one of the younger siblings, Gualberto did not form part of the core group that controlled his family's business. Fatima married Quito Beltran, an M.I.T. (Massachussets Institute of Technology) engineering graduate, who at that time had his own, albeit modest, business undertakings. Jasmin married Rosendo Tiu, who then had a freshly minted MBA degree. For the greater part of the 1970s, therefore, the AIMC board consisted of David, Carmen, Ernesto, Fatima and Jasmin, plus two professional managers. Several family members concurrently held executive posts, with David as President, Carmen as Treasurer and Vice President for the Real Estate Division, Ernesto as Vice President for the Manufacturing (Flour) Division, Gualberto Gomez (Carmen's husband) as Vice President for Sales and Administration and Rosendo Tiu (Jasmin's husband) as Head of the Corporate Development Office, although later he left for the United States.

In 1973, Bernarda herself passed away, succumbing to cancer. The year before, in 1972, Martial Law was declared, and the economy, just like the whole country, came to a standstill. Flour mill production declined and receivables piled up, forcing David to mortgage some of the company's property to avail himself of credit from the banks; officers even sàw themselves obliged to provide joint guarantees for loans (Ty, 1999: 34). There was a severe dollar shortage and, as a consequence, the government decided to fully regulate the flour milling industry (Ty, 1999: 38–43). Needless to say, millers like AIMC suffered immensely owing to inefficiencies in wheat shipment and flour allocation, leading to a contraction of sales and cash-flow problems. Nonetheless, AIMC managed to perform at par with its competitors despite functioning at only 65 per cent of its capacity. In its favour was a one-product focus allowing it to maintain low operating costs. Furthermore, because of its pioneer status, AIMC enjoyed a steady stream of clients loyal to the brand.

With the 1980s, the younger members of the brood, Horacio and Kosme, finally replaced the two professional managers, occupying their respective seats on the board (Ty, 1999: 36). Between 1983 and 1985, the country fell into recession and the flour milling industry was hit hard, having to contend with high inflation, currency devaluation and new taxes. Upon recommendations from the World Bank, the Philippine government finally decided to free markets and to deregulate flour milling in 1985. For the first time in years, AIMC, together with the rest of the industry, was able to turn up a respectable profit. However, AIMC began to lose competitiveness, sliding from third-largest producer in 1984 to sixth place in 1985 (Ty, 1999: 45). All the same, the next three years from 1986 to 1988 may be considered the 'boom years' for AIMC, with profit margins increasing by as much as 29 per cent and profit sharing figures running well into the millions of pesos (Ty, 1999: 38).

Also towards the end of the 1980s, major conflicts between two power groups within the AIMC board began to emerge. On the one hand was Carmen's group, which formed the majority, and on the other, David's group, constituting the minority, although he held the top executive post. The Simon family had full control of the company, since all of the board directors were siblings and the top executives were either one of the siblings themselves or their spouses (Ty, 1999: 47). Between the two older siblings, a decisive faction of 'swing voters' arose, composed of Jasmin, Ernesto, Fatima, Imelda and Gloria. For instance, at a certain point, Carmen wanted Kosme – sent abroad by David to study – to take over from David in running the company when David fell ill. Yet Kosme himself, recently returned from overseas, suddenly decided to marry, effectively turning his back not only on his studies, but on the company as well. The rift between them grew deeper as David fired Rosendo Tiu, Jasmin's husband, from the company, and sent him packing to the United States. As a former consultant remarked, observing the behaviour of the siblings as company directors during those years, 'they were only interested in the plans that would translate into money' (Ty, 1999: 47).

The decade of the 1990s was marked by AIMC's decline, motivated, above all, by the lack of understanding among family members on the board and in key executive positions. Foreseeing the entrance of new players and a more aggressive diversification by AIMC competitors, David proposed several strategic initiatives to the board. Among these were (1) a stock swap with Luzviminda Milling, then the second-largest in the sector, in order to forge an alliance, (2) a joint venture with Ralston Purina of the United States, which specialized in feedmilling, (3) integration with the top fast-food restaurant operators in the country, such as Jolibee or Goldilocks Bakeries, and (4) expansion into noodles and biscuit manufacturing (Ty, 1999: 48). Yet none of these plans materialized, since the other directors did not want non-family members on the board or with substantial stakes and influence in the company.

In 1992, David was forced to withdraw from the board, receiving a PHP2 million cheque as compensation for services rendered. Kosme was recalled to the company and, with Carmen's backing, he replaced David as president.

Yet scarcely two years had passed when AIMC entered a crisis, incurring a PHP30 million loss during the first half of 1994. Carmen had also resigned from the board because of mounting pressure from her siblings and fellow board members Jasmin, Ernesto and Fatima. It so happened that Carmen's husband and AIMC Vice President for Sales and Administration, Gualberto, was secretly doing business with AIMC for himself (Ty, 1999: 50). Gualberto was purportedly the silent owner of a company that supplied flour bags to an AIMC joint venture with a major distributor, on whom he lavished preferential treatment through lower prices and big discounts. He also showered favours on his daughter's pollard (a flour by-product) and marine insurance companies which engaged in business with AIMC. Thirdly, Gualberto somehow always managed to put AIMC's money market placements with his own family's Gomez Bank, of which he was a director, and not with China Bank, as the other board members had thought. Many of these grave issues were allowed to fester unnoticed because board meetings were often dedicated to discussing operational problems such as leaky pipes or defective glass doors in AIMC premises, as the minutes attest. Together with Carmen's exit came Kosme's departure from the AIMC presidency. The path was clear for David's return.

Once back as AIMC president, David made putting the house once more in order his top priority (Ty, 1999: 51, 54). He started by asking Gualberto, as the project's main proponent, to explain the decision to construct a third mill, despite the fact that the two existing mills were far from making use of their full capacity. Gualberto was likewise grilled regarding the 40 per cent pay rise that he gave himself without the board's approval. Neither were Gualberto's wife and David's older sister, Carmen, excused from having to give explanations. As the Vice President for Real Estate, Carmen was asked by David why AIMC still paid for the fencing, security, development and maintenance of 111 hectares of land in Cavite, south of Manila, after this had already been declared as dividends and was therefore the personal property of the owners. Furthermore, David interrogated Carmen as to why the Bernarda Tower II in Binondo, a 12-storey building constructed at a cost of PHP78 million and inaugurated in January 1994, only had five occupied lease units a full year later. Soon after, Gualberto Gomez was forced to retire in accordance with company policy. Carmen complained about the treatment her husband was receiving, but could do nothing to prevent his ousting (Ty, 1999: 53–4).

David had not forgotten his plans for strategic alliances, diversification and professionalization (Ty, 1999: 51–3). He reinitiated contacts with Luzviminda Milling and established new ones with Federal Flours, belonging to the Kuok Group, which controlled 50 per cent of the Malaysian market. However, none of these projects prospered owing to David's failure to gain the approval of his siblings on the board. David also wanted to inject new blood into the family enterprise by creating job opportunities for his younger siblings, yet the older ones refused to vacate their executive positions. Although the company's fixed compensation for executives was below standard, the non-fixed compensation (management bonuses, life/medical insurance, gasoline allowances and entertainment expenses) was significantly higher (Ty, 1999: 54).

Never mind that, upon David's return, AIMC registered remarkable improvements in performance. For example, by the end of David's first month in office, the company posted a profit of PHP3.7 million, compared to the loss of PHP6 million in the previous month. And, for the first quarter of 1995, AIMC reported a gain of PHP30 million, a figure even higher than the PHP25.6 million it earned for the whole of 1994 (Ty, 1999: 55). Exasperated by his siblings' uncooperative behaviour on the board, David drafted a letter of resignation, citing as reason his inability 'to secure the much needed harmony among the stockholders, directors and officers' (Ty, 1999: 55).

In the end, however, Jasmin succeeded in persuading David to stay on, if only to prevent the re-entry of the faction represented by Carmen and Kosme. David called, as a condition, for the reorganization of the board into operating committees that would review proposals together with the consultants before raising them for a decision. David would sit on all committees. Although family members would still be favoured in filling executive posts,

David would, first and foremost, require professionalism from them, meaning competence, commitment and dedication. This would mean 'setting aside personal considerations when attending to company matters' as well as 'maintaining regular office hours and open communication with their fellow officers and subordinates' (Ty, 1999: 56).

Shortly afterwards, David had to take leave for medical reasons and spent a couple of months overseas. Upon his return, in February 1996, he called for a long-range strategic planning session with the board members, the top management executives and some professors from the Asian Institute of Management in Tagaytay, a resort city near Manila. Neither Carmen nor Kosme attended (Ty, 1999: 56).

The companies belonging to the Simon family had always been run by more than one person at the topmost level, making them qualify, in principle, for either a corporate aristocracy or a corporate oligarchy. The bicephalous arrangement between Abelardo and Bernarda with which their group of companies was founded and experienced its initial flourishing was at first a big advantage, since they had very complementary skills and characters. They also always seemed to reach an understanding with no major conflicts between them, not even when it came to the involvement of Abelardo's first family and relatives in the business. Abelardo was very entrepreneurial, quick to spot business opportunities, while Bernarda was very persevering and prudent, enjoying an excellent credit record. Being a native-born Filipina, Bernarda, together with her brothers and sisters, provided the Abelardo group of companies with the necessary legal cover as the first directors of the board.

A large part of the success of the Simon family companies, however, may have been due to factors beyond their control or plain luck, as when the textile importation law caught them with huge inventories or when the government provided incentives for, first, paper and then, later, flour milling industries. Abelardo and Bernarda were not half as good managers or corporate governors as they were entrepreneur-founders. For instance, there was no clear separation between family property and company property, as evidenced by the fact that AIMC had to pay for the loans of Abelardo's friends which had gone bad or that company resources were used to support Abelardo's relatives. Neither were there any professionals in executive positions or on the board until the late 1960s; these slots were filled by Bernarda's siblings who had no further qualifications apart from this and their being Filipino citizens. These circumstances contributed to a lack of focus in the group which had sprawling interests in unrelated business concerns.

The succession by the second-generation Simons only served to highlight the oligarchical character of their style of corporate governance, insofar as any semblance of a common corporate good quickly faded from view. The Simons siblings, who never really got along well with each other when they were young, carried on with their rivalries in management and in the corporate board room. Once their parents were gone, they quickly broke up into warring factions, unable to manage their overlapping roles as family members, equity owners and corporate executives (Lee-Chua, 1997: 197–237). Bringing their respective spouses into the firms only complicated matters further, since their behaviour – at times, clearly inappropriate – severely added to the tension instead of lessening it. Consider, for example, Gualberto Gomez's several instances of double-dealing with AIMC, or the 40 per cent salary increase which he awarded himself without the board's approval.

David seemed to be the most enlightened among the brood and, as president, he had well-intentioned plans for the company's professionalization and growth through diversification, alliances and joint ventures. Yet none of these projects ever materialized because he always represented a minority within the board. Apparently, his other siblings did not see AIMC as a 'shared interest', but rather, as some sort of 'milking cow' from which each one should try to draw his or her own maximum personal benefit. Professionalizing corporate management or bringing non-family members into the business was obviously perceived as a threat in this respect. The Simon siblings banded with one another only so as to attain greater bargaining power over the rest, even at the expense of the good of the company itself.

II TWO HEADS ARE BETTER THAN ONE: THE VALLS BROTHERS OF BANCO POPULAR ESPAÑOL

At the board meeting of Banco Popular Español on 19 October 2004, Luis Valls, then co-chairman with his brother, Javier, announced: 'We have a problem that has become more pressing with the passage of time: people are worried with the succession and with what would happen to the bank when I retire. There is a whole wide range of answers to that question: some think that a peaceful continuity is assured, while others presage chaos, caused by a power vacuum and the ambition of the aspirants to the position. Regardless of whether they be right or wrong, we would certainly be doing the bank a disservice by not giving a timely solution, knowing about the problem beforehand. Given that I myself am part of the problem, let us now solve the succession issue while we still can: let me be relieved of the co-chairmanship by the actual chief executive officer [Ángel Ron], and let him be substituted by the actual chief operating officer [Francisco Fernández], in accordance with the system at present commonly used for covering vacancies in American and European firms' (Ballarín and Blázquez, 2005: 17). After his resignation, the only post Luis Valls retained in the bank was that of president of the shareholders' general assembly, while his brother, Javier, remained as co-chairman. José Luis Leal, president of the Association of Spanish Banks, had this much to say about the change of guard: 'The manner in which [Luis Valls] has organized his succession, knowing to strike a perfect balance between change and continuity, seems impeccable to me' (Banco Popular Español, 2004b: 62).

Luis Valls was considered to be the last of the 'magnificent seven', a term used to refer to the seven big Spanish banks and their respective chairmen which, under the tutelage or with the prodding of the Bank of Spain, carried out the financial transition in the country in parallel with the political one, from a 40-year dictatorship under General Francisco Franco to a democratic regime in the late 1970s (de Barrón, 2004b). Indeed, while all the other chairmen have come and gone, and several of the banks which they headed finally ended up merging with each other – take for instance BBVA, which resulted from Banco de Bilbao and Banco de Vizcaya, or BSCH, which came from Banco de Santander, Banco Central and Banco Hispanoamericano, and Banco Español de Crédito (Banesto), which in effect belongs to the BSCH group – only Luis Valls kept his place at the table for Banco Popular throughout the 32 years since 1972.

His survival at the very top of the bank is quite a feat, especially if one considers that not once did he (or the bank, for that matter) ever renege on matters of principle, despite the strong and shifty political and economic undercurrents. Way back in the 1950s, Luis Valls already formed part of the Private Council of don Juan de Borbón, then in exile, heir of the last King of Spain, Alfonso XIII (Fontán, 2006).

Luis Valls' father, Ferrán, was among other things a professor of history, who for a time worked in the Vatican Library. Reportedly, during the Spanish royal family's Roman sojourn, he taught d. Juan de Borbón Catalonian history in such an engaging manner that it led the latter to choose the title of 'Count of Barcelona', among several other options (Javier Valls, 2007). When Prince Juan Carlos wed Princess Sophia of Greece in 1962, Luis Valls spearheaded an effort, together with other civic leaders and nobles, to raise funds and present the young couple with a worthy gift on behalf of the Spanish people. In the early 1970s, Luis Valls provided funding and took an active part in the *FACES* (*Fomento de Actividades Culturales, Económicas y Sociales*) Society, meant to be a meeting place for people of all political persuasions outside the official one (de Juan, 2007). One of the Society's main achievements consisted in acquiring the newspaper *Madrid*, rescuing it from a faction of Franco's phalangists, and transforming it into a platform of independent thinking in preparation for Spain's future after the dictatorship. Unsurprisingly, this newspaper was closed down in 1971 by Franco's Information Minister at that time, Manuel Fraga.

Once the regime change had been effected in Spain, Luis Valls declared himself in favour of the legalization of the Communist Party and of the recognition of the workers' right to strike, 'because we all tend to abuse our position' (de Barrón, 2004b). Banco Popular even lent funds to the Spanish Communist Party, which Luis Valls considered one of the bank's best debtors. That fellow feeling was reciprocated by the Party's former Secretary General, Santiago Carillo who, in a television interview in May 1990, confessed to his being a Banco Popular client ever since his return from exile. Carillo said he had always been quite satisfied with its services and that he had no intention whatsoever of changing banks for half a per cent or 1 per cent more interest on his deposits (Boudeger and Ballarín, 1996: 4).

Regarding the failed military-sponsored *coup d'état* on 23 February 1981, Luis Valls was among the first of the chairmen of the big seven banks publicly to show support for the nascent Spanish democracy and condemnation of the uprising (Martínez Soler, 2006). This sent an unequivocal signal that helped dispel fears and rumours that the major bankers were involved in the civil apparatus of the aborted *coup* attempt.

However, Luis Valls merits our attention here not so much for his political role in Spanish society, especially during the transition period from a dictatorship to a democracy, but for his achievements at Banco Popular, which he co-headed between 1989 and 2004. Before the merger frenzy in which the big Spanish banks got caught in the 1990s, Banco Popular was the smallest in the leading pack of seven. But after the dust had settled and the whole financial sector had been restructured, Banco Popular ended up occupying third place. As Luis Valls ironically quipped, Banco Popular had scaled up the ranks in size 'without doing anything' (de Barrón, 2004a). Banco Popular simply stood its ground, not allowing itself to be obsessed with size, fending off unwanted suitors, ignoring the wave of expansion in Latin America and keeping cool with the Internet and dot-com investments.

Certainly, Banco Popular had always been a 'strange animal' within the Spanish banking industry. It is not one of the twin giants, represented by Santander and BBVA, but neither is it one of the small fry, among the likes of Sabadell or Bankinter (Ballarín and Blázquez, 2005). As a medium-sized bank, it seems to be in a league of its own.

Where Banco Popular truly stands alone is in terms of efficiency and profitability. Already in 1989, both local and international analysts considered Banco Popular to be the best managed bank in the country. The

Spanish financial daily *Expansión* applauded Banco Popular for producing above-average consolidated results and keeping focused on its business, rather than getting distracted by the personal issues of top executives and managers (Banco Popular Español, 1989: 48). Similarly, *Rating* magazine gave Banco Popular the highest mark among Spanish banks in accordance with 24 different variables, lending further credence to Luis Valls' opinion that the institution was right on track in balancing risk and profitability (Banco Popular Español, 1989: 68). In 1989, Banco Popular also came out as the best in terms of transparency, according to a study of the School of Business Administration of the Universidad Autónoma of Madrid and the weekly publication *El Nuevo Lunes* (Banco Popular Español, 1989: 31–2, 67–8). Banco Popular reports have always been held up as models in the presentation of financially significant data and have constantly been a favourite among academic researchers for their studies.

On the other hand, still in 1989, the British agency IBCA gave Banco Popular the highest rating among Spanish banks, an 'A/B' (Banco Popular Español, 1989: 48–9). This meant that the bank enjoyed an impeccable financial condition and bore a sound risk profile, consistently performing better than its peers. Banco Popular was found to be very conservative, with provisions exceeding those mandated by the Bank of Spain; its assets were likewise of high quality, with the lowest ratio of bad debts in the country. Regarding Banco Popular shares, the UBS-Phillips and Drew Research Group perceived them to be one of the most attractive bargains in Europe, given the quality of the bank's management team and the strength of its balance sheet; they even forecast a potential increase of 40 per cent in its price for the coming two years (Banco Popular Español, 1989: 49). Lastly, the American investment bank Salomon Brothers likewise agreed with this perception and strongly recommended the purchase of Banco Popular shares (Banco Popular Español, 1989: 49).

The December 1990 issue of *Euromoney* put Banco Popular at the top of the classification as the world's best bank thanks to its impressive earnings growth, stock growth, dividend yield, dividend growth, consistency and momentum.

When Luis Valls left the co-chairmanship 15 years later, in 2004, Banco Popular's fundamentals had not changed (Banco Popular Español, 2007). It managed assets worth almost €77.4 billion in total, a 19.2 per cent increase from the previous year, and declared €801 million in net profits, up by 12.1 per cent from 2003. Its profitability and efficiency were stellar, with an ROA of 1.59, an ROE of 24.55 and a cost/income ratio of 33.96, compared to the Spanish bank average of 1.13, 19.52 and 46.66, respectively. Because of the strength of its balance sheet, efficiency and recurrent profits, Banco Popular has earned and maintained since 1998 the long-term ratings of AA from Fitch-IBCA, Aa1 from Moody's and AA from Standard & Poors. For example, had an investor who bought shares in Banco Popular at the end of 1996 reinvested the dividends received since then, he would have earned an accumulated annual interest rate of 71.5 per cent by the end of 1997, 33.4 per cent by the end of 1998, 22.4 per cent by the end of 1999, and 21.2 per cent by the end of 2000. In the year of Luis Valls' exit, the British magazine *Banker International* belonging to the Lafferty Group gave Banco Popular the distinction of 'The Spanish Retail Bank of 2004' (Banco Popular Español, 2004b: 47).

In March 2007, the Banco Popular Group was composed of one nation-wide retail bank (Banco Popular), five regional retail banks (Banco de Andalucía, Banco de Castilla, Banco de Crédito Balear, Banco de Vasconia and Banco de Galicia), a mortgage lending bank (Banco Popular Hipotecario), an electronic bank (Bancopopular-e.com), a private bank (Popular Banca Privada) and banks in Portugal (Banco Popular Portugal) and France (Banco Popular France) respectively. It was also involved in portfolio management (Gestora Europea de Inversiones), factoring (Heller Spain and Portugal), life insurance (Eurovida), mutual fund management (Sogeval), pension plan management (Europensiones), renting (Popular de Renting), venture capital management (Popular de Participaciones Financieras) and stockbroking (Popular Bolsa).

How did the Valls brothers get into Banco Popular? Under the original name 'Banco Popular de los Previsores del Porvenir', the institution was founded on 14 July 1926 for the purpose of 'providing whomsoever avails itself of its services with the greatest facilities in all sorts of economic and banking affairs' (Banco Popular Español, 2007). The bank began opera-tions a few months later, on 14 October 1926, in the presence of King Alfonso XIII and the members of his government. During the first 20 years, the bank's evolution was highly subjected to the vicissitudes brought about by the Spanish Civil War and World War II. In February 1947, the bank changed its name to 'Banco Popular Español' and increased its capital to 100 million pesetas, thus gaining a nationwide presence. Only in the decade of the 1950s was the bank able to lay down firmly the foundations for its growth.

Luis Valls was born in the same year that Banco Popular was founded. Having finished law at the University of Barcelona, he first thought of dedi-cating himself to academic pursuits and, for this reason, he began working as a teaching assistant in the Chair of Political Economy. In 1953, his mother's cousin Félix Millet – then president of Banco Popular – invited him to come over to the bank and help sort out problems in the board, then perceived to be divided and inefficient. In his recollections many years later, Luis Valls himself admitted that 'there was no clear direction at that time' (de Barrón, 2004b). Once in the bank, he immediately gained everyone's trust and brought in allies in the persons of Camilo Alonso Vega, the chief of the Civil Guard and a minister in Franco's cabinet, Pedro Masaveu, the cement magnate, and Juan Antonio Bravo, who later on became members of the board (Javier Valls, 2007). Scarcely three years later, in 1957, Luis Valls was appointed executive vice chairman and, in 1972, he assumed chairmanship.

Javier Valls, four years his brother Luis's junior, also studied law at the University of Barcelona and, afterwards, he did graduate work in English at Columbia University in New York (Banco Popular Español, 1989: 179–80). He began working in Banco Popular in 1963 as an assistant to the chairman. In 1966, he was nominated to the board and, in 1972, he was appointed vice chairman. As stated earlier, Javier began sharing chairmanship duties at the bank with his brother Luis in 1989.

The history of Banco Popular may be divided broadly into four distinct periods and, throughout, the Valls brothers were heavily involved (Banco Popular Español, 2007). The first one covers the period from 1959, when the Spanish government put into effect a stabilization plan which made robust economic growth possible, throughout the decade of the 1960s up to 1974. The second is marked by the deep crisis which affected the whole Spanish banking sector in 1977 and the consolidation of the Banco Popular Group in its aftermath. The third spans Spain's entrance into the European Economic Community in 1986 and the spate of international alliances on which Banco Popular embarked thereafter. And the fourth is characterized by the adoption of telecommunication and information technologies, allowing Banco Popular to provide new and improved services to businesses and individual clients.

During the first period, Banco Popular, like the rest of Spanish banks, experienced rapid growth and expansion. Throughout those 14 years, deposits grew by 15 times, while assets increased by a multiple of 23 and net profits, by 24. In accordance with the specialization law which separated commercial banks from industrial banks, Banco Popular established an industrial bank, Banco Europeo de Negocios/Eurobanco, in 1964. That same year it entered into complementary businesses such as factoring (Heller Factoring), followed by mutual fund management (Sogeval) in 1965 and leasing (Iberleasing) in 1966. Banco Popular tapped into the market of Spanish immigrants in France by setting up a network of branches in the neighbouring country. In 1971, the Bank of Spain decided to put under the Banco Popular management umbrella five regional banks – Banco de Andalucía, Banco de Castilla, Banco de Crédito Balear, Banco de Vasconia and Banco de Galicia – in which it had considerable stakes through its real estate investment arm, Popularinsa.

The second period in Banco Popular's history began with the introduction of a new law in 1974 which made the separation of commercial and industrial banks no longer obligatory. Thus, on 31 May 1975, the general assembly of Banco Popular shareholders approved the plan to absorb the Banco Europeo de Negocios/Eurobanco, to be called Banco Popular Industrial from then on. In consequence, total assets increased by 85 per cent to more than 17.3 billion pesetas that year; nonetheless, it still managed to attain profitability of 13.35 per cent. Between 1976 and 1985, Banco Popular more than doubled its branch network all over Spain, from 229 to 885 offices. Once more, at the Bank of Spain's promptings, Banco Popular and Popularinsa were merged and the five regional banks together with Eurobanco became Banco Popular subsidiaries from 1987 onwards. Despite the surge in assets that year, to 97.3 billion pesetas, the bank was still able to chalk up an ROA of 1.4 per cent and an ROE of 24.79 per cent for a consolidated net profit of 24.29 billion pesetas.

In preparation for the unified European financial market beginning in 1993, Banco Popular elaborated a strategic plan in 1987 which reaffirmed its commercial retail banking focus, paying greater attention to profitability than to mere size. Its goal was to become something like a domestic bank for the whole of a united Europe. To achieve this, Banco Popular had to look for European partners with which it had complementary businesses and management styles. In 1988, it signed an agreement with the German insurance group Allianz through which it created Europensiones, Eurovida and Euroconsulting, holding 50 per cent of their capital. Subsequently, in 1989, two further alliances, with Hypobank from Germany and Rabobank from the Netherlands, were forged. Thanks to these arrangements, clients from any one of these banks could avail themselves of the services of the other two as if dealing with their own bank. Because of these partnerships, representatives from Allianz, Hypobank and Rabobank gained seats on Banco Popular's board. The year 1992 saw the founding of Banco Popular Comercial in France, as a joint venture between Banco Popular, which contributed its branch network, and Banco Comercial Portugués. Ties with the Iberian neighbour, Portugal, were further strengthened in 2003 by the purchase of 75 per cent of the Banco Nacional de Crédito Inmobiliario from Américo Amorim, the 'king of cork', in exchange for 4.5 per cent of Banco Popular and a seat on its board (El País, 2003).

The Valls brothers' final years in Banco Popular had their landmark the extensive use of net technologies to improve commercial transactions and customer satisfaction. In 1997, the Banca Telefónica platform was launched, providing electronic services to clients, and, in 2000, Bancopopular-e.com opened its virtual doors in cyberspace. Such was the success of home-grown digital technologies that a bank in Argentina even bought the rights to instal and maintain Banco Popular's operations and management software for itself.

Insofar as the Valls brothers had been performing both executive and board duties at Banco Popular for more than 40 years, it could be safely said that they were the chief architects of the bank's succesful strategy. In what does this consist?

Banco Popular's strategy is multi-pronged, touching on areas such as marketing, finance, operations and personnel (Boudeger and Ballarín, 1994). In marketing, Banco Popular tries to craft tailor-made solutions to its clients' different needs, converting itself into some sort of one-stop or global financial shop. This effort is coupled with a razor-sharp focus on target markets, usually composed of homogenous client groups or collectives. Whereas other banks aspire to be the McDonald's of the industry, Banco Popular sees itself more like the corner café, where the waiter would ask you exactly how you would like your coffee or your toast to be, said a former comptroller (Boudeger and Ballarín, 1994: 4). The restaurant comparison also serves to explain another facet of the bank's policy: it reserves the right to refuse admission and any prospective customer cannot just open an account automatically. Because of this, Banco Popular has the most loyal client base in Spain, allowing it to concentrate on its main business, retail banking – taking deposits and lending them out as loans to individuals and small and medium-sized enterprises – despite falling margins. Other competitors who do not have such loyal customers have had to resort to other sources of income, trying their luck in shares and bonds markets, peddling tax shelters or acquiring huge industrial portfolios and unrestrainedly involving themselves in the management of these companies. Banco Popular has eschewed all this or has kept minimal positions in these other businesses.

As for target markets, Banco Popular was the first to see the growth potential of the Spanish rural population which, in the 1950s, was grossly underbanked. It set up a network of around 4000 correspondents who acted as agents on commission, providing financial services throughout the countryside. Periodically, a Banco Popular representative would visit these correspondents for professional and technical support. In due course, these agencies were transformed into full-fledged branches where the volume of transactions had merited it. In the 1970s, Banco Popular followed Spanish immigrant workers to France and catered to their financial needs, just as it would do, in the 1990s, with northern European retirees resident in Spain. Careful segmentation and study of its client markets revealed important interrelations and synergies, such that, towards the end of the 20th century, Banco Popular served more than 80 per cent of Spain's travel agencies, about 50 per cent of the airlines and close to 75 per cent of the Catholic schools (Boudeger and Ballarín, 1994: 5).

Banco Popular's emphasis on profitability over market share has come under attack from time to time, but has somehow held on through the years. Analysts have claimed that too much attention was paid to profit ratios and too little to business volume, giving rise to an unsustainable situation. In the late 1980s, the liberalization of interest rates and the high yields on public debt prompted major Spanish banks (once again, Banco Popular was an exception) to offer annual interest rates between 11 and 13.5 per cent on 'super accounts' with huge balances. By remaining on the sidelines, Banco Popular saw the cost of its deposits increase, although by optimizing its asset structure it was still able to maintain above-average financial margins in the five years that this 'interest war' was waged. Banco Popular's decision was based on the fact that 'super accounts' were directed toward wealthy depositors, who had never been its stronghold in the first place. Furthermore, its value proposition had always rested on a complete custom-tailored package of products, rather than just a single 'super account'. Senior management thought that, while the choice between profitability or market share was an artificial dilemma because the two were not in contradiction with each other, quality of service and a steady growth in profit were more important than an increase in size alone. Becoming the biggest player in the market did not guarantee the satisfaction and balancing of client, shareholder and employee needs. In the end, quality of service and loyalty even trumped higher interest rates in the consideration of Banco Popular customers (Boudeger and Ballarín, 1994: 6–8).

As a final word on Banco Popular's marketing strategy, we add a few comments on its advertising policy. One could hardly call Banco Popular an aggressive advertiser, either in print or in broadcast media. Other banks spend a lot of money on grand campaigns while their employees sit pretty, waiting at branches; in constrast, Banco Popular workers have to be constantly on their heels, looking out for customers. As Rafael Termes, a former managing director and past president of the Spanish Bankers Association remarked, it is a customer-oriented rather than a product-oriented bank (Boudeger and Ballarín, 1996: 6). Moreover, two features of Banco Popular's culture make it especially media-friendly. One is its open-door policy, based on the conviction that 'the secret of Banco Popular's success is that it has no secrets', and the other, its executives' constant efforts in cultivating good public relations, drawing attention not so much to themselves but to the bank's achievements.

Luis Valls was a master of this craft, contributing articles regularly on a wide range of topics to magazines and dailies. One of his columns, entitled 'Spanish bankers on their way to the reservation' (*Los banqueros españoles caminan hacia la reserva*), a spoof on the then popular television series 'Centennial' and the current state of Spanish banks, raised eyebrows at the

Bank of Spain (Martínez Soler, 2006). He acknowledged, on a certain occasion, 'My first vocation was to become a banker, and second, a journalist' (Boudeger and Ballarín, 1994: 9). However, Luis Valls was not as able with the spoken as with the written word, and this is where his brother, Javier, came in. Fluent in English, French, Italian, Dutch and German, apart from his native Spanish, as co-chairman, Javier Valls took charge of external relations with banks and other institutions, accepting invitations to attend and actively participate in seminars and conferences. Being an extrovert, with a warm and affable character, he was Banco Popular's 'friendly face' and certainly gave the impression of enjoying himself while making presentations or simply attending social gatherings on the bank's behalf (Hoja de la Tarde, 2006). When he retired from Banco Popular in 2006, Javier Valls also sat on the international boards of Allianz AG and several other foundations.

A second dimension of Banco Popular's overall strategy under the Valls brothers refers to its financial policies (Boudeger and Ballarín, 1994: 9–12). The bank was very conservative and strict both in the kind and in the amount of the loans it made, assessing the credit-worthiness of each applicant individually, evaluating all aspects of the risks entailed and seeking to diversify them as much as possible. Its provisions for bad loans were always significantly higher than those mandated by the Bank of Spain. As a result, the ratio of non-performing loans to its total risks were less than half of the average of its closest competitors. Since the financial crisis of 1978, when inter-bank lending rates shot up to 60 per cent and more, Banco Popular had always pursued a policy of permanent liquidity and therefore independence from the money market. It has consistently preferred the security of being able to meet its clients' needs to the opportunity costs of excess liquidity.

On the face of it, Banco Popular's capital policy is one that has clearly evolved. Until the stockmarket crash of October 1978, the bank did not even keep a portfolio of its own shares, so as not to interfere in the workings of the market. But, because of the imminent danger of an unwanted takeover, it felt obliged to purchase sizeable holdings during the last three months of that year and tried to place them in the hands of what Luis Valls called 'friendly sharks'. This was the role that its select group of foreign partners – Allianz, Hypobank, Rabobank and Américo Amorim of the Banco Nacional de Crédito (BNC) of Portugal – eventually came to play. Similarly, before 1987, the members of the board of Banco Popular had negligible stakes in its equity; but by mid-1988, the 40 members of its newly expanded board already held more than 30 per cent of the bank's shares. In effect, what was formerly an institution very vulnerable to hostile takeover bids, had been transformed, in less than two years, into an ironclad and unassailable fortress. Another attractive feature of the ownership of Banco Popular shares was the policy of paying the highest dividends possible – without exceeding a 50 per cent pay-out – converting them into some form of 'shelter stock'.

Since the mid-1970s, when the Bank of Spain little by little eased regulations on reserves and interest rates, Banco Popular had always topped its class in profitability over average assets and over capital. But, for some observers, its Achilles' heel lies in that operating expenses as a percentage of total assets were invariably greater than those of competitors.

A third element of Banco Popular's strategy consists in its operations policies (Boudeger and Ballarín, 1994: 12–20, 1996: 9–13). Its organizational chart may be best described as lean, flexible and decentralized, definitely not bureaucratic. According to a former managing director, 90 per cent of decisions are taken at the branch level, a number indicative of the amount of delegation taking place. At the same time, for over a quarter of a century, each branch produced a 'monthly evaluation report' containing an account of the resources gained, their use and its contribution to the group income statement as if it were an independent bank. These reports arrived at the central office by the second day of each month so that superiors could promptly act on them. Subsidiarity was also practised in respect of the regional banks which, instead of being relegated to play second fiddle, always enjoyed full support from headquarters. In their home markets, these regional banks had reached a degree of penetration such that it made them unbeatable in retail banking.

Given the concerted focus that all Banco Popular units have on the operational objectives, since 1985, the group could even afford to do without an overall budget. As a former comptroller explained, 'We believe that a budget is very helpful when people are not in synch and don't know what to do. But once you have monthly reports and objectives are clear, a budget ceases to be indispensable' (Boudeger and Ballarín, 1994: 15). These operating procedures have been greatly enhanced by the judicious employment of new information technologies. Although the bank had been criticized in the past for failing to embrace cutting-edge technology quickly, the policy has always been to examine first the impact of computerization on the development of new products and on customer satisfaction, rather than just using it as a mere marketing tool.

And how about Banco Popular's personnel policy, as part of its general strategy? During its spectacular growth in the 1960s, the bank had no choice but to engage in massive external recruiting of professionals who already occupied relatively high positions, to the annoyance of the oldtimers who rose through the ranks and had fewer qualifications. The rift between the two groups was somehow healed with Luis Valls's recognition that the real money-earners were those occupying the frontline in the network of operations rather than the back-office executives (Boudeger and Ballarín, 1994: 19). In the 1980s, Banco Popular had a new opportunity to rejuvenate staff by offering early retirement. It then took the opportunity to take in computer-savvy, English-speaking university graduates with a nose for sniffing out risk. These new hires were given training through in-house programmes at its own Banking Institute. Some, however, got impatient, and were lured into working for other banks during this training period. Nonetheless, the bank believes it is always better to recruit highly-qualified people, although some leave, than to hire mediocre ones who stay.

Banco Popular employees have been expected to be flexible in their place of work, in the functions they perform and in their pay. It is not at all unusual that an information technology manager ends up in marketing or for a general manager from the Banco de Castilla to occupy the same position later in the Banco de Vasconia. Employees in managerial positions – nearly 50 per cent of the total – have individual compensation plans. And, furthermore, close to 60 per cent of the executives belong to the Banco Popular Managers' Association, a body established in 1977 to promote participation in the bank's governance by acting as a channel for the information, representation and defence of employee interests. Largely through the sale of Banco Popular shares to employees at a discounted price since 1968, the Managers' Association has become a significant shareholder group. Its representative sits on the board of directors and is consulted for appointments at the general management level.

Lastly, what could we say about Banco Popular's corporate governance style, specifically during its period of bicephalous leadership under the Valls brothers? Beginning in 1953, a clear separation was introduced between the supervisory functions of the board and the executive tasks of management, broadly following the German model. A chairman–president liaised between management and the board, besides exercising the bank's representation at the topmost level. When the Valls brothers began sharing leadership within the bank, in 1989, Luis took charge of the 'back room' operations, taking care of shareholders, employees and clients, whereas Javier busied himself with the 'front desk' and external relations (Boudeger and Ballarín, 1994: 20–22, 1996: 13–14). This division of labour between the siblings was the natural result of their complementary characters or personalities: Luis was a born organizer, who left nothing to chance; while Javier was more of an extrovert, the one who faced the public and travelled abroad.

In an attempt to explain the co-chairmanship, Luis Valls said: 'In fact, for the past 25 years, there has been a team working in the topmost position of the bank with the vision and mentality of a chairman. From this perspective, with this manner of doing, the chairmanship [taken] as a team has been able to fulfil its objective, correcting and complementing the limitations, including the physical ones, of its members. But experience has shown that this is insufficient. In a world of relationships, one's calling card is of utmost importance and the position stated therein could be just another limitation. In April 1989, the Madrid Merchantile Registry conditioned the approval of the co-chairmanship to its clear and unequivocal manifestation [. . .] Co-chairmanship is now reflected even in the business card' (Banco Popular Español, 1989: 28). Not only are two heads better than one, he added, but they can produce even more than double with the help of an efficient executive staff.

So convinced was Luis of the benefits of the co-chairmanship that, upon being asked by Cristina Johnson, an INSEAD professor writing an article on Banco Popular in 1991, whether he had fears regarding the continuity of the institution or about the future, he replied: 'If I were to die at this very moment, nothing at all would happen; no meetings would have to be called nor will anyone have to substitute me anywhere [. . .] The axis on which Banco Popular is built is not the person of the chairman. All the more so, ever since the time that there have been two co-chairmen' (Ballarín and Blázquez, 2005).

Luis had a legendary capacity for work and intense powers of concentration. During meetings with the loans committee, for example, it was clear that he had gathered a lot of information by himself on people and companies. Despite a gifted mind, he did not impose his ideas on other people, but rather made suggestions, so that, in the end, he did not even appear to be those same ideas' author. This happened with the bank's decision to limit loans to developing countries in Latin America and to concentrate on retail banking instead, for instance. Likewise, he was careful never to lose that personal touch: he would receive an average of 10 to 15 letters every month from clients, to which he would respond personally. Luis also retained a special concern for the employees, wary that there be no confrontations among them within the bank, that there be no ringleaders; besides, he always backed the Managers' Association. There was a widely shared opinion that Luis Valls was the one person most responsible for making Banco Popular what it is today.

Javier, on the other hand, played a key role in forging and maintaining the alliances with Banco Popular's European partners, in order to keep ownership in the right hands. Otherwise, it would not have been possible for the bank to keep its focus and, much less, its culture, despite their proven efficiency. To a large extent, his being named co-chairman was a mere formality. For more than 25 years he had been representing the bank at the highest levels and all major decisions have been reviewed by him together with Luis. It came as no surprise, therefore, that he was named co-chairman. It was a mere confirmation of something that, in fact, has been going on all along. He did not even have to change his agenda with the new designation (Banco Popular Español, 1989: 179–80).

In the mid-1990s, there was an understandable concern about leadership succession in the bank, since Javier was only four years younger than Luis, and the median age among the members of the executive line was over 55 years, many of them having worked in Banco Popular for more than 20. These fears were calmed, however, by the knowledge that the Valls brothers had, long since, taken care to train their close collaborators and probable successors properly. Future leaders coming from the ranks would have imbibed Banco Popular's corporate culture and were deeply steeped in it. There was no question whatsoever about the solidness of the institution's identity.

Perhaps the moment of maximum tension in Banco Popular's leadership came in 2002, when Fulgencio García Cuéllar was relieved of his duties as president and CEO (Ballarín and Blázquez, 2005: 4–5). García Cuéllar had worked for almost 30 years in the bank, scaling the ranks from investment analyst to regional director and head of human resources for the whole institution. We do not know for sure the reasons for his departure, but, within a few months, he assumed the same post in Banco Pastor. This would not have been striking, were it not for the fact that, soon afterwards, there was an exodus of 42 former Banco Popular employees, including a regional director and over a dozen branch managers, to Banco Pastor, with close to 50 more receiving unsolicited offers. Although these acts of piracy proper to a 'dirty war' were certainly a nuisance and caused quite some pain in terms of broken friendships, they never were a threat for Banco Popular. In the words of Ángel Ron, who succeeded García Cuéllar as the new president and CEO, they really could not engage in battle a bank that 'turned up only a tenth' of Banco Popular's profits. Despite the flight of former executives to Banco Pastor, Banco Popular's successful business model was, in all respects, one that could not be easily copied.

In December 2003, with the excuse of complying with the new Spanish corporate governance code, Luis Valls whittled down the size of the Banco Popular board by ten, leaving only 19 members (de Barrón, 2004a). Among those who lost their seats were Gabriel Gancedo, until then the sole vice-chairman, and Jesús Platero, former secretary to the board.

Banco Popular's success under the joint leadership of the Valls brothers, at this point, is well beyond doubt. They achieved this by crafting a solid strategy in line with the bank's corporate identity, sensitive and well-attuned to changes in the business and social environments, without succumbing, however, to the dictates of fads or fashions. They shunned mergers of convenience and kept their independence when everyone seemed bedevilled by size, but neither did this prohibit them from entering into fruitful alliances with other financial institutions. They stuck to retail banking in a domestic market, cautiously being enlarged to include Europe, when competitors took large positions in industrial holdings and made forays into Latin America. They adopted a 'wait and see' attitude on the development of the Internet while others plunged head-on into technological investments. But does this mean that Banco Popular under the Valls siblings was well-governed, that is, an institution that sought above all the common good of its corporate members?

Success does not necessarily imply good governance, to the extent that it depends on the time frame that one considers, but in the case of Banco Popular under Luis and Javier Valls, one could safely say that it did. Since 1998, the bank has been releasing yearly corporate governance reports in accordance with the recommendations of the Olivencia and the Aldama Commissions in Spain (Banco Popular Español, 2003: 3). Many of these recommendations were not at all new or foreign to the Banco Popular culture, as they had already been practised there for the past 30 years: the separation between ownership and control, the avoidance of speculation, balance in the composition of the board, reasonableness in directors' pay and transparency. Others, such as the creation of committees on nominations, compensation, audit and control, simply called for the slight tweaking of previously existing bodies within the board. In any case, the bank had always followed the 'comply or explain' principle enshrined in most codes of good corporate governance.

There are certain features of the composition and functioning of the Banco Popular board that are worth highlighting from the corporate governance perspective. Above all, there is just one class of common stock, which means that there are no stocks with 'special voting rights'. These shares are widely held among more than 70 000 shareholders, 90 per cent of whom are small shareholders, owning less than 4000 shares. There is no single controlling investor, individual or institutional. Despite Banco Popular's domestic focus, foreign shareholders represent a substantial share of the capital. And the board of directors controls a full third of the common stock, with members of the Banco Popular Shareholders's Syndicate as the biggest investor. The Syndicate is composed of investors who enter into a 'gentlemen's agreement' of always casting their votes on the side of management. Lastly, and once more, on this note the bank displays its maverick streak, members of the board do not receive compensation as such; only internal directors who double as full-time bank executives, that is, the chairmen and the CEO, do. Because of this moderation, board members earn substantially less than their counterparts in other comparable institutions. In 2003, Luis Valls earned €703 000 and his brother Javier, €656 000, while Francisco González, the chairman of BBVA, received €3.05 million (EFE, 2004). By the time Luis Valls retired, in 2004, the total pay package of the 19-member board was scarcely over €2.5 million (Banco Popular Español, 2004a: 17).

Since 2003, Banco Popular has also published a yearly corporate social responsibility report, largely in keeping with recommendations from the European Union and the United Nations Global Compact (Banco Popular Español, 2003; Banco Popular Español, 2004a). These reports cover the bank's relationships with each stakeholder group, including civil society at large, and initiatives it has undertaken in the area of sustainability. Banco Popular insists, however, that the most significant metric of its being a socially responsible corporation and contribution to the common good lies in the wealth it has created. In 2004, it generated a value of €2.3 billion – 3.9 per cent more than in 2003 and a 42 per cent increase from 1999 – equivalent to about 0.3 per cent of the Spanish GDP. It also provided jobs for 13 100 people, representing a net increase of 13.8 per cent from 1999, while the banking sector as a whole in Spain registered a fall of 12.2 per cent during the same period. With the Valls brothers as co-chairmen, Banco Popular has not only done well, it has also done well by doing good.

Between 1972, when Luis Valls was named chairman, and 2004, when he resigned, Banco Popular's net profit grew by 166 per cent and its assets by 200 per cent (de Barrón, 2004c). Its branches have multiplied eleven-fold while the number of employees has only doubled, from 6500 to 13 100, which is all of a record in productivity. Certainly this was not achieved simply by putting into practice the strategic imperative or the corporate governance directive *du jour*: among other reasons, Luis Valls himself was already 78 years old when he left the board. It was largely the result of the virtuous governance of one who seriously took the banking profession as that of 'taking care of other people's money'. He himself strove to be very austere. In his last will and testament, he wrote: 'Whatever I have, you can burn it: it's not worth anything', something readily confirmed by close sources (El Confidencial Digital, 2006). Furthermore, he pleaded: 'Please leave my friends in peace . . . Don't give publicity to the funeral nor to the interment, not to speak of obituary notices . . . Of course I would be most grateful that they pray, but nothing more . . . Let each one pray and ask others to pray as well . . . Beyond that which benefits the soul, no need whatsoever for social functions.'

III   CORPORATE OLIGARCHIES AND CORPORATE ARISTOCRACIES

An oligarchy is a form of government in which not only a few people rule, but also, these few people happen to be the wealthy ones. They rule with a view chiefly to their own particular interest, which is none other than to increase their private wealth. This describes quite accurately the situation within the AIMC board occupied by the Simon siblings and, for this reason, the firm could be appropriately called a 'corporate oligarchy'. The lack of cohesion among them, despite beings members of the same brood, was somehow transposed to their dealings with each other as directors of the family corporation. AIMC's mismanagement was, to an overwhelming degree, the mere result of the inability of the family members to get along well with each other and to go beyond their personal interests in an attempt to seek the corporate good. Furthermore, their only claim to a seat on the board was inherited wealth or 'blood equity', unaccompanied – for most – by any professional merit or 'sweat equity' in the business.

There were three main factions, led by David, Carmen and Jasmin, respectively, within the AIMC board. Although David was the eldest son and had twice occupied the chairmanship, his leadership was, for most of the time, carried out in isolation. Consequently, he could not even give the strategic changes he thought were necessary to improve the company's profitability and governance a try, since they all entailed a loss of family control and influence, both in ownership and in management. His siblings would simply have none of that, given that any such measure would significantly decrease or even prevent them from using AIMC for their own personal benefit.

Diametrically opposed to David and his leadership was the group formed by Carmen, the first-born daughter, her spouse, Gualberto, and Kosme, who was among the younger boys. Carmen had even tried to pit Kosme against David to become the company's chief executive, until the former's untimely marriage decision. They were the ones who best represented the culture of corruption within the company, secretly giving themselves substantial salary raises, not doing business at arm's length or misallocating funds for personal expenses.

Although the faction of 'swing voters' within the board, composed of Jasmin and the rest of the family members, did not engage in what could have been fraudulent transactions, neither did they take the corporate common good to heart. Instead, each one seemed fixated on not losing ground in terms of power and influence within AIMC, and using that to their own financial advantage. In truth, this group of directors did not really mind siding either with David or with Carmen, as long as it was beneficial to their monetary interests. They were against Carmen and her husband for the shady business deals and misappropriation of company funds, but neither would they support David in his strategic proposals for alliances. They knew they had the power of king-makers within AIMC, and they took advantage of this to the limit.

In the *Politics*, Aristotle speaks of four different kinds of oligarchies depending on the amount of property required, the basis of selection once the property qualification is satisfied, the role of heredity and whether the law or the group of oligarchs or magistrates is supreme (Pltcs, 1292a–b). In the case of AIMC we could say that it brought together all the worst features of oligarchies. A seat on the board required a huge amount of property stakes or shares, although all of it was inherited, either by oneself or one's spouse, and neither bought nor earned by hard work. Among the group of family members or corporate oligarchs who actually sit on the board, the leader is co-opted, not so much because of his excellence or merit, as would befit an aristocracy, but because of a broad sense of privilege. In the AIMC board, the most important criterion for leadership was one's willingness to cater to the whims and desires of the other directors, rather than one's preparedness for the job. And, lastly, it was also apparent that, in the governance of the Simon family corporation, the opinions of the siblings themselves who sat on the board and not any kind of 'law' had the last say.

Aristotle enumerates several causes for the overthrowing or 'revolution' of oligarchies (Pltcs, 1305a–1305b). These may be external, as when oligarchs oppress the people to such an extent that anyone is good enough to become their champion as long as he brings about change, but the majority are internal to the group of oligarchs themselves. A greater number of revolutions occur because oligarchs become very exclusive and even create a smaller oligarchy within the original one, fanning the flames of personal rivalries and divisiveness. An equivalent phenomenon to this would be the formation of the factions within the AIMC board. Aristotle also warns us that, owing to their inherent distrust of the people, oligarchs are inclined to hire and make use of mercenaries to advance their own purposes. This feature of oligarchies was somehow reflected in the attempt to bring in professional managers to AIMC, although it ultimately failed because of the unwillingness of the siblings and board members to cede control. Perhaps the most widespread cause of revolution in oligarchies is the extravagant living in which the rulers engage, so much so that they become no different from tyrants who rob the public treasury. This was sadly attested by conduct of Carmen's spouse, to which she appeared to have turned a blind eye. And, finally, it may also come as a surprise that Aristotle includes marriages and derivative lawsuits in the list of causes of the downfall of oligarchies, yet, on second thoughts, this becomes entirely reasonable, given the dependence of oligarchies on families.

What could be done, then, to prevent the collapse of oligarchies? Aristotle suggests that 'rulers [strive to be] on good terms both with the unenfranchised and with the governing classes, not maltreating any who are excluded from the government, but introducing into it the leading spirits among them' (Pltcs, 1308b). Above all, a fair and just treatment of the subjects, therefore, and a chance for the gifted among them to participate in the tasks of governance – characteristics that could be observed precisely in the 'corporate aristocracy' that the Valls brothers had established in Banco Popular – seem to be of utmost importance.

Aristocracies are often confused with oligarchies because, in both, a few rule, but the few who rule in each case do so for different reasons: in aristocracies, for the common good, in oligarchies, for a private good. Corporate governance in Banco Popular under the Valls brothers closely resembles the aristocratic regime described by Aristotle among the Carthaginians of his time (Pltcs, 1272b–1273b). In Carthage, leaders were chosen in accordance with merit, neither by chance nor inheritance: this accounts for the professionalism that was expected among the members of the Banco Popular board, who acceded to their position more for this reason than for the mere ownership of shares. Similarly, the magistrates of Carthage, just like the members of the Banco Popular board, carried out their functions without receiving any salary. What is vital for the establishment of an aristocracy is that excellence be reserved the first place.

Aristotle's observations on the perils that may haunt an aristocracy are also very enlightening (Pltcs, 1306b–1307b). He cites an overgrown ambition, either among those excluded from power who nevertheless deem themselves equal in excellence to those who rule, or in an original member of the governing party who desires to be greater and considers himself to have the right to rule alone as a tyrant. For this reason the Valls brothers had always endeavoured to work as a team, not only between themselves but also with their close collaborators in the board and in the executive committee. They valued collegiality as part of Banco Popular's corporate culture, and there was no better way of witnessing this than in the manner in which the co-chairmanship itself was lived, with a clear, effective and complementary distribution of tasks between the two brothers. As Luis Valls affirmed with conviction in an interview, even if he were to die in office, nothing at all would happen to the bank. Of course it was not necessary to wait for his demise in order to prove this. The smooth succession when he decided to turn over the sceptre of power to Ángel Ron in 2004 offered more than sufficient proof. Banco Popular did not depend more than it needed to on its chairman or its co-chairmen, for that matter.

Apart from an unwieldy ambition, the other grave danger for an aristocracy, in a state as in a corporation, is great inequality: when the poor are very poor and the rich, very rich. Certain measures were instituted by the Valls brothers in Banco Popular in order to avoid this. The first was the constitution of the Manager's Association, which in due time became one of the bank's significant institutional shareholders. This was a highly effective way of spreading hard-earned wealth among Banco Popular employees who, after all, were the prime creators of this value. It also added stability to the Banco Popular ownership structure, since the shares represented by the Manager's Association, together with those of the Shareholders' Syndicate, contributed to an invincible line of defence against hostile takeovers. The other measure consisted in the comparatively moderate and even modest salaries that the Valls brothers paid themselves while forming part of the executive committee. Non-executive directors on the board had no choice but to content themselves with the share price increases that good management and oversight had generated, since they were not entitled to compensation exclusively on this count. The transparency with which executive compensations issues were dealt with contributed largely to ensuring fairness and avoiding scandalous inequalities.

Inasmuch as aristocracies are akin to oligarchies, rulers in the former are bound to experience a strong temptation towards avarice and graspingness (Pltcs, 1307a). The Valls brothers would simply have no truck with this themselves, nor would they tolerate it in their fellow board members and executives. Perhaps the most eloquent statement in this regard was the frugality with which Luis Valls lived and the meagreness of his estate, considering the amount of wealth that he created and the money that passed through his hands.

IV   IN BRIEF

- The corporate governance regime at AIMC under the Simon siblings exemplifies a corporate oligarchy: only a few who possess a huge amount of wealth – albeit an inherited one – are entrusted with the task of ruling, and they do so, not with a view to the common corporate good, but to the particular, private good of each. This is the root of AIMC's poor governance and mismanagement, manifested in its mounting losses, eroding competitiveness and precarious viability as a business. Strategic initiatives to improve this situation were readily blocked by the different factions within the board, wary of losing control and the ability to make use of the company resources for their own private purposes. In the end, AIMC had been converted into the 'cookie jar' or the 'money bag' into which different board members dipped their fingers to help themselves.

- The outstanding success of Banco Popular may be attributed, in no small measure, to the aristocratic corporate governance regime instituted for over 30 years by the Valls brothers, Luis and Javier. This accomplishment could be measured, not by the bank's consistently top-notch operating results alone, but also by the superlative degree of satisfaction experienced by the different members of its corporate community: shareholders, employees, clients and civil society at large. Aside from manifestly seeking the common corporate good in the first place, often against the tide of fashion, the Valls brothers have also striven to use moderation and restraint in their compensation and lifestyles, setting an important example for the institution's corporate culture and identity.

- Both oligarchical and aristocratic corporate regimes are characterized by the government of only a few people. But while, in the former, the few are represented by wealthy individuals who above all pursue their own material benefit, in the latter, they are individuals distinguished by their excellence or virtue who seek the corporate common good. Corporate oligarchies suffer from the arbitrariness of whatever line of action may contribute to private material gain, while corporate aristocracies, in principle, are guided by the desire to uphold the law.

- The main dangers facing corporate oligarchies come from internal rather than external sources. They consist in the acquisitiveness of the oligarchs who are prone to extravagant living, their uncontrolled ambition that leads to factionalism and further complications arising from their dependence on family ties, such as inheritance and seniority.

- The continuity of corporate aristocracies is heavily premised on the just and proper treatment of those belonging to the governing as well as to the non-governing classes. With regard to the latter, this refers basically to the provision of opportunities for the better-suited among them in excellence or virtue to participate in the task of governance. Corporate aristocracies, therefore, require meritocracy, professionalism and an opportunity for continuing training.

REFERENCES

Aristotle (1990), *The Politics*, ed. Stephen Everson, Cambridge: Cambridge University Press.

Ballarín, Eduard and María Luisa Blázquez (2005), Banco Popular 2004, DG-147/ O-305-027, IESE International Graduate School of Management, University of Navarra, Barcelona-Madrid.

Banco Popular Español (1989), *Repertorio de Temas*, Madrid.

Banco Popular Español (2003), *Informe de Gobierno Corporativo. Informe de Responsabilidad Social Corporativa*, Madrid.

Banco Popular Español (2004a), *Informe de Gobierno Corporativo. Informe de Responsabilidad Social Corporativa*, Madrid.

Banco Popular Español (2004b), *Repertorio de Temas*, Madrid.

Banco Popular Español (2007), www.bancopopular.es (accessed 14 June 2006).

de Barrón, Íñigo (2004a), 'La retirada de un gran banquero. Una retirada preparada con dos años de antelación', *El País*, 20 October.

de Barrón, Íñigo (2004b), 'Un último magnífico. Con la marcha de Luis Valls se acaba la generación de banqueros que vivió la transición en España', *El País*, 20 October.

de Barrón, Íñigo (2004c), 'La metamorfosis del Popular bajo el imperio Valls', *El País*, 24 October.

Boudeger, Rose Marie and Eduard Ballarín (1994), 'Banco Popular 1996', 0-394-042/DG-1064-E/ Rev. 4/94, IESE International Graduate School of Management, University of Navarra, Barcelona-Madrid.

Boudeger, Rose Marie and Eduard Ballarín (1996), Banco Popular 1996, 0-397-077/ DG-1164-E, IESE International Graduate School of Management, University of Navarra, Barcelona-Madrid.

El Confidencial Digital (2006), 'Luis Valls y sus últimas voluntades: 'Ni entierro, ni funeral, ni esquelas. Lo que tengo, quemadlo; no vale nada', www.elconfidencial digital.com, 27 February (accessed 1 March 2007).

EFE (2004), 'Luis y Javier Valls, copresidentes del Popular, ganaron 1,36 millones', *El País*, 11 February.

Fontán, Antonio (2006), 'En memoria de Luis Valls', *ABC*, 27 February.

Hoja de la Tarde (2006), 'Javier Valls dimite a los 75 años de presidente del Banco Popular. Valls, la cara amable del Banco Popular', *Hoja de la Tarde*, 22 March.

de Juan, Aristóbulo (2007), 'Luis Valls Taberner, un año después', *Cinco Días*, 26 February.

Lee-Chua, Queena (1997), *Successful Family Businesses. Dynamics of Five Filipino Business Families*, Quezon City: Ateneo de Manila University Press.

Martínez Soler, José Antonio (2006), 'Adios al "cardenal" Luis Valls', *BLOGS.20.minutos.es*, http: //blogs.20minutos.es/martinezsoler/post/2006/02/27/ adios-al-cardenal-luis-valls (accessed 1 March 2007).

El País (2003), 'El Popular compra el BNC portugués y da entrada en su capital a Amorim', *El País*, 10 January (accessed 1 March 2007).

Ty, Wellington D. (1999), 'The professionalization of a family-owned flour mill: a case analysis,' Manila, The School of Management, University of Asia and the Pacific.

Valls, Javier (2007), 'A personal interview with the author', 12 December, Madrid, Spain.

7. Corporate polities and corporate democracies

At present there is a wide consensus on liberal democracies as the most desirable among all different political regimes. These are characterized by a commitment to liberal values, above all, to the rule of law, and the regular holding of free and fair elections among the members of the citizenry. Despite their limitations, liberal democracies are considered to come closest to the ideal of self-rule, through the wide participation of citizens in a government legitimized by their choice and consent.

Within the realm of business and the economy, one finds an increasing demand for a corporate democracy to complement the political democracy of states (Gates, 1998). It is believed that giving employees an ownership stake would enhance their motivation and commitment to the firms in which they work, inexorably leading to improved corporate performance. Employee ownership and participation in the governance of companies would defuse many instances of labour–management conflict. It would also broaden the distribution of wealth (a lot more would be able to benefit) and promote a more equitable distribution of the same: those who benefit would do so more equally. All of these factors would provide for greater cohesion, not only in the corporation but in civil society as well.

In the *Politics*, Aristotle presents us with two kinds of regimes wherein the many in a given constituency rule: democracies and polities (Pltcs, 1279a–b). We have democracies when the majority that governs pursues their own particular interests and, on the contrary, we have polities when the many that participate in governance seek the good of all, the common good. Next we shall examine an example of a corporate democracy and a corporate polity, respectively, through the case histories of United Airlines and IDOM Engineering Consultancy.

I   UNITED, WE FALL

United Airlines will always remember 11 September 2001 as its darkest day, when terrorists rammed flight 175 into the World Trade Center in New York and sent flight 93 on a tailspin to a farm in Pennsylvania, causing the death of 18 employees and 93 passengers. It was not, by far, the end of the company's suffering. Scarcely a year and three months later, on 9 December 2002, the company filed Chapter 11 bankruptcy protection and announced immediate pay cuts for all employees, as it struggled to develop a plan to address untenable debt, capital and cost structures (United Airlines, 2007).

A little more than a week after the terrorist attacks, on 19 September 2001, United furloughed 20 000 workers – its largest such action in history – owing to the company's dire financial situation. That measure did not seem to have helped much, since the airline ended 2001 with a record-breaking loss of $2.1 billion, nonetheless. After changing its chairman, president and CEO twice since the September 2001 crisis, United applied for a total of $1.8 billion in federal loan guarantees from the Air Transportation Stabilization Board (ATSB) on 23 October 2002. Despite promises of $5.8 billion labour cost reductions over the next five and a half years, $1.4 billion non-labour profit improvements annually and an additional $400 million in savings, the ATSB denied United's application on 4 December 2002, considering it unrealistic. From that moment on, the company had no choice but to seek court protection from creditors, while it tried to reorganize contractual and debt obligations in order to remain afloat.

United's failure brought with it a lot of collateral damage, not only to its various stakeholders and members of its corporate polity, but to the institution known as 'employee stock ownership plans' (ESOPs) as well. After all, when the United board of directors approved the proposal for 54 000 employees to exchange part of their salaries and benefits for company stock through an ESOP, it became the largest majority employee-owned firm in the world, on 12 July 1994 (United Airlines, 2007). The crash in United's performance, therefore, cast a long shadow of doubt both on the effectiveness of ESOPs as a form of equity-based compensation and benefit programme, and on the advantages of employee participation in a company's ownership and management.

We are often told that, the higher the rise, the harder the fall. Before analysing the reasons behind United's débâcle in 2002, perhaps we should first look into the causes of its once impressive ascent.

The passage of the Air Mail Act of 1925 allowed private operations, for the first time, to compete for the carriage of letters and parcels by air in the United States (United Airlines, 2007). Among the successful bidders was Walter T. Varney. His company's maiden voyage on 6 April 1926 between Pasco, Washington and Elko, Nevada marked the beginning of commercial aviation in the country. United Airlines itself was founded in 1931 as a holding company that included Varney's air mail service, Boeing Air Transport, Pacific Air Transport and National Air Transport.

In 1938, US Congress created the Civil Aeronautics Board (CAB), entrusting it with the comprehensive regulation of the airline industry. The CAB was given the authority to control route entry and exit, passenger fares and airline mergers. In such a heavily regulated environment with highly restricted competition, unionized airline employees grew accustomed to generous pay packages despite largely inflexible work arrangements (Bergstresser, Froot and Smart, 2006: 2).

It was not until October 1978 that the Airline Deregulation Act was passed and the CAB phased out. Airlines were at last allowed to compete on the basis of price and to enter and exit routes without government intervention. These developments favoured the birth and expansion of new players in the industry armed with innovative business models, such as Southwest Airlines and People Express.

Overall, the decade of the 1980s was a disastrous one for the airline industry in the US, which witnessed the bankruptcy of established companies such as Braniff, Frontier and Eastern. To blame were increased competition which led to lower fares, rising fuel costs and heightened labour unrest, all set against a background of a general economic slowdown. In 1985, United suffered a crippling strike at the hands of its pilots (Kochan, 1999: 2). Management at United wanted pilots to accept a long-term, two-tier wage agreement, permitting the company to compete on short-haul flights, particularly to the US West Coast. However, United's pilot union rejected this proposal and forced the company to shut operations down. This made pilot union leaders fully aware of their considerable strength at the bargaining table and left management deeply scarred, with a lingering distrust of employee associations. Not long thereafter, then United CEO Richard Ferris initiated an effort to transform the company into a diversified 'full service' travel business, buying Hilton Hotels and Hertz Rent-a-Car as a first step. Once more United's pilot union opposed this move and began with their attempt to buy the company. Although this initial bid failed, it nonetheless triggered a shareholder revolt against Ferris and his diversification strategy, ultimately leading to his ouster. In due course, both Hilton and Hertz were sold, and United was again forced to refocus on its airline business, as its pilots desired. In fact, between 1987 and 1993, three other tries for an employee buy-out of United took place.

The beginning of the decade of the 1990s was once more fraught with turbulence for the US airline industry, due to the Gulf War and an economic recession. Pan Am, TWA and Continental went into bankruptcy and, although United managed to avoid such a drastic move, it was nevertheless obliged to restructure. After declaring consecutive record losses of $332 million in 1991 and $957 million in 1992, United adopted a strategy of strict cost containment that included a hiring freeze, the grounding of older aircraft and the sale of flight kitchens (United Airlines, 2007). Management, however, remained fearful that the $400 million operational savings from these measures still would not be enough to change the company's fortunes in 1993. For this reason it engaged in a round of intense negotiations with employee unions in order to cut down labour costs and ensure United's survival. The centrepiece of these restructuring plans was precisely the ESOP agreement brokered with the Air Line Pilots Association (ALPA), the International Association of Machinists (IAM) and the non-union employees at United, resulting in their purchase of 55 per cent of the company. Conspicuously, the Association of Flight Attendants (AFA) did not take part in this deal.

The ESOP at United included six major provisions (Kochan, 1999: 1; Bryant, 1994a). First, pilots, machinists and non-union employees accepted pay cuts of 15.7, 9.7 and 8.25 per cent, respectively, for six years. There was no guarantee, however, that salaries would be restored before 2000. Second, in exchange for these wage concessions, workers were guaranteed job security during this period. Thirdly, pilots agreed to a two-tier compensation plan which allowed lower salaries for those flying the United Shuttle, a low-cost and no-frills service about to be launched. Fourthly, market rates – that is, at 50 per cent below prior rates – would from then on be used in the future hiring of non-union non-management staff members. In fifth place, newly recruited workers would be expected to contribute 25 per cent to their own medical plans. Finally, the ALPA, the IAM and the non-union employees each gained the right directly to appoint one member out of the 12 who constitute the United board of directors. Together with the CEO, these employee representatives on the board would then jointly select another four, external, independent directors. These governance measures would remain in effect for as long as the employees owned at least 20 per cent of United; that is, foreseeably, until 2019.

The United ESOP transaction, valued at $4.5 billion by the company and $5 billion by the unions, was over twice the price of the next largest employee buy-out (Jurek, 1994). And although it involved only 54 000 from a total of 75 500 United employees, it was already the country's second-biggest in size. It was also in the works for almost ten years before finally getting off the ground. Remarkable as it was, United was not alone among the US airlines, however, in embarking on the ESOP adventure. At that time, TWA, Northwest and Continental were already 45, 38 and 9 per cent ESOP owned, respectively; Eastern and Pan Am likewise had considerable ESOP holdings, although by then they had already gone bust.

Just the same, there was no lack of congratulatory words the moment the United ESOP deal pulled through. Indeed, the Clinton administration had long encouraged employee ownership as a way to preserve jobs and to lower business costs. Thus, Labour Secretary Robert Reich commented, 'Inevitably, other companies will stand up and take notice. From here on, it will be impossible for a board of directors not to consider employee ownership as one potential business strategy' (Bryant, 1994a).

Neither was there an absence of naysaying Cassandras, the most vocal of whom was Lee Iacocca, the former Chrysler chairman. 'Somebody's crazy. It can't work. What do you think will happen when it's a choice between employee benefits and capital investment?' (Bryant, 1994a). The immediate effect for shareholders was that they received $84.81 in cash for every share they held and a proportionate fraction of 45 per cent of the new company. United's balance sheet was weakened by the withdrawal of $1 billion from reserves and an increase of about $1.15 billion in debt in order to finance the buy-out. Consequently, the company's share price fell by $1.625, to close at $128.125 on the day the news was released (Bryant, 1994a).

Before we analyse the details of United's particular ESOP and its effects on the company's performance, we should first try to understand what an ESOP in general consists of.

A truism of human nature is that we take better care of that which we own. By contrast, whatever is held in common becomes prone to neglect, decay and abuse. This reasoning constitutes, in fact, one of the major defences of the institution of private property. Within the American context, this principle found an echo in the Jeffersonian ideal according to which every citizen, to preserve his freedom and autonomy in a democratic republic, needed to own some property, needed to have a stake (Rosen and Quarrey, 1987: 4). In agricultural societies, such property usually took the form of land, but in industrial societies, ownership of shares in a corporation have become more important as a source of wealth and a basis of economic independence. ESOPs were then invented expressly as instruments that enabled workers to work for themselves by owning shares in the company where they laboured.

Concretely, ESOPs came into existence with the passage of the Employee Retirement Income Security Act (ERISA) by the US Congress in 1974 (Reinbergs and Crane, 2000: 1). Government then enacted a series of tax incentives to encourage their use as retirement plans. Further tax reforms such as those of 1986 have only made recourse to ESOPs more attractive: businesses can deduct contributions to ESOPs from corporate income taxes; banks can deduct 50 per cent of their interest income from ESOP debts; when ESOPs buy stocks in a closely held firm, owners can defer taxation on the sale; and so forth (Rosen and Quarrey, 1987: 4–5). ESOPs, therefore, are tax-qualified, defined-contribution retirement benefit plans, similar to 401(k) plans, named after the US Internal Revenue Service code section, in which companies make annual contributions to employees' accounts. All participants in an ESOP deal, such as the selling shareholders, the company and its employees, unambiguously receive tax benefits under certain conditions.

ESOPs allow employees to own shares indirectly in the company where they work by investing their retirement contributions, for example, through a separate non-profit entity called an ESOP trust. The ESOP trust buys shares in the company and holds them for the employees until the time when options can be exercised. Over time, employees acquire an increasing right to company shares. For instance, an employee qualified to receive 100 shares in a company after five years may receive 20 shares after three years, 30 shares after four years and still another 50 shares by the end of the fifth year. When employees leave or retire from the company, they are entitled to receive the entire cash value of their stock.

As we have seen, the underlying reason for an ESOP is to motivate and reward employees by giving them a share in the ownership and control of the company. However, ESOPs have also proved to be a tool flexible enough to serve other purposes (Reinbergs and Crane, 2000: 3). They have provided owners of closely held companies – where 90 per cent of ESOPs are found – with an exit strategy through which they could obtain cash for their shares without looking for an outside buyer. All they have to do is transfer ownership to their employees in controllable phases. Another use of ESOPs is for outright corporate funding. A company issues new shares which it sells to an ESOP in order to raise capital; or the borrowing capacity of an ESOP is employed to refinance debt, acquire other companies and so forth. Since the late 1980s, ESOPs are already known to have been used as last-ditch efforts to save failing businesses, to prevent hostile takeovers and even to extract wage concessions from employees (Rosen and Quarrey, 1987: 5). Understandably, these latter uses have had direct negative effects on employees' pension plans.

Before setting up an ESOP, a company has to make sure that it has sufficient cash flow to fund the initial advisory and annual administrative fees, the yearly contributions to the ESOP trust and the obligations to repurchase shares from the employees who leave the company (Reinbergs and Crane, 2000: 3–4). For these reasons, ESOPs are generally too expensive for companies with fewer than 20 employees. Typically, the number of employees of companies with ESOPs range from 20 to 500, and the ESOPs themselves own between ten and 40 per cent of the company. Only ten to 15 per cent of ESOPs own a majority or controlling interest in their firms, although there have also been cases of companies 100 per cent owned by an ESOP trust.

As a consequence of ownership, corporate governance rights similarly accrue to ESOP members (Reinbergs and Crane, 2000: 4). Employees are represented on the company board by ESOP trustees who owe them fiduciary obligations. Apart from the employees themselves, ESOP trustees may also be chosen from external institutions, such as a bank. Trustees then have a right to vote on major corporate issues, such as mergers and liquidations. Like all board members, ESOP trustees may sometimes have to face difficult choices. For instance, if a majority shareholder wishes to sell the company, they may be torn between getting a good price for the ESOP shares they represent and impending job losses were the deal to be pushed through.

What was the situation at United when the ESOP was agreed? In retrospect, it is fairly easy to affirm, as some authors do, that the United ESOP was 'doomed from its inception', since it 'was adopted under duress, rejected by a major segment of the workforce, and soon opposed by new management' (Rosen, Case and Staubus, 2005: 1). Indeed there were solid grounds for this set of claims ever since the beginning.

By the mid-1990s, like most players in the US airline industry, United did not have much of a choice in turning to an employee buy-out (Jurek, 1994). The alternatives of engaging in a radical downsizing or filing for bankruptcy were equally unpalatable. United had no option but to bite the ESOP bullet as it was seething under competition from low-cost carriers, notably Southwest. A major competitor of United on many domestic routes, Southwest enjoyed much lower operating costs because it operated only one kind of airplane which flew 11 per cent more hours a day than United. Southwest employees also worked on longer shifts with less pay and on a wider range of duties. Furthermore, Southwest did not serve meals, nor did it have to pass baggage on to other carriers; neither was it part of any new computerized airline reservation system. The sum of all these factors was that, on many domestic routes, it cost United an average of 9.35 cents to fly one seat one mile, while Southwest's tab was a mere 7.21 cents (Bryant, 1994a). Hence the insistence of United management on a second-tier pay structure for pilots who would be flying the shuttle service for distances of less than 750 miles.

To be sure, almost 30 per cent of United employees did not form part of the employee buy-out, and a considerable number of those who participated in the ESOP did so very reluctantly; they were simply forced into it by their unions. Some 17 000 flight attendants who occupy the front lines of customer service never joined the bargain (Bryant, 1994c). Their union, the Association of Flight Attendants (AFA), said that the company was unwilling to negotiate the necessary job security provisions for its members. That is why, in stark contrast to the marketing slogans the company then employed – 'the employee-owners of United invite you to come fly our friendly skies' or 'thank you for calling United Airlines; please hold and one of our owner-representatives will be with you shortly' – some flight attendants simply wore buttons which said, 'We just work here' (Wikipedia, 2007).

At the forefront of the United ESOP deal were its unionized pilots, also known as 'flying vice-presidents', both for their high salaries and for the control they have over the company (Bryant, 1994b). There are a couple of reasons why pilots tend to think they have greater ties to their airline and know better how to run it than any other group of workers – including managers – and even shareholders. Firstly, because their skills are industry-specific and, more importantly, because their salaries are closely tied to seniority. When their company fails and they are forced to transfer to another carrier, they know they have to start at the bottom of the heap in terms of wages. On the contrary, a pilot with seniority could arrange his flying schedules in such a way that he could work for only three days during two months in a year. Furthermore, being well educated and many being former military officers, they normally have huge egos which lead them to think they always have the best solution to any problem.

On the other hand, precisely because pilots are trained to look for very quick and complete answers, they may have a hard time grappling with ownership, where 'there is so much gray and so much haze', as Robert Iverson, a former pilot who became president of an airline, retorted. Just before the ESOP deal materialized, for instance, the pilot union at United sent a memo encouraging all employee groups to continue to pursue its narrow interests and compete with each other in negotiations or arbitration (Bryant, 1994b).

In any case, from the very beginning, there were already deep divisions regarding the buy-out, even among the pilots themselves. Pilot union leaders agreed to pay millions of dollars in fees to their staff lawyers or those on retainer without proper disclosure to their board or to their rank and file (Wikipedia, 2007). After the failed ESOP attempt in 1989, Frederick Dubinsky, United ALPA chairman, secretly handed over $375 000 to Charles Goldstein, a staff lawyer. And, in 1994, Roger Hall, Dubinsky's successor, also gave Goldstein another $2 million in an under-the-table deal. That was on top of a $4.12 million 'success fee' Hall dished out to the legal firm Cohen, Weiss & Simon, apart from its hourly billing. These lawyers could hardly have been objective in their advice to the union, knowing that the huge amounts of their pay were subject to the success of the ESOP. It also seemed grossly unfair for them to receive these bonuses covertly, while the pilots they represented were taking pay cuts under the ESOP agreement. The mere fact that the ALPA, together with the IAM, accepted a $4.8 billion discount on prospective wages and benefits in return for equity was, in itself, an oddity. This took place in less than 2 per cent of all ESOPs (Rosen, Case and Staubus, 2005: 3). Many of their respective members opposed such huge concessions, saying 'you can't eat stock'.

Even from the perspective of United management, there never was full support for the ESOP transaction. Stephen Wolf, the United Chair and CEO under whose mandate the ESOP was negotiated, immediately stepped down as soon as it was passed and took a consulting job with Lazard Freres, the investment bank which advised the board during the process (Wikipedia, 2007). He was replaced by Gerald Greenwald, who initially tried to transform United culture from one of 'command and control' to one based on high employee involvement. Owing to disagreements over the concessions, the pilot union members also voted out the leaders who brokered the ESOP only a few weeks later and replaced them with new ones who had hardly any interest in employee ownership. Meanwhile, the machinists, who were perhaps the most sceptical group, increasingly got distracted by challenges from a rival union (Rosen, Case and Staubus, 2005: 3).

The surprising thing, however, was that the ESOP on the short run produced very positive results, despite all these obstacles (Rosen, Case and Staubus, 2005: 3). After its first full year in operation, by the end of 1995, employees seemed to enjoy working for the 'new' United, with grievance rates falling by 74 per cent and sick time by 17 per cent; revenue per employee had also risen by 10 per cent. Cost per seat-mile were down and on-time arrivals were up. United stock outperformed the Standard & Poor's 500 index by 67 per cent and shareholder value rose by more than $4 billion.

By March, 1996, United became the nation's number one airline in market share, operating margins and share price, which had more than doubled since the pre-ESOP days (Chandler, 1996). Part of the success was due, undoubtedly, to the robust surge in air travel, generating $2 billion in profits for the whole industry in the previous year, against the $13 billion in losses for the previous five years. But much of the merit also lay in the new Chair and CEO Greenwald's efforts to increase employee participation and devolve decision making to them. He launched a couple of initiatives to serve as catalysts for the transformation of United's workplace culture, such as 'Culture Leadership Training', a culture-change workshop, and 'Mission United', a programme meant to improve communications (Kochan, 1999: 3). In fact, he even promised to devote half of his working week visiting employees and listening to both their problems and proposals (Bryant, 1994c).

Pilots were given more freedom in setting air speed, improving punctuality in arrivals. They reciprocated, among other things, by hiring a consultant to help them think more like managers. As a result, they even suggested that United reduce the number of pilots in reserve for the start-up operation of the shuttle service to the US West Coast, contrary to what could have been expected (Bryant, 1994b). During a pilot shortage in the summer of 1995, the union agreed to extend working hours instead of forcing the company to cancel flights, as would have been their contractual right (Chandler, 1996). Perhaps the greatest proof of a more cooperative atmosphere between pilots and management was Greenwald's decision to shelve the merger talks with US Airways in October 1995. The main reason was the difficulty of combining the two union seniority lists, and the rights that came with them.

Relationships between United management and other worker groups also showed marked improvements (Chandler, 1996). Ramp workers brainstorming with pilots and flight managers figured that the company could save up to $20 million in fuel costs a year by using electricity to power planes idling at gates: all they needed were longer ladders to be able to plug cables into the aircraft. Another employee team took charge of rolling out the electronic ticketing system, explaining it to travel agents and customers on tours with so much success that United became the first company to put it into practice, in 1995. Aircraft cleaners had long asked for ashtrays to be soldered, since smoking was prohibited, anyway, but hardly got any attention. When United president John Edwardson began working with cleaning crews once a month and had to dig a hunk of wet chewing tobacco from an ashtray, these got shut immediately. Even the flight attendants, whose union did not sign up for the ESOP, have been getting their share of management's ear. For one, annoying regulations concerning body weight limits, the height of their heels or the closure of their shoes had all been waived.

However, a lingering thorn in United's side was its no-frills high-frequency shuttle service – in imitation of Southwest – to California (Chandler, 1996). Initially, it was projected to generate 20 per cent of United's revenue and $1.5 billion in savings throughout 1996, but that target was not met because Southwest reacted by offering even larger fare cuts. Instead of the 7.4 cents per seat-mile objective, United was registering a cost of 8 cents, far above the 7.1 cents of Southwest. In consequence, the shuttle service was losing a considerable amount of money.

By its third year, in 1997, the goodwill surrounding the ESOP agreement at United began to show cracks (Kochan, 1999: 3–6). Management and the ALPA could not agree on wage increases after some very profitable years, and the pilots' representatives on the board announced that they would no longer cooperate with management in joint initiatives. Neither did management know how to handle a new union of passenger service agents which, although formed under the wing of IAM, was itself not a signatory of the ESOP deal.

In the first half of 2000, contracts with the ALPA and the IAM were due for negotiations (Arndt, 2000). Under the ESOP agreement both pilot and machinist wages should snap back to 1994 levels. However, while United's owner-employees were working with reduced pay in the past six years, their colleagues at other airlines experienced substantial wage increases. For this reason, pilots demanded a 6.7 per cent increase in pay, and machinists 16 per cent more, to at least achieve parity with other carriers. Because of higher fuel costs and rising interest rates, however, management rejected the unions' demands, which it qualified as an extortion. During the summer of 2000, pilots then refused to do overtime work and forced the cancellation of some 30 000 flights and delays in several thousands more (Belton, 2000). United hubs looked like refugee camps, and its chair and CEO James Goodwin had to apologize publicly. In the end, management caved in to the pilots' claims and took a $116.5 million hit in the third quarter. Yet Goodwin took a jab at his pilots by announcing his decision to take over US Airways despite their opposition shortly thereafter. The merger was finally vetoed by regulators on antitrust grounds and United gained nothing from it but bad blood. Such was the state of affairs at the company when the 11 September 2001 attacks took their toll.

On the run-up to United's filing for bankruptcy protection in December 2002, management and the different worker unions frantically behaved like passengers on a sinking ship. Mechanics of the IAM reiterated their claims for a 37 per cent pay increase in February, under threat of a strike (Bernstein and Arndt, 2002). In November, pilots of the ALPA said they would be willing to give up another $2.2 billion worth of concessions, but only in exchange for 20 million stock options or roughly 12 per cent of United's equity (Bernstein, 2002). Options could be exercised as soon as they vest, and, that way, pilots could cash in on their company's eventual success, whereas ESOPs could only be exercised when pilots leave or retire. Meanwhile, United shares, which were selling at $30 when the ESOP took effect, nose-dived to $3, having traded at more than $100 in 1997 (Flanigan, 2002). At that point, among the strongest suggestions made to United's chief, Glenn Tilton, in order to resuscitate the airline was that of dumping the ESOP altogether (Arndt and Zellner, 2002).

During the years that its ESOP was in place, United became a clear example of what we call a 'corporate democracy'. It was a company in which many (a significant majority) of its workers owned a controlling stake through their respective labour unions. The problem, however, was that United was an employee-owned and controlled firm largely only in form or structure, but never really in substance or culture. Each of the parties involved in the ESOP continued to think and behave primarily in terms of its own narrow interests instead of the corporate common good.

The United ESOP deal was commandeered mainly by investment bankers who focused more on the financial issues, without giving the people issues of collective bargaining and relationships among parties due consideration (Kochan, 1999). Management and the different labour unions were under the mistaken impression that the ESOP, by itself, would be sufficient to change attitudes and behaviours automatically. Each of the groups involved had a different motive for signing up to the ESOP agreement, one that did not necessarily contribute to the corporate common good. Management had used it to wangle wage concessions from workers; the ALPA was interested in gaining a voice in the governance process as well as certain control over strategic decisions; the IAM had the intention of achieving job security above all. As for the non-union workers, they did not even have representatives in the ESOP negotiations, so there were grounds for their resentment that the deal was simply foisted on them. The flight attendants' union was never brought on board from the very beginning. The only points of agreement on the part of the workers was that they did not want United to be broken up into regional carriers, nor did they want it to diversify from the airline business; neither did they want jobs to be outsourced to non-union members. These were not sufficient or valid reasons to enter into an ESOP.

Relationships among the mechanics, flight attendants and pilots were further strained because each of these worker groups considered itself the most important player in the airline's operations (Bryant, 1994a). The mix between blue-collar and white-collar workers, as well as the enormous wage differences among them, was fertile ground for all sorts of conflicts to arise among their respective unions, despite their shared equity interests.

As for the management initiatives on corporate culture transformation, they were neither systematic nor reinforced in day-to-day operations; they were also abruptly cut short, much too early for that delicate wildflower to dig in its roots (Kochan, 1999; Bryant, 1994a). Likewise, management had seriously overestimated the employees' commitment to the ESOP while it underestimated the power of their labour unions. Labour unions have their own interests, which do not necessarily coincide with those of the workers they represent.

Bankruptcy proceedings were further complicated because the United ESOP trustee, State Street Bank, was in principle obligated to sell the stock it held to collect at least $37 million for the employee-owners (Hopkins, 2002). But that would trigger an ownership change which would prevent United from availing itself of the $1.4 billion in tax write-offs to which it was entitled. The dilemma was whether the ESOP subscribers should give up their $37 million in order to provide the $1.4 billion due to United's creditors.

The perception of the ESOP among the parties involved proved to be far more important than its actual existence. The labour unions at United never seemed to have comprehended the benefits of the ESOP, nor did they trust management to deliver the goods (Cohen, 2001). Despite having financial ownership of the company, United employees did not seem to have what Charles O'Reilly – a human resources and organizational behaviour professor at Stanford's Graduate School of Business – called 'psychological ownership': a feeling that one's personal fate is tied to that of the company (Manjoo, 2002). There are several probable reasons for this. On the one hand, the unions may have served as an extra layer that isolated individual workers from management, instead of bringing them closer. There have also been suggestions that, once employees have turned into owners, labour unions, premised on the opposition between work and capital, have lost their reason for being (*The Economist*, 2003). Labour unions at United should have ceased to defend pay rises and onerous work conditions at all costs, with hardly any consideration for the financial situation of the firm. On the other hand, United's sheer size as well as its being a publicly traded company may have also contributed to the employees' indifference to their company's future.

Some have criticized excessive union control in United's board, despite their occupying only three seats (Rosen, 2002). Indeed, labour had veto power over the company's strategic decisions, but this was also the case with Southwest, which had even broader employee ownership and greater employee influence over daily operations, yet was doing very well. It would be better to pin the blame, then, on faulty ESOP design and an even lousier implementation of an ownership culture. After five years, the company would make no further contributions to the ESOP and new employees would never get to participate, nor would older employee-owners acquire new stock. This sent the unequivocal message that the ESOP in United was something ephemeral, a fad that would pass in due time. Certainly, this was not the best way to elicit a long-lasting commitment from the various interested parties. Such a commitment, however, was crucial to an ESOP's success.

An authentic ownership culture vital to a successful ESOP, on the other hand, requires several conditions (Rosen, Case and Staubus, 2005). A significant portion of the workforce and the majority of full-time employees should be able to own shares. These employee-owners should also be convinced that the amount of shares they hold can considerably improve their financial standing. Management, in turn, should put in place practices and policies that reinforce this sense in employee-owners, such as providing them with timely profit-and-loss information and giving them a chance to participate in daily decision-making processes. Only then would employee-owners fully assume their responsibilities to the company, and act in a manner that is cooperative and loyal, with a willingness to undergo some amount of self-sacrifice for the corporate common good. Under these conditions of worker participation combined with employee ownership through an ESOP, robust corporate growth and success come as a foregone conclusion (Rosen and Quarrey, 1987). Ownership and participation strengthen a worker's identification with the firm, provide him with a chance to put his talents and ideas to use, and create an incentive for him to work more productively.

Therefore we should be wary of conflating United's fate under an ESOP and the validity of an ESOP itself as part of corporate strategy for improving performance. Rutgers University professor Douglas Kruse, in his testimony before the US Congress shortly after United filed for Chapter 11, declared that firms with 'significant' (over 5 per cent) and 'widely-dispersed' (more rank-and-file workers than bosses own shares) employee ownership are more productive than others (Kruse, 2002). In the first year of an ESOP, productivity jumps by 4 to 5 per cent – double the average of American firms – and this higher trend continues on through the years. Employee-owned companies also enjoy higher stockmarket returns and stronger growth without making a dent in profits. It is true that ESOP corporations have their share of risks, arising from the employees investing a large portion of their capital in a single company, albeit their own. Yet this could be overcome by offering, besides the ESOP, more traditional defined-benefit pension schemes. What is indubitable is that workers experience greater motivation and a stronger identification with an employee-owned company.

In the case of United, it was not the ESOP per se, but a host of other factors, mainly the lack of an ownership culture, that caused the company's downfall. A union pilot heavily involved in the ESOP negotiations used the following metaphor to explain the failure (Mackin and Rodgers, 2003). He likened it to a multibillion dollar gift, tied with a red ribbon, and delivered to a stadium where the more than 80 000 United workers were found. The box had been sitting on the ground for several years, yet, unfortunately, no one figured out how to untie the ribbon and open the box.

Sharing ownership among the many workers was not the decisive element for success, as the tens of thousands of subscribers to the United ESOP, qualifying it as a corporate democracy, discovered. Rather, it lay in worker participation, in a true ownership culture, where each of the employee-owners earnestly sought the corporate common good instead of defending his own narrow interests.

United did not emerge from Chapter 11 bankruptcy protection until 1 February 2006, in what was the largest and longest airline bankruptcy case in US history.

II THE ASSOCIATIONAL COMMITMENT AT IDOM ENGINEERING CONSULTANCY

The Guggenheim Museum rises on the banks of the Nervión River in Bilbao as a titanium-clad sea monster, according to some, or a marooned sea-going vessel, according to others, that has thrust its bow against the Salve Bridge. This unique creation by the American architect Frank O. Gehry has indisputably put the city on many a tourist's itinerary and has certainly served as an effective economic catalyst for a region which, in the 1980s, was reeling from the decline of its steel mills and shipyards. Shortly after its inauguration in October 1997, corks were popping at a party not too far away, at the headquarters of IDOM Engineering Consultancy, the project managers for the construction of the museum. Apart from the obvious, a major cause for celebration was the absence of any death or major casualty during the five years that IDOM took charge of the building project. Much was owed for this to the concern, or one could almost say the obsession, with safety that Rafael Escolá, IDOM's founder and first president, had bequeathed to the firm.

IDOM began its existence as DOM, an acronym for *Dirección de Obras y Montajes* ('project management and installations') in 1957 (Cardenal and Vilallonga, 2004: 65). Escolá was then a middle-aged engineer who had just been hired as a consultant to set up a cold strip rolling steel mill worth a billion pesetas for a company called Basconia in Etxebarri, near Bilbao. His previous experience consisted in working for a construction firm called *Edificios y Obras, S.A.* (*EOSA*), where he took charge of both technical and commercial aspects, and however briefly as director of *INAR*, an academy for Engineering and Architectural students in Madrid (Cardenal and Vilallonga, 2004: 42, 49). In answering Basconia's call for an independent consultant, Escolá took a first step towards fulfilling his dream, that is, engaging in the practice of engineering as a liberal profession. At that time, practically all engineers in Spain were employees either of state or of privately-owned companies.

By temperament and, later on, by conviction, Escolá had always greatly valued the autonomy or independence that came with the practice of a liberal profession, even for engineering (Escolá, 1993: 8–10). He felt greatly attracted by the idea of not having bosses or, at least, of not working for them, in the sense of having to please them in order to advance in one's own career. Often, this entailed being unduly diplomatic or calculating both in one's words and deeds, for fear of upsetting superiors. Being one's own boss, he thought, one could offer a better service to clients, with whom one would have no choice but to deal directly; one would have to sell his ideas to them and not to any other intermediary. The professional independence of an engineer would then be better safeguarded and possible conflicts with the commercial or financial interests of third parties kept at bay. Even then, the independent professional should know when to seek advice and, to the extent possible, keep in close contact with others in a similar situation. Partly for this purpose, Escolá co-founded with Mario Romero ASINCE, the Spanish associations of engineering consultants, in 1975 (Cardenal and Vilallonga, 2004: 206).

Yet this idyllic vision immediately vanished as soon as Escolá realized that he could not do the steel mill project alone and that he would be needing help. What was available then was a group of specialists who more or less tried to coordinate their activities; but what Escolá needed and wanted was a team specialized in project management. He himself had to create that team. Apart from himself, the first team member whom Escolá drafted was Luis Olaortúa, then a 25-year-old engineering senior who in due course would succeed him as the head of IDOM. Despite not having finished his studies, Olaortúa would already figure as Escolá's co-author in the cold strip rolling steel plant project. This was a consequence not so much of Escolá's generosity, as his original vision and desire of sharing the authorship, reputation and merit of an enterprise with his collaborators (Cardenal and Vilallonga, 2004: 91). Olaortúa, together with the few others who would join DOM in its initial stage, simply received payment for services rendered from the proceeds of Escolá's honoraria as an external contractor for Basconia. There was no labour contract and, therefore, there were no employees. Strictly speaking, there was no engineering consultancy firm yet; there was only an independent engineering consultant – Escolá himself – who enlisted the help of a team composed of a few young engineers or engineering students, draftsmen and so forth, in meeting the requirements of an external contract.

So pleased was Basconia with the results of its working relationship with Escolá that many other contracts followed after the steel mill was finished, in 1959. Escolá's team started to gain quite a reputation in the Bilbao area so that several important consultancy projects were offered to him. That same year, DOM was inscribed in the Register of Patents and Trademarks with Escolá as the sole proprietor and a book value of 100 000 pesetas (Cardenal and Vilallonga, 2004: 65). This situation would continue for a couple of years more, with Escolá working as an independent consultant together with a 16-member team that depended on his earnings. At that time, DOM won the tender for the lighting installations of the San Mamés football stadium, home of the Bilbao Athletic Club, among its projects. In 1961, DOM had already booked sales amounting to 1.25 million pesetas (Cardenal and Vilallonga, 2004: 92).

Two important events occurred in 1962, ushering in the second stage of DOM's trajectory. First was a change of name, with the addition of an 'I' which stands for '*ingeniería*' (engineering) to the trade mark or brand (Cardenal and Vilallonga, 2004: 92). The other was IDOM's transformation into a firm that offered engineering consultancy services. Albeit reluctantly, Escolá had to abandon his dream role as a freelancer and assume that of an entrepreneur. With the fees he charged clients as an external contractor he had to hire people, pay them salaries and shoulder general operating expenses. However, he did not fully renounce his objective and settled into the practice of engineering as a 'semi-liberal' profession instead (Cardenal and Vilallonga, 2004: 72). As sole owner and manager of IDOM, he avoided naming other superiors and shunned all forms of hierarchy within the firm. His motto seemed to be 'let each one do his thing' in order to ensure the greatest amount of professional freedom possible. He reckoned that, instead of being appointed to a position, workers should gain the prestige and honour they deserved from their colleagues for the quality of the work they carried out.

Reality checks did not take long in coming, nonetheless. Some projects required the close coordination of a great number of members of the team. But, since they had no regular office hours, sometimes clients could not contact the persons they needed, much less receive proper service. The lack of punctuality was also rife. It then became necessary to implement a minimum of formal systems of authority, schedules, norms and regulations to allow for work in common. 'An engineer who works for a firm should submit himself to the rules and to whatever his superiors may indicate to him', Escolá would write later on in his ethics manual for engineers (Escolá, 1987: 182). Some balance had to be struck between legitimate personal and professional freedom, on the one hand, and order in the business organization, on the other.

At this moment it became utterly clear in Escolá's mind that, unlike other business ventures that delivered goods, an engineering consultancy firm had nothing else to offer its clients but the engineers themselves. IDOM's final product was not some raw material transformed by the incidence of capital and labour; there was no raw material in the first place: apart from the engineer's creativity, the means of production were virtually inexistent and the capital needed reduced to a minimum (Cardenal and Vilallonga, 2004: 92–3). Meditating on this fact Escolá decided, on 1 January 1962, to distribute the ownership of IDOM among the engineers who had already worked for at least four years in the firm. Olaortúa was the first to qualify, in 1963, and since then, whatever yearly increase there was in the value of the firm was proportionally divided among the different co-owners and co-workers. Shares in the firm took the form of 'shares in value' (*participaciones en valor*), which reflected the yearly increments in IDOM's value. Escolá had devised a system for the yearly valuation of IDOM as a whole and for calculating the 'shares in value' that were to be distributed, also on a yearly basis. Half of the 'shares in value' was to be destined for IDOM's former owners – until 1963, it was Escolá alone – in proportion to their 'ownership shares' and the other half was to be distributed among the new owners, in proportion to their salaries. Granted that, from the legal viewpoint, Escolá continued to be the sole proprietor of IDOM, the distribution of these 'shares in value' had to be consigned to purely private agreements (Cardenal and Vilallonga, 2004: 94). IDOM was on its way to becoming a 'corporate polity', an organization in which all worker-members took part both in ownership and in management or governance.

Apart from Escolá's own particular vision of the engineering profession and of an engineering consultancy firm, the distribution of 'shares in value' among his professional colleagues at IDOM was also largely motivated by the trust that he had in people. He liked to say (and acted accordingly) that everyone was trustworthy, unless proven otherwise. And even when there was sufficient cause for disappointment, he did not lose trust rashly, giving the other person a chance to make amends instead (Cardenal and Vilallonga, 2004: 82–4). In the early days of IDOM, for example, a young administrative clerk was given the responsibility of working as cashier. Once, however, the young man decided to take some money from the till in order to buy himself a pair of shoes, saying that he would pay back the money at the end of the month. But instead of doing so when the day arrived, he opted to take out more money for other purposes. These small thefts went on for months, until the clerk was finally discovered. The office manager then recommended that the employee be dismissed, but Escolá suggested that he be given a chance to redeem himself. The clerk was asked to return the money he had stolen in small instalments and was allowed to keep his job.

Escolá even went further in building an atmosphere of trust in IDOM. He refused to take other people's failings all too seriously. 'Even in cases in which a person may objectively do us wrong, we have to open for him a credit line of time and trust', he wrote (Escolá, 1987: 83). He was also very wary of judging other people's intentions, since these cannot be fully gleaned from the observation of their actions alone. Escolá's ability to confide in other people made him an excellent listener (Cardenal and Vilallonga, 2004: 84–5). The IDOM pioneers, most of whom were fresh out of engineering school, warmly recall the weekly meetings in which Escolá would consult them on how best to go about the technical and operational issues confronting the firm. He was a master of the art of 'management by listening'. By earnestly listening to his collaborators, they engaged in a shared deliberation and decision-making process. Because of this, it was difficult to pinpoint in retrospect who the original author of a proposal concerning the firm was, for everyone had a chance to participate; neither was this, in truth, very important. By confiding in his colleagues despite their youth and inexperience, by listening to them and allowing them to participate in decisions, Escolá ensured that responsibility over IDOM fell squarely on each and everyone's shoulders and not on his alone.

This style of operating and managing that Escolá had instilled in IDOM from the very beginning meant that no one working there ever considered himself just a mere employee: 'There are no bundy clocks. Everyone knows the difference when asking for permission for something important or for something urgent. However, I don't think we'll ever get back to the point – in 1962 – when people left work simply to play football. Perhaps that was just an excessively youthful interpretation of the principle of "working without fetters"', Escolá said in his memoirs (Cardenal and Vilallonga, 2004: 86).

For all of the above-mentioned reasons, the distribution process of ownership and participation in management in IDOM did not stop with the inclusion of college graduates or professionals. Absolutely everyone working in the firm who complied with the requisite conditions ought to be given a chance to join as a full-fledged member of the corporate polity. This is exactly what happened in 1965, when IDOM experienced a second founding moment, and non-college graduates among its workers were welcomed into the fold. It was also the year in which the first version of the 'associational commitment' (*compromiso associativo*) in IDOM was drafted and adhered to (Cardenal and Vilallonga, 2004: 94–6). The first people to avail themselves of this opportunity to become part-owners of IDOM and somehow participate in its management were Juan Mario Pero-Sanz, who started working in the firm at the age of 14, and Ana Zubiaur, a secretary. This move was completely coherent with Escolá's idea (later shared by the young engineers working with him) that IDOM's output did not depend on the contribution of the college graduates alone; the efforts of the clerical and support staff were also vital. The logical conclusion, therefore, was that they too should be allowed access to the ownership of the firm.

The first 'associational commitment' in IDOM was written over a couple of week-ends in Muñatones, a small country inn (Cardenal and Vilallonga, 2004: 95). It was a private agreement in which the 'founding fathers' decided that IDOM should always be the collective property of its workers, regardless of their professional qualifications. Hence, there would never be 'external owners', nor would there be a basis for a distinction between 'mere employees' and owners. Should an IDOM co-owner and co-worker decide to leave the firm, he ought to sell his shares back to IDOM.

This change certainly brought with it significant consequences. From then on, the signatories of the 'associational commitment' would no longer be receiving salaries, but 'retributions from current earnings', an expression that does not connote any difference in classes among workers (Cardenal and Vilallonga, 2004: 98–100). Aside from these 'retributions', co-owners and co-workers would also be receiving 'complements' based on performance or job evaluations and personal circumstances, such as family size or number of dependants.

How did the signatories of the 'associational commitment' actually share in the management and governance of IDOM? With the coming into effect of this foundational document, Escolá ceded all his political rights over IDOM to the newly-constituted board of directors (Cardenal and Vilallonga, 2004: 102–3). The directors, however, were conscious that their role consisted above all in representing their fellow workers and owners in seeking the good of the firm. Reserved for the general assembly of co-owners and co-workers of IDOM were the rights to approve any modification in the rules affecting the value or the distribution of ownership, and that of confirming whoever has been nominated by the board as president. The distribution of ownership and the participation in the management and governance of the firm did not translate into an egalitarian regime for IDOM, nonetheless. The fulfilment of executive roles had to be limited to a few (a president, a managing director and a head for each territorial group) mainly for practical purposes. An engineering consultancy firm needed a certain agility in its decision making, lest business opportunities be lost as a result of prolonged consultations and deliberations. Thanks to a culture of reciprocal trust, co-owners and co-workers of IDOM could delegate certain powers to executives and directors, and these, in turn, making use of that same trust, could also delegate specific tasks to other members of the firm.

Given the benefits of participation in any human enterprise, it is perfectly understandable for everyone to desire it in theory. What is not so easy is to go ahead with participation down to its last consequences, which includes a willingness in the founder to give up his privileges and be just one more among the other members of the group. In the case of Escolá, this would not have been possible were it not for the confluence of three conditions (Cardenal and Vilallonga, 2004: 97). First was his extremely high regard for the value of human work, definitely in a place above financial capital; second was his acute sense of justice, of giving each person his due; and third was his detachment from power and material things: of course he knew of their importance, but he did not have his heart in them. If only he did not have the caring for a score of families that depended on IDOM for their welfare, Escolá would most certainly have chosen for himself the career path of a freelance engineer.

With its 'associational commitment' first written in 1965, IDOM embarked on putting into practice a different relationship between capital and labour (Cardenal and Vilallonga, 2004: 107–10). In essence it could be understood as Escolá's version of 'the third way': one found between liberal capitalism, in which owner-capitalists always held the upper hand in relation to workers, and socialism, in which labour unstintingly acquired a predominant stake over capital providers on surplus value. Its similarities to the principles of Church Social Doctrine lie in plain view, although Escolá himself was hesitant to claim such a filiation for his invention (Pontifical Council for Justice and Peace, 2004). However the case may be, the fact is that IDOM to date has never experienced any labour unrest, not even during the times in which the economy underwent serious recessions and offices had to be closed and workers laid off.

Inevitably, IDOM's corporate culture did not agree with many conventional business terms, and substitutes had to be found more in keeping with its home-grown ideas (Cardenal and Vilallonga, 2004: 110). Escolá even came up with an equivalence table for this new lexicon: IDOM was an 'engineering firm', not a 'business'; there were 'people working in IDOM', not 'personnel'; these 'begin to form part of IDOM', and are not 'hired'; they occupy a 'functional level', rather than belonging to a 'category'; for their efforts they receive a 'retribution', 'shares in value' and 'retribution to shares in value', instead of a 'salary', 'stocks' or 'shares', and 'dividends'; and, finally, co-owners and co-workers or IDOM are called to a 'consultation', not a 'votation'.

Long before laying down an organizational credo became fashionable, IDOM already had its own which could be summarized in the following statement: 'In works of engineering, the human person is everything, and the firm is but a means to carry out an activity' (Cardenal and Vilallonga, 2004: 111). In the realm of ends, the people who worked in IDOM occupied the first place and, in consequence, whatever referred to their care or attention, training, evaluation and retribution was top priority. Next came the clients, who were the beneficiaries of the service that IDOM provided. And only in third place were profits considered. The hierarchy of goods was then clearly established: first, people, then, service and last, profits. The belief was that, if the people in IDOM were enthusiastic about their work, if they were united amongst themselves and disposed of the means necessary for their development, they would be able to offer their clients a great service, and the firm would stand on solid financial grounds. Escolá's affirmation that 'we value the human person more than the engineering firm' did not at all ring hollow in IDOM (Cardenal and Vilallonga, 2004: 112).

Although, from the viewpoint of internal corporate culture and practice, issues regarding IDOM's identity as a work community may have been resolved, not the least with its 'associational commitment', from a legal perspective, it very much continued to be a 'strange animal' (Cardenal and

Vilallonga, 2004: 106–8). On the one hand, it could not be a 'partnership' (*asociación profesional*), as was often found among medical doctors, lawyers and architects, because, according to Spanish law at that time, only university degree holders could form part of such an association. On the other hand, neither was it a 'joint stock company' (*sociedad anónima*) because, apart from its special way of understanding the relationship between labour and capital, members did not have to contribute or invest financial capital initially to join; their main capital was their work, not their money. And thirdly, neither could IDOM be considered a cooperative in the strict sense, since not all members enjoyed full political rights over the firm. Instead of every owner-worker having a direct hand in the management and governance of the firm, such powers were delegated to the executive committee and board of directors. Owner-workers reserved certain rights, however, as previously mentioned.

There has never been a perfect fit, therefore, between IDOM's corporate culture, as laid down essentially in its 'associational commitment', and its juridical status or legal figure. After all, the 'associational commitment' was simply a private agreement between the firm and the person concerned. That is why, between 1967 and 1971, IDOM adopted the legal figure of an 'atypical joint stock company' (*sociedad civil de carácter atípico*); and when tax laws changed thereafter, so that engineers no longer paid their dues through their professional college but directly to the state, it reverted to a loose body of 'engineers in the free exercise of their profession' distributed among ten territorial groups (Cardenal and Vilallonga, 2004: 115). It was clear in everyone's mind, however, that this was not going to be a permanent solution. Once more, when tax and operational pressures increased in 1974, IDOM finally decided to turn itself into a 'joint stock company' (*sociedad anónima*), with the majority of the territorial heads as incorporators. Escolá and the core group had resisted from the very beginning IDOM becoming a 'joint stock company' (*sociedad anónima*), for they reckoned that that would put in jeopardy the very substance of their 'associational commitment'. So, in order to reduce this risk to a minimum, the incorporators of IDOM, S.A. agreed to sign a public document before a notary in 1984 by which they became mere fiduciaries of the firm, and declared that assets in fact belonged to the signatories of the 'associational commitment' (Cardenal and Vilallonga, 2004: 116–17).

Since then, the status quo has been maintained, with IDOM externally being a 'joint stock company' (*sociedad anónima*) although, internally, the 'associational commitment' guides its functioning. This dual system has held on throughout the firm's soul-searching during the first half of the 1990s, when it considered implementing structural and strategic changes to better respond to the needs of an evolving market (Calvo and Ricart, 1995).

Until then, IDOM had been organized into territorial groups so that its professionals could work more closely with clients, but industry trends seemed to be pointing in the direction of organizing the consultancy according to areas of technical expertise. By the end of this period, the board of directors had decided to adopt a matrix-like structure, in accordance not only with territorial groupings and areas of technical expertise (industrial engineering, civil engineering, architecture and construction, energy, the environment, and so forth), but also with the necessary general support functions (legal, financial, marketing and learning departments). These structural modifications undoubtedly introduced their own share of challenges in internal communication, the coordination of activities and the widening of the firm's international outreach (Prado and Ricart, 1996).

In 2000, IDOM's 'constitution' once more underwent a revision which introduced the figure of the 'member' (*socio*), different from that of the mere 'associate' (*asociado*) (IDOM, 2002). While stating clearly that there are no qualitative differences between members and associates in terms of property rights in IDOM, nevertheless, members have a greater hand than associates in management and oversight. In order to become a member, one first has to become an associate. Just like the associates, therefore, members come from all the ranks of workers in IDOM; but a longer tenure (12 years) and a greater commitment to its corporate philosophy and involvement in its management is required of them. Members are also expected to possess certain moral authority and professional prestige both within IDOM and externally. Individually and through their assembly, members are entrusted with the advisory function and supervision of the IDOM Board and Executive Committee, naming their constituents and exercising the right to introduce items in their respective agendas.

There are two major reasons for which we think that the corporate governance regime in IDOM qualifies as a corporate polity. The first refers to the level and degree of participation among its workers, both in the ownership and in the governance of the firm. The second derives from the establishment of the corporate common good as the guiding light for the whole of IDOM's operations.

IDOM as a service-provider has no other assets to offer its clients apart from the work of its professionals. In the beginning, it did not even count on any financial capital and its 'means of production' were negligible. However, the service it gave did not depend solely on the work of the engineers and other university graduates then in association with Escolá; its delivery would not have been possible without the collaboration of the support staff, composed of draftsmen, secretaries, administrative clerks and so forth. In other words, IDOM's output resulted just as much from the work of the engineers as from the work of the other members of the firm who had not received a college education. If that work were the 'property' or the means through which IDOM was able to satisfy its clients' needs and thereby earn an income, it was only logical that everyone who contributed to it be accorded a 'share in ownership'.

Granted that there was hardly any capital in IDOM but work, and everyone who contributed to it was entitled to a share in ownership, then the separation between owners or (financial) capitalists and workers within this context had no reason for being. Everyone who worked in IDOM could become a part-owner according to the 'associational commitment' precisely because of his work. In consequence, workers would no longer be receiving a salary from an employer in exchange for their labour – they would no longer be employees – but, instead, they would be receiving a 'share in value' from the work they carried out in conjunction with others. There would be hardly any distance between workers and the fruits of their labour: 'There is no employment contract between us [. . .] Neither are there two parties, one which hires and pays the other' (Cardenal and Vilallonga, 2004: 261).

The share in ownership and the participation in profits in IDOM, however, are not egalitarian but proportional. As Escolá himself explained, 'Some time back, I went down a road that led me to distribute 90 per cent of the property among you from the 100 per cent that I owned. You don't have to thank me for it because you've earned it. But logically, some of you have already earned much and others still not as much [. . .]. Those who do not have much yet [. . .] may experience the tendency to diminish the importance of these shares in value in IDOM. To these I say, "Get rid of that tendency!" I would have nothing of egalitarianism when it comes to this, because those who have spent their lives in IDOM would consider it utter foolishness. The time and effort they have put into it make them see IDOM as something very much their own and no one has the right to take that away from them' (Cardenal and Vilallonga, 2004: 260).

Not all workers are given an equal share in ownership or receive the same income. As explained earlier, a worker's income in IDOM depends on his professional level, the tasks he carries out, the scope of his responsibility, his job objectives and accomplishments, seniority and family allowance (Alcázar and Melé, 1996: 4). Part of the income is given in cash and another part is destined to increase a worker's 'share in value'.

There is also a proportionality in the involvement of different workers in the management and governance of the firm. Although all signatories of the 'associational commitment' have an equal say in approving or rejecting modifications regarding the ownership structure of the firm and its valuation, as well as approving or rejecting the presidential nominees presented by the board, they do not enjoy the same power and authority in the rest of the matters concerning the firm. In these other issues the votes of associates are weighted according to the number of years transpired since they signed the 'associational commitment'. As explained earlier, members have more 'political rights' of control and oversight although they share the same 'economic rights' of ownership as associates (IDOM, 2002).

Positions of power and authority in IDOM, however, are not conceived as objects of ambition from which one could take advantage of the work of subordinates for one's own benefit. Rather, they are above all perceived as opportunities – demanding no small amount of self-sacrifice – to serve others. The first point of Escolá's testament upon leaving the presidency in 1979 reads: 'You should see in whomsoever carries out executives functions . . . just one more among the people in this engineering firm who tries his best to fulfil an assignment entrusted to him. Thank him for the service that he renders to you. He does so even when he goes about the arduous task of evaluating each one and determining that person's retribution: someone else has to do it since it wouldn't be logical that each one set his own income. Responsibility is a heavy burden and giving orders is never pleasant, much less when it is not one's professional goal; I am certain that those who do so right now would very much rather work exclusively as engineers. Help them to fulfil their executive function without compromises. They should truly govern and make whoever does not obey see the damage he inflicts on the rest of the group. If you make governing too difficult for them, or if they themselves were to become too soft and not concretize whatever they have to concretize, I assure you that, in spite of everyone being excellent professionals and human beings, IDOM would disappear in a few years (and if you weren't all that good, in less than a year)' (Cardenal and Vilallonga, 2004: 258–9).

If Escolá had insisted so much on building an atmosphere of trust in IDOM, all the more so with respect to those who govern: 'one should always think that they wish one well, and that what they say corresponds exactly to what they think, and nothing more. As for them, they should always behave this way and appear to do so' (Cardenal and Vilallonga, 2004: 259). It certainly helps to know that executives and directors are not attached to the prerogatives of their position – like Escolá himself, they would simply prefer to be working as engineers. It is only out of necessity that they assume the job of governing IDOM, and they try to do so with a spirit of service, for the good of the whole.

Proof of the detachment of those who govern from their executive positions is that Escolá, in his lifetime, witnessed the voluntary and peaceful handover of the reins of power in the firm twice: first, to Luis Olaortúa in 1979 and, later, to Felipe Prósper in 1995. Furthermore, those who feel a greater attraction to wield power than to exercise their engineering profession normally end up leaving IDOM in due time, by some natural process of self-selection (Alcázar and Melé, 1996: 11). Participation in the management and governance of IDOM is likewise facilitated by the autonomy or independence of the different territorial groups (*agrupaciones*). In his testament Escolá admonished them 'never to make a common fund, since that would induce each group not to fight its own battles and depend instead on a centralized economic organization. Keep your independence, but neither should you be aloof when one of the groups is having difficulties and deny it your help, albeit at the cost of your own savings. Otherwise, the rest of the groups would treat you with the same indifference. Everyone could have a hard time, sooner or later: when your turn comes, you would then wish you had been more generous with your help to the others in the past' (Cardenal and Vilallonga, 2004: 262).

In this regard, Escolá was talking from experience, not from mere theory. Between 1967 and 1968, the Bilbao group experienced severe cashflow problems (Cardenal and Vilallonga, 2004: 132–4). As an initial measure, workers had to renounce part of their monthly retribution in order for the office to survive, but, later on, it also became necessary to let go of a fourth of the 100 workers in the office. Of the redundant workers, 23 were afterwards relocated at other IDOM groups, while the remaining two made monthly trips to the Bilbao office to collect the difference between their unemployment cheques and what would have been their normal retribution. In the end, the Bilbao group was saved, thanks to the help it received from the workers themselves and the assistance from the Zaragoza and Barcelona offices.

In this same vein, the Gijón group, a decade later, had to be closed down owing to the coal mining crisis in the region, but half of its engineers were relocated to other offices and half granted generous severance payments (Cardenal and Vilallonga, 2004: 127–30). Nevertheless, the workers of the Gijón office before it closed sent Escolá a moving letter expressing their thanks and their pride in having formed part of IDOM (Cardenal and Vilallonga, 2004: 213). This mutual help among IDOM workers and groups was part of a tradition that stretches back to the early 1960s, when there was no money for the two extra months' pay, nor for the Christmas bonus (Cardenal and Vilallonga, 2004: 131). The executive committee tried to keep everyone informed of the situation (lest he or she spend that money beforehand) and, when finally, the financial problems were overcome, there was great joy and relief for all.

What indicators could we cite in support of the idea of the common corporate good as the primary aim of those who govern IDOM? We could begin by eliminating what could be its strongest contender, that is, wealth maximization. As Escolá himself confessed, 'We never really earned much money, and because of that, we had to make maximum use of profits, directing as much as possible to reserves' (Escolá, 1993: 16). Coupled with the zeal with which IDOM guarded its independence, never were there attempts to source capital externally and all growth had to be organic.

Certainly, one could earn a lot more money outside IDOM, if that is what one were after. As one engineer admitted, regarding the system of retribution through 'shares in value': 'In practice, it doesn't mean much money until one has been in the firm for about fifteen years, but we're proud of it: it's one of the pillars of our identity as an "association of professionals" in the long term, although, in the short term, it may not seem like it. Moreover, it's one of the reasons for which people, in the long term, identify their personal interests with those of the firm' (Alcázar and Melé, 1996: 5). Others do not share such a rosy view and think that 'shares in value' are not that valid an incentive, either in the short or in the long term. For one, they are very widely distributed and they benefit most the more senior members of IDOM, regardless of their performance and contribution to the development of the firm. Instead, these other members welcome the introduction in the mid-1990s of another variable component in the pay package, related to performance and the fulfilment of objectives, rather than mere 'shares in value' (Alcázar and Melé, 1996: 10).

Another limit to the amount of money that IDOM professionals take home comes from Escolá's absolute prohibition that they accept anything apart from their honoraria: 'in order to preserve the independence we now have with regard to external proprietors and with regard to financial and commercial entities, it is necessary that you reject whatever invitation to accept anything other than your professional fees. The day that you think you could accept some other form of payment (over and above our project cost, and so forth) since it wouldn't affect your independent judgment anyway, you would have crossed the threshold over to a different kind of engineering firm and you would have lost the main kind of clients that we now have' (Cardenal and Vilallonga, 2004: 259). Escolá was uncompromising in his belief that this was the cost of IDOM's professional independence and, ultimately, of its prestige or good name.

If people remain in IDOM despite opportunities to earn greater wealth elsewhere, what other things of value could the firm offer them in exchange? First is the chance for continued professional development, inasmuch as IDOM has always been conceived from the very beginning, by Escolá and his associates, as a place for lifelong learning. No doubt this feature of IDOM's corporate culture was heavily influenced by Escolá's own personal experience, having been director of the INAR Academy for engineering and architectural students and an associate professor, first at the school of engineering in Bilbao, where he taught 'Complementary installations of factories' between 1959 and 1964, and later on in Saint Sebastian, where he took charge of the subject of 'Engineering ethics' between 1984 and 1992. He had also written scores of books and monographs related to engineering and character formation, including *Deontología para ingenieros* ('Deontology for Engineers') which has, since then, undergone many editions and translations. Between his forays into academe, he also set up a 'graduate school of engineering' within IDOM itself in 1968 (Cardenal and Vilallonga, 2004: 163–6). During the 25 years that this school was operational, over 300 young engineers went through the programme and it served as an excellent recruitment channel, albeit serendipitously, for the firm itself, which always had the first choice among the graduates. The school likewise fulfilled the function of some sort of informal 'placement agency' where many different firms in need of engineering professionals would come to hunt for talent.

Despite the understandable difficulties of intergenerational conflict between the seniors and the juniors in IDOM, Escolá always insisted on what both parties stood to gain from a symbiotic relationship. The senior engineer would certainly be obliged to put his ideas in order and to clarify concepts, since he would have to put things down in writing for a junior partner, but then again he could count on the help of this younger person for tasks which might seem more tedious or repetitive. The younger engineers would engage in a process of 'learning by doing' under the seniors' tutelage, but at the same time, they could contribute youthfulness and vitality to the older partners' problem-solving scenarios. A fulfilling professional career is very much a possibility within IDOM, as the experience of Pero-Sanz bears out (Cardenal and Vilallonga, 2004: 170). As mentioned earlier, Pero-Sanz began working in IDOM in 1961, at the age of 14, and became one of its first non-professional associates. He then compatibilized his work with engineering studies until he graduated in 1972. At that time he received an offer which bettered that of IDOM. Two years later, however, Pero-Sanz returned to IDOM because Escolá told him that he was needed.

This emphasis in IDOM on life-long professional development even above profit maximization as a better way to contribute to the corporate common good seems to contradict its very high turnover rates, which at times reached the alarming figure of 50 per cent (Cardenal and Vilallonga, 2004: 167–9; Escolá, 1993: 30–32). The threat to IDOM from such a drain on its human capital was clear. Some executives suggested including a clause in the contracts with clients, prohibiting them from making job offers to IDOM professionals. Because of his love for freedom Escolá felt inclined to oppose such a move from the outset. Yet what carried the day was typically an engineer's argument, based on the quantification of processes. Escolá calculated that, since half of the engineers eventually leave IDOM – a fourth in the short and another fourth in the medium to long terms, they would have to take in 200 in order to be able to keep at least 100. The solution, therefore, lies in creating a huge flow of engineers in and out of IDOM. That way, an individual's right to seek a better job opportunity would be safeguarded, while IDOM would be able to keep the engineers it needed. At the same time, the firm would also be able to contribute to the common good of society by providing well-trained engineers for the job market.

Just in case the message in this respect was not sufficiently clear, Escolá wrote down in one of IDOM's corporate documents, 'If the opportunity to pursue further studies were to arise which would entail a part-time dedication to work, the interested party will be advised independently of the convenience or inconvenience that such a move would mean for IDOM' (Cardenal and Vilallonga, 2004: 168). Furthermore, instead of retaining people through clauses in their contracts, Escolá was of the opinion that IDOM should enrich their job profile, present them with tasks that are attractive and challenging, provide them with a nurturing environment, and so forth. In other words, the firm should only resort to means that fully respect a person's freedom to choose his place of work.

Notwithstanding IDOM's interest in the continuing formation of its professionals and the respect it shows for their choice of place of work, there are some discordant voices in the practical application of such principles (Alcázar and Melé, 1996: 8–11). One engineer thought that a number of senior engineers had been allowed to get left behind and out of date in their knowledge and skills, owing to excessive 'protectionism', tolerance and complacency. If the firm had really considered their full professional development in the first place, then it should have prodded them to seek it, either within IDOM or without. Some other engineers expressed their opinion that IDOM's policy of separating technical or professional expertise from management positions or positions of authority may be responsible for the feeling of dissatisfaction that push people out of the door. When one begins at IDOM as a young engineer and is told that his overriding purpose is to develop his technical expertise, usually he has no problem accepting that. But as one approaches middle age – say, between 35 and 40 – a person often finds himself confronted with a choice between his love for engineering and a certain desire for power. Those who choose the latter and see their strategic options in IDOM severely limited, pack their bags and go.

Leaving is never an easy decision, all the more so in IDOM. A signatory of the 'associational commitment' who leaves IDOM is obliged to sell his 'shares in value' back to the firm. He is then reimbursed the nominal value of his shares, multiplied by a progressive coefficient depending on the number of years spent in the firm (Alcázar and Melé, 1996: 9). If he had spent more than 18 years in IDOM, he would recover the full value of his shares. However, if the financial status of the firm recommends a delay in the pay-out, the sale is put on hold and the person concerned has to wait.

Apart from the churn rate of around 50 per cent among professionals, another potential trouble sign in IDOM comes from the proportion of signatories of the 'associational commitment' with respect to the total, which in 1996 stood at a little more than half, or 280 out of 500 workers (Alcázar and Melé, 1996: 1, 9). These associates include professionals, such as engineers, and members of the support staff, composed of secretaries, draftsmen and so forth. Whereas, in the beginning, a couple of years were enough for one to take part in the 'associational commitment', the time requirement has been raised to a minimum of eight years. The proportion of associates with respect to the other workers in IDOM is, of course, closely related to the turnover rates and proper career planning. The attrition rate among workers until the first three or four years is quite high, although it falls sharply afterwards. In this respect, IDOM behaves much like other professional consultancy firms where recent graduates simply earn their wings to spread them out to fly elsewhere.

Nonetheless, this essential element of IDOM's identity, its retention rate, has been undergoing certain revision in recent years. A former president explained that only those truly committed to the 'philosophy' and development of the firm should form part of the 'associational commitment' and, with this in mind, 'there are many associates who shouldn't be here' (Alcázar and Melé, 1996: 9). Another executive remarked that membership in the 'associational commitment' should depend on the strategy that IDOM wishes to pursue. If it wanted to be a high value-added service firm, then perhaps associates should be limited to university graduates only, but if the offer basically consisted in the work-hours of project managers, draftsmen and so forth, then the current set up may be adequate.

What one may draw from all these considerations concerning the professional development opportunities, the turnover rate and the proportion of associates to the total number of workers in IDOM, is that the firm sets very high levels of professional demands and commitment, thereby constituting an extremely selective work environment. IDOM definitely is not the ideal working place for everyone, not even for the majority; and this is so for reasons other than one's technical expertise or professional competence. The firm has a well-determined set of values requiring an almost unconditional commitment, turning it into quite an exclusive work community.

IDOM mirrors the Aristotelian ideal of a corporate polity not only because of the participation of its associates in ownership and management, but also because of their earnest desire to seek the corporate common good in the first place. This means paying attention, above all, to the full development of workers. However, apart from a professional or technical dimension, as we have just considered, this also entails a distinctively human or ethical one, pertaining to the practice of the virtues. Throughout this narration we have seen how Escolá and those who joined him as well as their successors fostered the growth of human virtues in the IDOM work environment: a love for freedom together with the assumption of attendant responsibilities, professional competence and a continuous effort to improve, honesty and truthfulness, a desire to help others and to be of service, teamwork, generosity and magnanimity towards the faults and defects of others, candour or a trusting attitude, and so forth. And all this has been achieved without neglect of the discipline imposed by running a business in the form of an engineering service firm.

IDOM as a whole and each and every one of its members bears the mark of trustworthiness, as the following story reveals (Cardenal and Vilallonga, 2004: 131–2). In 1965, the consultancy sector was undergoing rough sailing and IDOM's treasury was unable to meet its monthly obligations towards workers. Given its short credit record and low capitalization, any loan it could obtain from the bank would be insufficient. Escolá and Olaortúa then asked for an appointment with Joaquín de la Rica, the managing director of *Turbos Forjados*, a client firm. They explained their predicament to de la Rica and asked for 300 000 pesetas as advanced payment for future services. After making the pertinent consultations, de la Rica handed out the sum to Escolá and Olaortúa, who were then able to pay workers. Although, because of its youth, IDOM still did not enjoy a good credit standing before banks, it already had a sterling reputation of trustworthiness among its clients. For a professional services firm, that is an invaluable asset.

None of this means, of course, that IDOM as a firm or any of its constituents is perfect. It never made such claims in Escolá's time, nor has it since then. That is precisely the reason behind the following lines in Escolá's farewell letter: 'I ask pardon from all of you for the roughness of my character and for the lack of patience with which I have so often dealt with many of you. To those who have known me, I'd like you to know that you're what I value the most. I thank you for this mix of respect and trust that you have always shown me – I hope that you don't change in the future – with such good humour, besides. I have worked with you for almost 40 thousand hours (and I intend to add up four to five thousand more, if I don't die earlier). During all of this period, aside from earning a living, I have been able to fulfil my professional aspirations to such an extreme that, if today, I had to begin again, I would have no doubt in choosing to work with you again, you who have been my collaborators, work mates and friends. I hope that when you reach the age of 60, all of you could say something similar' (Cardenal and Vilallonga, 2004: 251).

III   THE MORE THE MERRIER?

Aristotle raises the issue of the advantages and disadvantages of having a multitude govern by citing Homer, who 'says that "it is not good to have a rule of many", but whether he means the corporate rule, or the rule of many individuals, is uncertain' (Pltcs, 1292a). That is, it was not really clear whether Homer referred to a government of various individuals who acted in unison (corporate rule) or to a multitude of individuals each of whom advocated his own manner of governance (rule of many individuals). Aristotle himself felt quite inclined to favour the rule of many over the rule of the few. 'For the many, of whom each individual is not a good man, when they meet together may be better than a few good, if regarded not individually but collectively [. . .]. For each individual among the many has a share of excellence and practical wisdom, and when they meet together, [. . .] they become in a manner of one man, [. . .] with regard to their character and thought. Hence the many are better judges than a single man [. . .] for some understand one part, and some another, and among them they understand the whole' (Pltcs, 1281b).

Aristotle expressed his confidence in that, precisely because of their number, although the individuals in themselves may not possess a high degree of excellence, they end up complementing each other and make up for each other's deficiencies and even faults. 'If people are not utterly degraded, although individually they may be worse judges than those who have special knowledge, as a body they are as good or better' (Pltcs, 1282a). Indeed, in unity there is strength, for even the small excellences all add up. That is why 'the many may urge their claim against the few; for, when taken collectively, and compared with the few, they are stronger, and richer and better' (Pltcs, 1283b).

There are two kinds of government by the many, democracies and polities. In a corporate setting, democracies have been exemplified by United Airlines, particularly during the period in which its ESOP took effect in the middle of 1994, until it filed for bankruptcy protection towards the end of 2002 and its ESOP became worthless. Although 'the many' among its workers had a share in ownership and indirectly participated in governance through their labour representatives, a true ownership culture was never put in place and each of the parties involved continued to seek its particular interest in the first place, even at the expense of the corporate common good. Polities, on the other hand, have been represented by IDOM Engineering Consultancy, beginning the time in which its associational commitment was formalized in the early 1960s. In IDOM, unlike the situation in United Airlines, an authentic culture of ownership and participation even preceded the legal mechanism through which 'shares in value' were distributed among the qualifying workers. IDOM's corporate culture was put to the test several times by the inevitable vagaries of economic life and its constituent members always rose to the occasion, clearly sacrificing their individual interests for the good of all in the organization.

Relatively, Aristotle had little to say about polities in contrast to democracies. He even used a generic name to refer to them ('constitutional government'), because 'one man or a few may excel in excellence; but as the number increases it becomes more difficult for them to attain perfection in every kind of excellence' (Pltcs, 1279b). Most of his comments on polities were reserved, instead, for the 'mixed rule' – a combination between an oligarchy and a democracy – which represented for him the best attainable political regime, not in theory, but in practice.

More references could be found in the *Politics* to democracies, especially in their comparison to oligarchies. Aristotle acknowledged that the difference between these two types of regimes lay not so much in the numbers, the many versus the few, as in certain qualities of those who rule or govern. Democracies represent the rule of a majority who are poor and who value equality and freedom greatly, whereas oligarchies are the government of the wealthy. 'The number of the governing body, whether the greater number, as in a democracy, or the smaller number, as in an oligarchy, is an accident due to the fact that the rich everywhere are few, and the poor numerous. [. . .] For the real difference between democracy and oligarchy is poverty and wealth. Wherever men rule by reason of their wealth, whether they be few or many, that is an oligarchy, and where the poor rule, that is a democracy' (Pltcs, 1279b–1280a).

In a democracy, therefore, the note on poverty simply arises from the observation that there are always more poor people than rich ones in any given society. How, then, are the two other characteristics of a democracy, freedom and equality (Pltcs, 1317b), related to each other? In its extreme form, citizens in a democracy think that justice consists in a strict equality, such that, being equal in one sense, they should also be equal in all others. For them, 'that equality is the supremacy of the popular will; and that freedom means doing what one likes. In such democracies everyone lives as he pleases, or in the words of Euripides, "according to his fancy". But this is all wrong; men should not think it slavery to live according to the rule of the constitution; for it is their salvation' (Pltcs, 1310a). Being equal, every citizen in a democracy should be able to do as he pleases, even to the extent of disregarding the law or the constitution. But this idea of freedom is what brings such a democracy's downfall. True freedom consists in living in accordance with the law and the constitution. Therein lies democracy's salvation.

These characteristics of democracies, poverty, equality and freedom, give rise to a series of operational procedures (Pltcs, 1317b–1318a). First, the election of officers should be made by all out of all, by lot, and hardly requiring any property qualification: if ever, only a very low one. Second, there should be payment for the services rendered to the state. And thirdly, no magistracies or offices should be perpetual and, instead, all citizens should govern and be governed in turn.

All these elements of procedural democractic justice are easily traced in the functioning of United's corporate governance during the period in which its ESOP was in effect. Board representatives from each of the labour unions could be elected from any one of its respective members, without further requirements. They could vote and be voted into office in turn, and they were entitled to remuneration while carrying out their official duties. Not so in IDOM, where board and executive committee membership was limited to a certain class of workers – some professional, and indirectly, property qualification was required – and was not subject to universal suffrage. Even here it becomes clear that the governance in IDOM did not exactly fit into the democratic mould.

In the *Politics*, Aristotle considered at least two different ways of classifying democracies. One attended to the population, its predominant mode of living and other features ensuing from this (Pltcs, 1291b–1292a). By virtue of this classification, Aristotle distinguished among states where the majority were farmers, artisans, labourers, merchants, and so forth, assigning to each its own ideal of democratic justice. One was based on strict equality, another, on a low property qualification, and such like. Interestingly, Aristotle set apart demagogies as the worst form of democracies. These are regimes in which the multitude, and not the law, bear the supreme power. However, the multitude referred to here is one subject to the impassioned appeals to prejudices and emotions by the demagogue, not one that jointly engages in any rational consideration. Rhetoric, not reason, carries the day. 'For in democracies which are subject to the law the best citizens hold the first place, and there are no demagogues; but where the laws are not supreme, there demagogues spring up' (Pltcs, 1292a). This may well describe the situation at United when its ESOP unravelled. Not only did the leaders of each of the parties prefer their private good – for instance, keeping the bargaining power of the labour unions – to that of the whole company, they also employed every effort to convince their constituents that the stance adopted was to their best advantage.

The other classification of democracies focused on the manner in which the legislative, the executive and the judicial powers of the state were exercised (Pltcs, 1317a). Because of this, IDOM, which is a polity or a constitutional rule, may mimic a democratic regime. Take for granted the manner in which IDOM's head is subject to confirmation by the vote of the members of the associational commitment, or the way in which this same assembly could choose to approve or reject proposed changes in the valuation and distribution of 'shares in value'.

Finally, Aristotle's musings on the mechanisms of regime change or revolutions in democracies also shed light on corporate settings. By and large, because democracies generally allow citizens to do whatever they like, they are the most tolerable – and stable – among perverted regimes (Pltcs, 1289b). The stability of governments depends on whether those who desire the maintenance of the status quo outnumber those who wish for a change, and each of the two groups is usually formed on the basis of the 'quality' – that is, freedom, wealth, education, good birth – of its members. Revolutions occur as a result of significant changes in both the quantity and the quality of states, as when the number of the poor exceed a certain proportion and transform the regime into a democracy, for example. Once more, this phenomenon helps explain what occurred at United when the pilots' labour union, the ALPA, gained enough strength to sabotage the whole of the airline's operations through a strike and forcibly extract their demands from management.

IV   IN BRIEF

- United Airlines may be considered a corporate democracy because, through its ESOP, large swathes of workers (though not all) were able to gain ownership stakes in the company. Indirectly, ESOP subscribers were also granted a say in corporate governance through their representatives on the board. However, a true ownership culture was never implemented. It did not take long for each party to the ESOP to start looking after its own interest exclusively: management sought lower wages, pilots wanted power over strategic decisions and mechanics pursued job security. Mainly for this reason, compounded by other external factors such as the 11 September 2001 terrorist attacks, United was forced to apply for bankruptcy protection and its ESOP became worthless.
- IDOM Engineering Consultancy exemplifies a corporate polity because, through its 'associational commitment', workers had a chance to participate in the ownership and in the governance of the firm. For extraneous reasons, IDOM's legal status does not strictly correspond to its internal practice, which is guaranteed only by private agreements. Neither does every IDOM associate vote on equal footing with the rest on all governance issues. There is no doubt, however, that the common good of the firm takes precedence

over the particular interests of its constituents, as proved by their willingness to sacrifice personal gains during periods of crisis. Likewise, there are sufficient proofs of the respect and support of the firm for the professional and moral growth of its members.

● Aristotle looks kindly on the rules of the many, insofar as the multitude could water down individual faults and magnify individual excellences. Nonetheless, he still insists on differentiating democracies, which strive after particular interests, and polities, which pursue the common good. Compared to democracies, he hardly expounds on polities.

● Democracies are further characterized by their emphasis on justice as equality and freedom, understood as conformity to the law in the best, and doing whatever one likes in the worst, of cases (demagogy). This entails certain principles of procedural justice regarding the terms and conditions of being elected into office. This voting system, however, is not immune to the influence of demagogues. They make use of their rhetorical prowess over their fellow citizens' feelings and emotions to provoke a regime change or revolution to serve their own particular interests.

REFERENCES

Alcázar, Manuel and Domènec Melé (1996), *La Filosofía de IDOM*, TD-40/O-391-010, IESE International Graduate School of Management, University of Navarra, Barcelona-Madrid.

Aristotle (1990), *The Politics*, ed. Stephen Everson, Cambridge: Cambridge University Press.

Arndt, Michael (2000), 'Employee ownership isn't buying labor peace at United Airlines', *Business Week*, 10 April.

Arndt, Michael and Wendy Zellner (2002), 'How to keep United flying', *Business Week*, 13 December.

Belton, Beth (2000), 'United's James Goodwin: "We didn't cave" ', *Business Week*, 2 November.

Bergstresser, Daniel D., Kenneth A. Froot and Darren R. Smart (2006), 'UAL, 2004: Pulling Out of Bankruptcy', 9-205-090, Harvard Business School, Boston.

Bernstein, Aaron (2002), 'Stock options: fuel for United's revival', *Business Week*, 8 November.

Bernstein, Aaron and Michael Arndt (2002), 'United may fly around a strike', *Business Week*, 14 February.

Bryant, Adam (1994a), 'After 7 years, employees win United Airlines', *The New York Times*, 13 July.

Bryant, Adam (1994b), 'Pilots with a management attitude', *The New York Times*, 2 September.

Bryant, Adam (1994c), 'Company reports; a down-to-earth view at United', *The New York Times*, 28 October.

Calvo, Marcos and Joan Enric Ricart (1995), *IDOM, S. A.*, DG-1122-E/O-395-067, IESE International Graduate School of Management, University of Navarra, Barcelona-Madrid.

Cardenal, Ana and Gabriel Vilallonga (2004), *Rafael Escolá. Ingeniero*, Madrid: Fundación Rafael Escolá.

Chandler, Susan (1996), 'United we own', *Business Week*, 18 March.

Cohen, Susan I. (2001), 'United Airlines' ESOP woes', *Risk Management*, **48**(6), 9, 1 June.

The Economist (2003), 'A capital idea', 27 March.

Escolá, Rafael (1987), *Deontología para Ingenieros*, Pamplona: Eunsa.

Escolá, Rafael (1993), *Cómo nace y se hace una empresa de ingeniería*, Bilbao: Escuela Superior de Ingenieros Industriales y de Ingenieros de Telecomunicación de Bilbao.

Flanigan, James (2002), 'United is a poor model for employee ownership', *Los Angeles Times*, 4 December.

Gates, Jeffrey R. (1998), *The Ownership Solution: Toward a Shared Capitalism for the 21st Century*, Reading, MA: Addison-Wesley.

Hopkins, Marc (2002), 'United Air case pits employees stk rights vs co's future', *Dowjones Newswires*, 20 December.

IDOM (2002), 'Compromiso Asociativo y Gobierno en IDOM', *DB-105*, 7 February.

Jurek, Walter (1994), 'Airlines and employee ownership', *Corporate Growth Report Weekly*, 3 January.

Kochan, Thomas A. (1999), 'United Airlines', *Rebuilding the Social Contract at Work: Lessons from Leading Cases*, Task Force Working Paper #WP09, Institute for Work Employment Research, Cambridge, MA: MIT Sloan School of Management.

Kruse, Douglas (2002), 'Research evidence on prevalence and effects of employee ownership', *Testimony before the Subcommittee on Employer-Employee Relations, Committee on Education and the Workforce, U.S. House of Representatives*, 13 February, www.nber.org/~confer/2002/lss02/kruse.pdf (accessed 9 May 2007).

Mackin, Christopher and Loren Rodgers (2003), 'But what about United Airlines? Answering tough questions', *The ESOP Report*, January.

Manjoo, Farhad (2002), 'United's ESOP fable', *Salon.com*, 12 December, http://dir.salon.com/story/tech/feature/2002/12/12/esop/index.html (accessed 8 May 2007).

Pontifical Council for Justice and Peace (2004), *Compendium of the Social Doctrine of the Church*, Rome: Librería Editrice Vaticana.

Prado, Jaime and Joan Enric Ricart (1996), *IDOM (B)*, DG-1176/O-397-115, IESE, International Graduate School of Management, University of Navarra, Barcelona-Madrid.

Reinbergs, Indra A. and Dwight B. Crane (2000), *Note on Employee Stock Ownership Plans (ESOPs) and Phantom Stock Plans*, 9-201-034, Harvard Business School, Cambridge, MA.

Rosen, Corey (2002), 'United Airlines, ESOPs, and employee ownership', National Center for Employee Ownership, November, www.nceo.org/library/united_esop.html (accessed 25 April 2007).

Rosen, Corey and Michael Quarrey (1987), 'How well is employee ownership working?', *Harvard Business Review*, September–October, 4–7.

Rosen, Corey, John Case and Martin Staubus (2005), 'Every employee an owner. Really', *Harvard Business Review*, June, 1–8.

United Airlines (2007), 'United history', *Company information*, www.united.com/
    page/middlepage/0,6823,2286,00.html (accessed 2 May).
Wikipedia (2007), 'United Airlines', http://en.wikipedia.org/wiki/United_Airlines
    (accessed 7 May).

8.   Governance as praxis

So far, we have gone through the different political regimes described by Aristotle and we have seen how they apply to various corporate governance contexts. The time has come for us now to identify and expound on what could be the Stagirite's main contribution to this ongoing discussion: the understanding of governance as a kind of an activity that comes under the name of praxis.

In their work on the corporate governance practices in Flemish family businesses, Van den Berghe and Carchon (2002) designed a framework that could prove to be very helpful in our study. They distinguished among five different perspectives from which the exercise of corporate governance could be analysed. Corporate governance could be understood at (1) the level of the board of directors, from (2) the so-called 'corporate governance tripod' that brings together shareholders, directors and management, from (3) the angle of a firm's direct stakeholders, such as its employees, suppliers and customers, from (4) the viewpoint of a firm's indirect stakeholders – that is, government, the environment and society at large – and finally, from (5) an all-encompassing global angle that accounts for the economic and legal systems apart from the culture, values and norms in which a business organization is embedded. The majority of studies concerning corporate governance focus exclusively on a single one of these levels, inadvertently ignoring the others which, nevertheless, could also be very significant. Van den Berghe and Carchon's framework possesses the additional merit of being quite intuitive or readily understandable in its proposed widening of the corporate governance landscape.

Firstly, corporate governance studies carried out at the board level are undoubtedly the simplest ones. As Gevurtz (2004: 93–5) has reminded us, there are other governance options apart from the board-centred model. In a partnership, for instance, the partner-owners themselves may manage the firm, whereas this possibility is not open to a corporation's shareholders. By virtue of being shareholders, these people only have rights to elect directors and to vote on matters that directors submit for their approval; they have no right to manage the corporation themselves. There are, of course, various justifications for a board-centred model of corporate governance, such as the need for central management, the benefits of group decision making, the demands for the representation of corporate constituents and

215

for the mediation of their claims, and the exigency of management oversight (Gevurtz, 2004: 95–102).

Second-level corporate governance research broadens its scope by considering not only the dynamics within the board but also the relationships among directors, shareholders and management. However, these relationships are discussed almost solely in terms of the principal–agent theory, which unfortunately is too abstract, elementary and untextured. Without necessarily abandoning the principal–agent paradigm, third-level corporate governance studies nonetheless signify an improvement on the former, because they advocate a more holistic view of the firm as a networked organization operating in a distinctive socioeconomic environment. This means that not only the interests of shareholder-principals as expressed through their representative corporate directors and those of manager-agents matter, but so do the concerns of other direct stakeholder groups, such as workers, clients and suppliers, for example. Here is where deliberations referring to corporate social responsibility and corporate citizenship finally come to play. Yet again the prevailing corporate governance mandate of 'balancing stakeholder interests' seems too difficult, if not impossible, actually to put into practice. The same could be said with far greater reason when the range of stakeholders is expanded to make room for the indirect ones, like the state or the environment, as the fourth-level corporate governance analysis suggests.

Van den Berghe and Carchon (2002) cannot be more on the spot in affirming the importance of the economic, legal and cultural – including ethical – environments in corporate governance studies, but they err in thinking that these are just another dimension that adds up to all the previous ones, somehow completing them. Rather, what they consider to be the fifth or the global perspective in corporate governance research already needs to be taken into account, in fact, from the very beginning. That is to say, even when we situate ourselves only in the first-level corporate governance studies focusing on board dynamics, we should already be mindful of the economic, legal, cultural and ethical baggage of the different players. Another way of expressing this is, of course, that corporate governance is a political activity that necessarily takes into account all these different dimensions of human agents and of the groups they form or inhabit, particularly those of the corporation and of society as a whole. As Gevurtz remarks, 'human beings, even in the business context, do not divorce their notions of how to run a business from their broader political and cultural ideas' (Gevurtz, 2004: 172–3).

In their research on the global history of corporate governance, Morck and Steier (2005) have reminded us that practically every country is organized in a different way, with regard to its economic, legal, cultural and ethical environments. Even if a capitalist system may generally be presupposed among countries, such that production and the distribution of rents were organized on the basis of individual savings, it so happens that there are still several varieties of capitalism to choose from. Family capitalism, bank capitalism, state-guided capitalism, managerial capitalism and shareholder capitalism are just some of the different versions found in the world today. That a representative sampling of corporations in any given country prefers to adopt one strand of capitalism over another is a phenomenon that the principal–agent theory, by itself, would be hard pressed to explain. The motivations of the different actors, both individual and institutional, are far too complex for agency theory alone to make sense of. Given the diversity of capitalisms that reflects a similarly diverse panorama of corporate governance environments, it becomes very difficult indeed to find measures or mechanisms that would prove universally effective.

Oftentimes we encounter detailed prescriptions to enhance board effectiveness for governance (Lawler and Dysart, 2007). In the United States, with regard to board composition and structure, there are supposed to be age and term limits for directors as well as limits in the number of boards where they may serve; it is also advisable to have independent directors and to have one of them, or at least a non-executive or external director, to act as chair, we are told. Boards are likewise admonished to hold regular executive sessions and strategic retreats (keeping an information channel independent of management notwithstanding), carry out periodic visits to company operations and receive a continuing education. As for the thorny issue of executive compensation, there also appears to be a consensus that it should be linked to company performance and that a mandatory shareholder approval of remuneration packages would be helpful in containing it.

Within Europe, while leaving a margin for differences in board structure, that is, the two-tier management and supervisory boards found in German-speaking countries and the full unitary boards dominant in countries such as the United Kingdom and Spain, some form of convergence, nonetheless, is sought in what may be understood as good governance style (Heidrick and Struggles, 2005). For instance, boards are encouraged to constitute committees specializing in audit, compensation and nomination; membership, internationalized and diversified; and transparency and disclosure, especially on pay, increased.

However, despite all these efforts, we still have to come up with a foolproof set of corporate governance guidelines or best practices. As has already been insinuated, this is because of the significant differences in the environments of countries, each of which is characterized by its own unique legal, economic and cultural or ethical systems. For any given country, therefore, a truly effective corporate governance system would have to be, in large measure, 'path-dependent' (Morck and Steier, 2005: 4). This means that much of the good corporate governance practice in any particular country environment is an 'accident of history' (Morck and Steier, 2005: 18), hardly applicable to a different setting.

Just the same, we should not conclude that, because corporate governance systems are 'path-dependent', 'accidents of history', varying from one country to another as a function of political tradition, there are no universal guidelines available for good corporate governance. That would be tantamount to falling into some sort of unrestrained relativism. Instead, as Aristotle would recommend, we should look for certain universal elements in the practice of governance that would stand the tests of time and place. These, in short, are what he calls virtues.

How do the different Aristotelian virtues apply as excellences in the practice of corporate governance? As we have had the chance to examine, most studies in effective corporate governance propose that boards constitute committees specializing in nomination, compensation, compliance and audit functions, for example. The nominations committee would be entrusted primarily with the recruitment of suitable board candidates. To carry out its task, Aristotle would exhort the members of this committee to search for candidates who display the following character traits or virtues: 'first of all, loyalty to the constitution; then the highest administrative capacity; and excellence and justice of the kind proper to each form of government' (Pltcs, 1309a). Then again, 'for if the ruler is intemperate and unjust, how can he rule well?' (Pltcs, 1260a). Loyalty, administrative capacity and justice are the characteristics that should count as truly relevant merits, rather than considerations born out of a purported birthright, the possession of superior material wealth or a favourable stroke of luck or good fortune. Included in these merits are foresight and mastery in knowledge; yet most important of all is excellence of character. For, as Aristotle states elsewhere, 'a ruler ought to have excellence of character in perfection, for his function, taken absolutely, demands a master artificer' (Pltcs, 1260a).

With respect to the compensation committee, assigned with the function of determining the pay of top management and of directors, Aristotle insists on the value of moderation or temperance. The objective for which the members of the remuneration committee should aim is to enable the ruler not only to live temperately but also liberally; for this he must therefore possess a sufficient amount of property. When faced by the lure of material things and pleasures, moderation or temperance means self-mastery, while liberality requires generosity or the inclination to give and share freely what one has with others who may experience greater need. But to live both temperately and, beyond that, liberally seems to be more a matter of education or training in the virtues rather than of ownership of a specific amount of resources. No given quantity of resources by itself could guarantee either temperance or liberality, yet, having been appropriately educated in these virtues, the exact amount of property owned seems to matter less. We should be more preoccupied with providing the chance to cultivate the requisite virtues when determining directors' and executives' pay than with arriving at a fixed amount or formula. The pay structure and limits that we set only represent means that could facilitate the practice of temperance or moderation and liberality on the part of top managers and board members.

Precisely in the name of moderation, Plato in the *Laws* forbade citizens from possessing more than five times the minimum property qualification; thinking that virtues were more important than setting any fixed amount, Aristotle in the *Politics*, however, did not wish to go that far (Pltcs, 1266b). For Aristotle, temperance and moderation does not mean setting an equal amount of possessions for all, 'for it is not the possessions but the desires of mankind which require to be equalized, and this is impossible, unless a sufficient education is provided by the laws' (Pltcs, 1266b). Instead of embracing egalitarianism, Aristotle advocated the education of desire, particularly with regard to material possessions, such that people would not crave more than what they actually need.

Nonetheless, Aristotle was also concerned that governors or the members of the ruling class received adequate pay, lest they become badly-off and readily prone to bribes. More importantly, those who decide on compensation matters should take care that rulers do not illicitly enrich themselves by taking advantage of their office. Normally, 'people do not take any great offence at being kept out of government – indeed they are rather pleased than otherwise at having leisure for their private business – but what irritates them is to think that their rulers are stealing public money; then they are doubly annoyed, for they lose both honor and profit' (Pltcs, 1380b). In fact, in the best viable regime in practice or polity, which is a cross between democracy and aristocracy, holding offices does not translate into instant riches, since 'all would be able to hold office, which is like the aim of democracy, and the notables would be magistrates, which is the aim of aristocracy' (Pltcs, 1308b–1309a). Pay is certainly a powerful motivator, but, for a good governor, it should neither be the only nor the most powerful one. If that were the case, organizations would always be under the threat of losing their governors to the highest bidder. It is in the remuneration committee's interest that the top executives' and directors' pay should be more than adequate to allow for a liberal lifestyle, but it should even be more concerned that they practise moderation and temperance.

A third body within the board, the compliance committee, takes care that the conduct of directors be in accordance with the rules and principles it has set for itself. Largely because these rules of conduct have been determined and imposed by the board of governors upon themselves, Aristotle underscores the importance of obedience to them, even in what could otherwise be considered as trifles. He explains, 'in all well-balanced governments there is nothing which should be more jealously maintained than the spirit of obedience to law, more especially in small matters; for transgression creeps in unperceived and at last ruins the state, just as the constant recurrence of small expenses in time eats up a fortune' (Pltcs, 1370b). Note that he requires a 'spirit of obedience to law', rather than the mere compliance with its letter. He also calls for such an attitude particularly in reference to apparently 'small matters', for that is where menacing behaviours or vices tend to run unchecked, until they have already caused huge, sometimes irreparable, harm or damage. Apart from the exemplary role that rulers are supposed to set for their constituents on these matters, it likewise is the case that small errors or faults are always easier to remedy or rectify than bigger ones. This is certainly true for all organizations, states as well as business firms.

Lastly, most recommendations for good corporate governance tend to include the formation of an audit committee within the board, entrusted with supervising the gathering and flow of information, especially financial ones, about a company. In this respect, Aristotle argues in favour of what we would nowadays call 'transparency', achieved through the convocation of some sort of general meeting of all the concerned parties, accompanied by diligent and meticulous record-keeping practices. With respect to states – although in a manner completely applicable to business corporations – Aristotle indicates: 'In order to avoid speculation of the public money, the transfer of revenue should be made at a general assembly of citizens [of "corporate citizens", we could say] and duplicates of the accounts deposited with the different brotherhoods, companies, and tribes' [that is, leaving them open to scrutiny by anyone interested] (Pltcs, 1309a). In addition, Aristotle likewise recommends that those magistrates or rulers who have managed to gain a reputation for ruling without illicit personal gain be awarded special public honours (Pltcs, 1309a). This reward could constitute yet another incentive for rulers to foster the virtues of honesty, integrity and trustworthiness.

The basis for Aristotle's understanding of the task of governance, which we have applied analogously to the corporate setting, lies in the distinction he establishes between the categories of '*praxis*' (action) and '*poiesis*' (production) (Metaphysics, 1048b, Pltcs, 1254a). Both praxis and poiesis refer to changes produced by human beings acting on concrete, individual and contingent realities; that is, they signify practical activities that human beings carry out, making use of their freedom and reason. They do not result from engaging in a purely theoretical exercise; rather, they represent specific kinds of activities that bring about material changes. They are not concerned with simply knowing, reflectively, the world that surrounds us, but with changing it through a conscious intervention.

In praxis, the end of the activity is internal to the activity itself. Think of the act of consciously looking at something, at any given object such as a tree, for example. The end of looking at a tree is not the tree itself but the image of the tree as I see it. My sight does not produce the tree: it was already there before I saw it, nor will it cease to exist once I draw my sight away from it. The only thing that my sight produces is the image itself of the tree. Now where could that image be found? Nowhere else but in my visual faculty, insofar as it is operational; in my own seeing capacity as I exercise it, focusing on a particular tree. This is what 'the end of the activity is internal to the activity itself' means. Because of this, the change wrought by praxis is one that primarily affects the agent himself. Returning to our example, I would have gained the characteristic of being able to see a specific tree, something that I did not have prior to my decision to look. Praxis also entails that there is hardly any time lapse or distance between the performance of an action and the attainment of its end. As soon as I look at a tree I am already seeing it: either I see it or I do not, but I do not have to wait for any time to pass before I actually see the tree.

In the case of poiesis, on the other hand, the end is said to be external to the activity itself. Consider the construction of a house. The end is the finished house and it is clearly external to the various activities carried out by the architects, engineers, carpenters, masons, electricians and so forth. The finished house is to be found not in any of these agents, nor in their respective activities, but outside of their activities as a product. Unlike praxis, therefore, the change brought about by poiesis is observed mainly in the outside world, external to the agents themselves. In particular, the change consists in the newly constructed house that was not there before. Compared to praxis, in poiesis there is a time lapse or a distance between the moment in which the different workers involved in the construction of the house began their activity and the time when their objective is achieved; that is, that specific instance when the house is already finished and ready to be inhabited. It may take several weeks, months and even years. Throughout this period, there is no guarantee that the house will reach its completion, and there is always a faint possibility that it remain only partially built.

As a distinct and special form of politics, corporate governance refers to an activity that belongs to the category of praxis rather than of poiesis. It is an instance of action, rather than of mere production. As such, corporate governance should be analysed and evaluated on the basis of the changes it introduces in the agent himself, rather than in the agent's surroundings or physical environment. This means that, in order to govern well, one needs above all to cultivate the excellences, character traits or virtues (*aretai*) proper to a ruler. These are far more important than the rules, principles or laws that he may set down later on. Not that a good governor could totally dispense with the rules, but they only become secondary once excellent character traits or virtues are in place. After all, granted that 'rules are meant to be broken', only the ruler's virtue can ensure in the end that the goods rules are supposed to protect are actually kept safe, even when the rules themselves have been overrun. Furthermore, rules by themselves are useless or could even be harmful, unless they are properly interpreted and implemented. And it so happens that the proper interpretation and implementation of rules depend on the moral and intellectual dispositions (ultimately, the virtues) of the governors or the people entrusted with these functions.

Most other approaches consider governance as an activity belonging to the category of poiesis or production. In consequence, they are more concerned with the formulation of some sort of rule-book, as the corresponding external product or object on which the success of the activity rests or should be judged. Their aim seems to be the creation of a foolproof instructions manual on the task of good governance. Similarly, there is an undue emphasis on the setting up of structures and the design of processes as if these carried the key.

They tend to forget that the outcome of good governance cannot be separated from the internal or personal dispositions – in other words, virtues – of the agent, so much so that it is impossible to perfectly codify a set of rules and institute certain structures and processes, then pretend that their observance alone would guarantee the desired results. To perform a praxis such as governance well, beyond following the rules, the right intention and moral dispositions aside from the appropriate circumstances also have to be assured. For this there is nothing better than the holistic education of the ruler in the virtues of mind and character. It is not that Aristotle holds written laws or principles in disdain. They certainly form a necessary bulwark against arbitrariness in the governor and exert a powerful influence in moulding habit and custom amongst a people. He still thinks that habit and custom are superiour to the law, however, for, except in the case of physical coercion, it is only from habit and custom that the law could draw force and strength. Whereas the excellence of poiesis is called technique or art, the right reason in production, such as the one used in the crafting of governance laws, structures and procedures, that of praxis is called prudence, the right reason in action, the paramount virtue of the ruler or governor.

Indeed, prudence or practical wisdom is a character trait acquired through habit, appropriate mentoring and discipleship, as well as a broad experience. Notwithstanding the doctrine regarding the 'unity of the virtues', according to which any particular excellence in character requires all the others for its full development, prudence is said to encompass all the human virtues. Prudence therefore includes moderation or temperance, truthfulness, courage, and so forth, character traits indispensable for a good governor. It is demonstrated in the ability of individuals to judge particular situations on their merits and to act accordingly; it should never be confused with the mechanical application of impersonal, purportedly general, rules (Nicomachean Ethics, NE, 1141b). Such rules or laws would be valid perhaps in the realm of the physical and mathematical sciences, but not in human behaviour which, being free, is messy and unpredictable. If the good in human action is nevertheless to be sought, it should be done with an eye or certain sensitivity to the particular good of the people involved and to the contingency of circumstances (NE, 1143b). None of these could be adequately covered by the supposedly universal laws.

As Kane and Patapan (2006) have pointed out in their reflections on managerial reform, the development of prudence has been thwarted in most institutions and organizations 'first, by the imposition of artificial external disciplines on decision making, such as those provided by a market [. . .]; second, by a general technocratic approach to decision making [. . .]; and third, by attempts to approach the problem in a counterproductive, piecemeal fashion [. . .]' (Kane and Patapan, 2006: 712). Furthermore, they diagnose an even deeper cause for the current flaws in governance that finds its roots in Weber's analysis of bureaucracy: the replacement of prudence by the rational–legal structures of a purely instrumental form of rationality (ibid.). These are defects glaringly present in the majority of corporate governance codes and literature on best practices. Emphasized are techniques, theories *du jour* on human behaviour and decision making and short-term, tunnel vision objectives while the virtues are completely ignored.

We began this work by clarifying that good governance should be understood primarily as the proper exercise of power and authority at the topmost level of an organization, such as the business firm. We should now add that it refers, not so much to the 'how?', to the ways and means, the rules, structures and procedures to be implemented when exercising power and authority, as to the 'what for?', to the purpose or end of whoever exercises them. Such a question warrants a response based on a 'good', particularly on the specific contribution to the 'common good' of society as a whole that any corporation is meant to deliver. Here we find the ultimate justification for the existence of corporations.

In previous sections we had already explained how the goods and services produced by the community of persons working in a firm figure in the whole, complex range of material and spiritual goods, internal and external goods, goods in themselves and instrumental goods, the one final good or end and the common good. We have to say, furthermore, that, in order to recognize or 'perform' such goods and to assign them their proper place in the hierarchy in cases of conflict, virtue – pre-eminently, prudence – is needed. A merely physical or mechanical recognition and production or performance of these goods is not enough, if they are to be articulated and seamlessly woven into the larger fabric of societal common good. That is why certain people, at one point or another, sometimes fail to acknowledge and therefore heed the 'calling' of a good yearning to be realized. More than anything else, it may be due to their lack of virtue. Excellence of character not only enables one to do things properly, technically and ethically speaking. It also allows one to detect the convenience or need for that good, when many other people of inferior virtue would nonchalantly pass it by, oblivious even of that good's existence. Virtue makes one perspicacious of goods to be achieved in any given circumstance.

Because virtue is needed not only to interpret and implement properly the rules of governance, but also to correctly identify and produce the goods involved, it becomes clear that the key to good governance ultimately lies in the education of the governors or rulers. Even the kind of regime dominant in an organization just amounts to a host of formal conditions that best allow for the proper education in the virtues of the governors or rulers. Unless this principle is sufficiently acknowledged, all attempts at corporate governance reform will be, at best, superficial or cosmetic, and at worst, ruefully ineffective, as witness the already long list of reforms that have preceded it.

REFERENCES

Aristotle (1971), *Aristotle's Metaphysics*, trans. and notes C. Kirwan, Oxford: Clarendon Press.
Aristotle (1985), *Nicomachean Ethics*, trans. Terence Irwin, Indianapolis, IN: Hackett Publishing.
Aristotle (1990), *The Politics*, ed. Stephen Everson, Cambridge: Cambridge University Press.
Gevurtz, Franklin A. (2004), 'The historical and political origins of the corporate board of directors', *Hofstra Law Review*, **33**(Fall), 89–173.

Heidrick & Struggles (2005), 'Corporate governance in Europe: what's the outlook?', *Heidrick & Struggles 2005 Study*, www.heidrick.com/NR/rdonlyres/B1A816CD-0E51-4605-B22C-40CB1B50561D/0/HS_EuropeCorpGovOutlook.pdf.

Kane, John and Haig Patapan (2006), 'In seach of prudence: the hidden problem of managerial reform', *Public Administration Review*, September/October, 711–24.

Lawler, Edward E. and Theodore L. Dysart (2007), '10th Annual Board Effectiveness Study 2006–7', *USC Marshall School of Business/Heidrick & Struggles*, www.heidrick.com/NR/rdonlyres/723D125E-9746-4486-829A-D49A8AF0832B/0/HS_BoardEffectivenessStudy0607.pdf.

Morck, Randall and Lloyd Steier (2005), 'The global history of corporate governance: an introduction', *NBER Working Paper No. W11062*, http://ssrn.com/abstract=652361.

Van den Berghe, Lutgart A.A. and Steven Waldo Monique Carchon (2002), 'Corporate governance practices in Flemish family businesses', *Corporate Governance: An International Review*, **10**, 225–45, http://ssrn.com/abstract=314293.

Index